Vanessa De Wilde and Claire Goriot (Eds.)
Second Language Learning Before Adulthood

Studies on Language Acquisition

Series Editors
Luke Plonsky
Martha Young-Scholten

Volume 65

Second Language Learning Before Adulthood

—

Individual Differences in Children and Adolescents

Edited by
Vanessa De Wilde and Claire Goriot

ISBN 978-3-11-152398-9
e-ISBN (PDF) 978-3-11-074304-3
e-ISBN (EPUB) 978-3-11-074313-5
ISSN 1861-4248

Library of Congress Control Number: 2022941001

Bibliographic information published by the Deutsche Nationalbibliothek
The Deutsche Nationalbibliothek lists this publication in the Deutsche Nationalbibliografie;
detailed bibliographic data are available on the internet at http://dnb.dnb.de.

© 2024 Walter de Gruyter GmbH, Berlin/Boston Typesetting: Integra Software Services Pvt.

This volume is text- and page-identical with the hardback published in 2022.

www.degruyter.com

Contents

Vanessa De Wilde and Claire Goriot
Introduction —— 1

Sara E. N. Kangas and Megan Cook
Learning disabilities as external individual differences in second language acquisition —— 9

M. J. H. Van Koert, N. L. Leona, J. E. Rispens, J. Tijms, M. W. Van der Molen, V. H. P. van Daal and P. Snellings
The role of memory in the acquisition of vocabulary and grammar in the first language and in English as a foreign language —— 31

Ferran Gesa and Maria del Mar Suárez
Individual differences and young learners' L2 vocabulary development: The case of language aptitude and exposure to subtitled TV series —— 65

Vanessa De Wilde and June Eyckmans
'In love with English': A mixed-methods investigation of Flemish children's spontaneous engagement with out-of-school exposure —— 87

Claire Goriot and Roeland van Hout
The relation between out-of-school exposure to English and English vocabulary development in Dutch primary school pupils —— 109

Rosa M. Jiménez Catalán
Lexical profiles of children and adolescent EFL learners in the semantic domain of animals —— 133

Ágnes Albert, Brigitta Dóczi, Katalin Piniel and Kata Csizér
The contribution of motivation and emotions to language learning autonomy in the Hungarian secondary school classroom: The results of a questionnaire study —— 155

Mark Christianson and Kota Ohata
Effects of authentic communication experiences on linguistic self-confidence: Individual differences in perceptions among Japanese primary school students —— 177

Susan Sayehli, Rakel Österberg and Jonas Granfeldt
Emotion and motivation in younger learners' second foreign language acquisition —— 203

Debora Carrai
Secondary school pupils' language choice satisfaction in the L3 classroom: The roles of teaching, motivation, language choice and language classroom anxiety —— 225

Index —— 261

Vanessa De Wilde and Claire Goriot
Introduction

Researchers have looked into the role of individual differences in second language learning and found that differences between learners in areas such as language aptitude, language learning motivation and exposure to the language influence second language learning (Dörnyei 2014; Dörnyei and Skehan 2003; Muñoz 2012). Many of these studies investigated second language learning in adults. Recently, researchers have started taking an interest in the role of individual differences in young second language learners, but still far fewer studies have addressed the role of individual differences in second language learning of young learners compared to studies which have investigated these variables in adult learners.

However, the group of young second language learners is by no means a small group. Many children are speaking a language / languages at home which is not the school language, foreign language learning programmes tend to start earlier than before (Enever 2011; Mourão and Lorenço 2014), and many children are frequently exposed to a foreign language in social settings such as online games and social media (De Wilde et al. 2020; Zhang et al. 2021). Previous studies already showed that there are large individual differences between children, for example in the extent to which they are proficient in the first and the second language (Goriot et al. 2018), their socio-economic status (Cummins 1979), and their motivation to learn a second language (Mihaljević Djigunović and Lopriore 2011; Muñoz and Tragant 2001). Research has also shown that these individual differences may influence children's developmental outcomes in various domains such as their cognitive development, and educational success (Goriot et al. 2018; Prevoo et al. 2016). As said, however, research on the role of individual differences in second language acquisition in child learners is fairly limited. Therefore, studying the role of individual differences in young learners can contribute both to SLA-theories and to evidence-based L2 education.

This volume aims to discuss recent findings concerning the role of individual differences in language learning found in studies concerning young learners (pre-primary, primary and secondary school age). The chapters in the book concern different topics linked to *internal* individual differences such as language aptitude, motivation, attitude and *external* individual differences such as out-of-school exposure and type of instruction, the relative contribution of internal and external factors to language learning, and the interplay between various individual differences. The chapters cover both topics related to foreign language learning (in a formal and an informal setting) and topics related to second language learning (such as language learning in children with a migrant background). The studies took place in various European countries, the United States and Japan and thus give insights into aspects which might influence second language acquisition in many different contexts. The common denominator in the book is the young age of the participants in the study. All studies have been conducted with learners who were either in primary or secondary education. The individual difference variables under investigation are very diverse and the results of the various studies show that many different aspects can play a role in language learning, possibly also depending on the language learning context (such as the prevalence of the foreign language in society, the teaching methods, the place of the foreign language in the curriculum, etc.).

The chapters in this volume will add to the existing knowledge of individual differences in second language learning – which mainly concerns adult learners – by bundling research on individual differences in child second language learners. It is thereby a source of information for researchers studying children who learn a second language, but also for educators working with these children, as it shows that the language learning process and outcomes are influenced by a variety of factors that differ between learners.

1 Structure of the book

The book consists of ten chapters which each discuss an empirical study done with young second language learners. Some of the chapters have adopted a quantitative, others a qualitative, and still others a mixed-methods approach. Consequently, the chapters in the book give a varied view on how individual differences might impact young learners' second language acquisition. Below, we give an overview of the structure of the book by laying out the individual differences under investigation in each chapter.

Chapter 1 reports on an ethnographic multiple-case study with second language learners with learning disabilities. Kangas and Cook discuss how learning disabilities can be an external individual difference in 10–13 year-old Spanish- / Urdu- / Greek-native children acquiring English as a second language. Through classroom observations and interviews with students and school staff they found that children with learning disabilities are often placed in a linguistically poor environment, separated from their peers who are proficient in English. Furthermore, in the classroom environment behavior-management rather than language learning seems the priority. At the same time, educators attributed the lack of growth in pupils' English proficiency to pupils' learning disabilities, instead of to the sub-optimal environment they were educated in.

In Chapter 2 van Koert, Leona, Rispens, Tijms, van der Molen, van Daal and Snellings investigate whether and how working memory and phonological processing contribute to the acquisition of vocabulary and grammar learning in young (9 to 11 years old) learners' first language (Dutch) and English as a second language. With respect to L2 learning, it was found that both individual differences in English phonological processing – measured with a non-word repetition task – and Dutch vocabulary were positively related to English vocabulary knowledge. English phonological processing was also positively related to performance on receptive and productive grammar tasks in English. Contrary to the expectations, however, working memory did not play a role in grammar performance.

Chapters 3 to 5 examine L2 acquisition through factors that are maybe especially important to young learners, that is through media and social settings. In Chapter 3 Gesa and Suárez describe a study in which 11–12-year-old Catalan/Spanish learners of English were exposed to subtitled television programs. In a randomized-control experiment the authors investigate how this exposure might impact vocabulary learning while also considering learners' language learning aptitude. The results show that over the course of eight weeks, pupils' English vocabulary knowledge significantly improved and that language aptitude positively influences pupils' English vocabulary learning, regardless of whether they were in the experimental or control condition.

De Wilde and Eyckmans report on a mixed-methods investigation of 10–12-year-old Flemish children's spontaneous engagement with English outside the classroom in Chapter 4. By combining quantitative questionnaire data and qualitative focus group data, they examined *when* and *why* children engage with English in their free time. It was found that children mainly use English 1) on holiday to communicate with those who do not speak the same mother tongue, 2) at home, even though family members usually share the same first language, 3) at school with friends, although they also speak the same first language, 4) during online gaming or while texting and posting on social media, and 5) when singing songs. Although children seemed to find it hard to tell why they do so, they seemed to find English 'fun', and to think it sounds better than Dutch (their mother tongue).

Goriot and van Hout discuss how young learners' (age 4 to 12) out-of-school exposure to English impacts English receptive vocabulary knowledge in Chapter 5. They compared a group of children who receive English lessons from the start of primary school with a group of children who receive English education in the upper grades only, while also comparing older and younger pupils. They investigated to what extent out-of-school exposure to English differs between pupils from the different groups, and how individual differences in out-of-school exposure are related to English vocabulary acquisition. It appeared that older children engage more in English activities outside school than younger children, and that both groups of children also engaged in different kinds of activities. The starting point of English education was not related to exposure to English outside the school environment. Whereas younger children were mainly exposed to activities that were meant to learn something, pupils in the upper grade of primary school engaged in gaming and watching English movies. In both groups of pupils, however, individual differences in out-of-school exposure to English were positively related to English vocabulary development.

Chapter 6 (Catalán) investigates second language learning in both children (11–12 years old) and adolescent learners (17–18 years old). The chapter maps how age differences impact young learners' lexical profile. The Spanish learners of English were subjected to a lexical fluency task in the domain of animals. It was found that the older participants generated more words and more clusters of groups of animals than the younger children. Both groups mostly formed clusters of two animals, but older children tended to generate larger clusters than younger children. Furthermore, children partly generated different words than adolescents.

Chapter 7 looks into the way in which learners' motivation and emotions influence language learning autonomy. Ágnes Albert, Brigitta Dóczi, Kata Csizér and Katalin Piniel shed light on this matter by measuring over 300 Hungarian secondary school pupils' autonomous learning behaviour, autonomous use of technology, L2 motivation and emotions. Students were subjected to a questionnaire measuring these constructs. The results showed that students' curiosity positively influenced their sense of autonomy, both with respect to learning behaviour and use of technology. Furthermore, students' motivation and enjoyment were positively related to their autonomous learning behaviour, while learning experience showed a negative relationship with autonomous learning behaviour. Other emotions (the ideal L2 self, pride and boredom) showed a positive relationship with the use of technology, while a negative relationship was found with confusion. These results show that autonomy is a complex construct, and that various internal and external factors relate to this construct in different ways.

In Chapter 8 Mark Christianson and Kota Ohata discuss how authentic communication experiences resulting from an international exchange program can impact Japanese primary school children's linguistic self-confidence. More than 100 Japanese pupils (who were 11 to 12 years old) participated in an exchange visit with students from the United Kingdom. The UK-students came to Japan, and the Japanese students spent a week with them, in which they needed to communicate in English with the exchange students. Many Japanese students indicated afterwards that the contact they had with the UK-students positively influenced their linguistic self-confidence and motivation for learning English.

The two final chapters (Chapters 9 and 10) are concerned with learning a second foreign language (L3). In Chapter 9 Susan Sayehli, Rakel Österberg and Jonas Granfeldt investigate young Swedish learners' emotion and motivation towards learning a second foreign language. The data of a questionnaire, distributed amongst 120 Swedish secondary school pupils, revealed that pupils' motivation showed a relation with the second language they choose to learn: pupils who learned Spanish as a second foreign language showed more external, pragmatic reasons to do so than pupils who learned German or French. Furthermore, the motivation to learn a second foreign language and the emotions associated with it, differed between boys and girls, such that boys show higher levels of willingness to communicate, whereas girls showed higher levels of foreign language classroom anxiety. Sayehli et al. also showed that internal individual differences were associated with willingness to communicate: pupils with lower levels of foreign language classroom anxiety and a more developed ideal self for the foreign language, were generally more willing to communicate. Carrai's study in Chapter 10 is devoted to learners' satisfaction in the L3 classroom. The study investigated learners' satisfaction with regard to their L3 language subject choice, and looks into the role of teaching, motivation, language choice and language classroom anxiety on young Norwegian learners' satisfaction when learning a second foreign language. More than 1500 students filled in a questionnaire. The results showed that individual differences in students' perception of teaching, learning, and intrinsic motivation, and, to a lesser extent, their perceptions of teachers' adaptation, the teacher herself, and the learning environment, were positively related to satisfaction with L3 choice.

2 Future studies with young learners

Although this volume provides an overview of many factors that influence second language learning in children and adolescents, questions remain. Throughout the volume, the chapter authors formulate possible directions that research investigating individual differences in young second language learners could take. We will discuss some of their suggestions here. They might serve as an inspiration for researchers aspiring to do research with young L2 learners.

Overall, there is a call for studies with young learners in different contexts (as suggested by Van Koert et al., Gesa and Suarez, De Wilde and Eyckmans,

Albert et al. and Carrai). These could be studies with learners learning a language in contexts in or outside the classroom, learners receiving different amounts of exposure to the target language or learners learning a language which is linguistically more closely related or more distant from their L1. These contextual factors might play a role in the contribution of several individual differences in L2 learning and future studies should be done in various contexts so the results can be compared across contexts.

Furthermore, some authors state the importance of doing more research that can inform classroom practice and/or educational policy. Kangas and Cook for example suggest that more research needs to be done on child L2 learners with learning disabilities that looks into the interplay between internal and external individual differences in other school contexts. Catalán suggests more research should be done in word learning in other semantic domains to detect difficulties in understanding and producing texts that might occur for learners in the classroom.

Some chapter authors also formulate methodological recommendations for future studies with young learners. Gesa and Suárez and Christianson and Ohata stress the need for more studies done with a larger number of participants. Goriot and Van Hout suggest refining some of the variables that are considered in studies which look into language learning through out-of-school exposure (e.g. distinguishing between different types of computer games depending on their purpose). Albert et al., Christianson and Ohata and Carrai suggest supplementing survey studies with teacher and student interviews to be able to also interpret the data qualitatively. Finally, some chapter authors (Albert et al. and Christianson and Ohato) call for more longitudinal studies in order to get more insight in the role of individual differences over a longer period of L2 learning.

3 Conclusion

All in all, the research in this volume shows that individual differences in young learners play an important role in second language acquisition, their motivation to learn a second language, and their linguistic confidence. On the one hand, these individual differences can be internal, that is, coming from the learner herself. One of these internal factors is *age*. Within a given time limit, older L2 learners retrieve more words in the second language that belong to a specific category than younger learners (Catalán). Older children also tend to engage more in informal activities in the foreign language than younger children

(Goriot and van Hout). Other internal individual differences that play a role in young language learners are *motivation* and *emotions*, and both of these factors seem to play a role in learners' sense of autonomous learning behaviour and their use of technology to learn a foreign language (Albert et al.). Students' intrinsic motivation is also positively related to their satisfaction with the language they chose to learn at school (Carrai), and to their willingness to communicate in the foreign language (Sayheli et al.). With respect to emotions, pupils' foreign language classroom anxiety is negatively related to their willingness to communicate (Sayheli et al.) *Language aptitude* plays a role, too. Gesa and Suárez show that language aptitude is positively related to pupils' vocabulary learning in the foreign language. Finally, van Koert et al. show that internal cognitive differences, and more specifically phonological processing, are positively related to vocabulary and grammar knowledge in the second language. Taken together, these studies provide evidence that internal individual differences in young learners should be taken into account when working with this population either in education or research. At the same time, individual factors are sometimes linked to learners' L2 performance, although such a relation may not necessarily exist. As Kangas and Cook show, teachers thought students' learning disabilities were the cause for their limited foreign language skills, while they tended to overlook the poor linguistic environment these pupils were educated in.

Next to internal individual differences, external individual differences play a role in young second language learners, too. If children learn a new language in a formal way, the *learning environment* can be seen as such an external factor. Students' perception of the teacher and the learning environment, for example, positively influence their satisfaction with the language students chose to learn (Carrai). Furthermore, an exchange program in which students need to communicate in the foreign language with students from another country seems to positively influence students' linguistic self-confidence (Christianson and Ohata). In an informal environment, individual differences in exposure to English, for example via games, television, or on holiday, may positively influence children's knowledge of English (De Wilde and Eyckmans; Goriot and van Hout; Gesa and Suárez).

This volume is a good starting point for researchers to get insights into the possible contribution of various individual differences in the language learning process of young second language learners. This book may also be of interest to policy makers and practitioners working with young L2 learners as it will give an insight in the role of different variables which impact L2 learning at a younger age.

References

Cummins, J. 1979. Linguistic interdependence and the educational development of bilingual children. *Review of Educational Research* **49**(2). 222–251.

De Wilde, V., Brysbaert, M., & Eyckmans, J. 2020. Learning English through out-of-school exposure. Which levels of language proficiency are attained and which types of input are important? *Bilingualism: Language and Cognition* **23**(1). 171–185.

Dörnyei, Z., & Skehan, P. 2003. Individual Differences in Second Language Learning. In C. J. Doughty & M. H. Long (Eds.), *The Handbook of Second Language Acquisition*, 589–630. Oxford: Blackwell Publishing Ltd.

Dörnyei, Z. 2014. *The psychology of the language learner: Individual differences in second language acquisition*. New York: Routledge.

Enever, J. 2011. *ELLiE – Early language learning in Europe*. UK: British Council.

Goriot, C., Broersma, M., McQueen, J.M., Unsworth, S., & van Hout, R. 2018. Language balance and switching ability in children acquiring English as a second language. *Journal of Experimental Child Psychology* **173**. 168–186.

Mihaljević Djigunović, J., & Lopriore, L. 2011. The learner: Do individual differences matter. In Janet Enever (ed.), *ELLiE: Early language learning in Europe*, 29–45. UK: British Council.

Mourão, S., & Lourenço, M. (Eds.). 2014. *Early years second language education: International perspectives on theory and practice*. New York: Routledge.

Muñoz, C. (Ed.). 2012. *Intensive exposure experiences in second language learning*. Bristol: Multilingual Matters.

Muñoz, C., & Tragant, E. 2001. Motivation and attitudes towards L2: Some effects of age and instruction. *Eurosla Yearbook* **1**(1). 211–224.

Prevoo, Mariëlle J. L., Malda, M., Mesman, J., & van Ijzendoorn, M.H. 2016. Within- and cross-language relations between oral language proficiency and school outcomes in bilingual children with an immigrant background. *Review of Educational Research* **86**(1). 237–276.

Zhang, R., Zou, D., Cheng, G., Xie, H., Wang, H.L., & Sheung, O.T. 2021. Target languages, types of activities, engagement, and effectiveness of extramural language learning. *PloS one* **16**(6). e0253431.

Sara E. N. Kangas and Megan Cook

Learning disabilities as external individual differences in second language acquisition

Abstract: Although cognitive aptitude has been examined as an individual difference in second language acquisition (SLA; for overview, see Dörnyei and Ryan 2015), there is a dearth of research on the influence of learning disabilities (LDs) in second language (L2) learning for children. In fact, LDs are seldom researched as an influential individual difference in SLA for young bilingual children. Thus, this chapter will focus on a study that examined LDs as an individual difference in SLA for English learners (ELs), bi- and multilingual children who are acquiring English as an additional language in U.S. schools. In doing so, the study asks the following research questions:

(1) What are the external individual differences (IDs) in the SLA of ELs with disabilities?
(2) How do these external IDs contribute to internal IDs for ELs with disabilities?
(3) In what ways do these individual differences represent deficit thinking?

The study utilized a multiple case study design (Stake 2006) of two U.S. middle schools. The participating students were 11 ELs with LDs. The ethnographic data included 74 classroom observations; 53 interviews with students and staff; and school records. Data were analyzed through hybrid inductive–deductive coding (Fereday and Muir-Cochane 2006). For its theoretical underpinnings, the study utilized *deficit thinking* (Valencia 1997), which argues the underperformance of children is attributed to their supposed innate deficiencies, instead of external factors within schools.

The analysis revealed the LDs of ELs were linked to limited L2 learning opportunities. As a result of their LDs, ELs were placed in classrooms where they were (a) isolated from their English-proficient peers, (b) restricted from collaborative language learning tasks, and (c) primarily exposed to behavior-management teacher discourse. Yet, ELs' LDs – not the linguistically poor learning environments – were positioned by educators as the cause of ELs' plateauing English proficiency. The study illuminates how individual differences in SLA for ELs with LDs are, in part, shaped by learning conditions in the school.

Keywords: external individual differences, English learners with disabilities

Despite empirical evidence that points to the contrary, there has long been a perception among parents and teachers that children with cognitive disabilities cannot and should not be bilingual (see Bialystok 2001; Hakuta 1986; Kay-Raining Bird et al. 2005; Paradis et al. 2021). Rooted in the apprehension that bilingualism would be too cognitively demanding for children with disabilities, those who adhere to this belief are concerned that child second language (L2) learners' cognitive aptitude will inhibit their L2 attainment. In short, they understand second language acquisition (SLA) as a process that is determined by *individual differences* (IDs), traditionally thought of as those internal cognitive, affective, and other personal attributes that L2 learners possess (Ehrman et al. 2003). Reflecting the larger social turn in SLA (see Block 2003; Firth and Wagner 2007; Gregg 2006), however, there have been calls for research to conceptualize IDs in broader instructional and sociopolitical contexts (DeKeyser 2012; Dörnyei 2009; Paradis 2011; Pfenninger 2017). In light of this reconceptualization, IDs can be understood as both internal, existing within L2 learners, and external, laden in the physical and sociopolitical environments surrounding L2 learners (Dörnyei 2009; Ushioda 2009).

Mirroring SLA's predominant orientation toward adult L2 learners – in ways that obscures understanding of child SLA (Oliver and Azkarai 2017; Paradis 2007) – there has been a dearth of research on the interplay of internal IDs and environmental contexts for child L2 learners. Yet, probing this interplay is exigent for children with disabilities, given the pervasive concern about the cognitive capacities of child L2 learners with disabilities, which stems from the understanding that these children's internal IDs limit their L2 attainment. Addressing this gap in child SLA research, this chapter seeks to examine IDs – both internal and external – of school-aged L2 learners with disabilities through an ethnographic multiple case study conducted in two schools in the United States.

1 Literature review

To situate the present study, we draw upon two interrelated bodies of literature on IDs of child L2 learners with disabilities. First, we explore internal IDs, contrasting pervasive beliefs about the cognitive and linguistic aptitude of child L2 learners with disabilities with empirical evidence. Second, we provide an overview of research on external IDs, illuminating how L2 learning environments in schools create suboptimal conditions for child L2 learners, particularly those with disabilities. Given the context of the study, the literature addresses the interplay of internal and external IDs in connection to child L2 learners with disabilities in the United States.

1.1 Internal IDs: Beliefs and evidence

For some time, literature has documented the long-standing belief about the cognitive abilities of bilingual children with disabilities, namely that acquiring two languages as a child with a disability is harmful (see Cheatham and Barnett 2017; Genesee et al. 2015; Kangas 2017; Kay-Raining Bird et al. 2012; Kay-Raining Bird et al. 2005). Described as the *limited capacity theory of bilingualism* (Paradis et al. 2021), this belief presupposes children with disabilities have limited cognitive aptitude and thus will become overtaxed by exposure to more than one language. Critically, this belief understands internal IDs for children with disabilities in terms of limitations and deficiencies – assuming bilingual aptitude is stymied by their cognitive disabilities. However pervasive this belief is, it is baseless, even for children who have more significant cognitive disabilities, as Genesee (2015) describes: "Practically speaking, there is no empirical evidence at present to justify restricting children with developmental disorders from learning two languages" (p. 12).

Indeed, a number of studies have examined the first language (L1) and L2 development of children with various developmental disabilities, finding evidence of greater bilingual gains when exposed to two languages. For instance, Simon-Cereijido and Gutiérrez-Clellen (2013) examined the effects of the bilingual intervention, Vocabulary, Oral Language and Academic Readiness (VOLAR), on preschool children with speech or language impairments. The children in the study had an L1 of Spanish and reportedly had limited prior exposure to English in the home. The VOLAR program uses shared book reading and accompanying activities to build the children's oral language development and lexicon. The program was administered in 45-minute increments four days per week, over the course of nine weeks. The findings indicated that compared to children who did not receive the intervention, children who participated in VOLAR made significant gains in both English and Spanish. Gonzalez-Barrero and Nadig (2018) similarly examined the effects of exposure to two languages on the lexical and morphological skills of children with autism spectrum disorders, with non-verbal IQ scores of at least 80 (i.e., low average or higher). Through a regression analysis, they found that the amount of exposure to the languages was the primary predictor of children's lexical and morphological skills. These findings align with an investigation by Kay-Raining Bird et al. (2005) into the bilingual skills of children with Down syndrome. Measuring their L1 and L2 skills on several language measures, the researchers found that the children with Down syndrome who were exposed to two languages scored comparable to monolingual children with Down syndrome who were only exposed to English.

Examining the effects of bilingual exposure on academic outcomes, Thomas and Collier (2012) compared students with speech or language impairments and learning disabilities (LDs) enrolled in dual language programs to otherwise similar peers with disabilities who were not. Although the sample was relatively small ($n = 86$), the findings showed that students with disabilities served in dual language programs outperformed their peers on the standardized reading assessments at each grade level. Across the literature, evidence suggests that bilingual children with disabilities perform similarly to their monolingual peers with disabilities, but as Kay-Raining Bird et al. (2016) underscored in their review of literature on bilingualism and developmental disorders, external IDs in terms of the amount of bilingual exposure and access to bilingual programs are critical.

Despite the above evidence, educators often adhere to the limited capacity theory of bilingualism for one particular group of child L2 learners in United States' schools – English learners (ELs) with disabilities (Cioè-Peña 2020; Kangas 2017). In Cioè-Peña's (2020) ethnographic study, both educators and mothers of ELs with disabilities believed that bilingualism was beyond the cognitive capabilities of the children. Kangas (2017) also found this assumption active in a bilingual elementary school wherein ELs with disabilities received less bilingual instruction than their peers without disabilities. Educators rationalized underservicing ELs with disabilities, citing that students would be overwhelmed by bilingual instruction. The above literature not only highlights an apparent juxtaposition between common beliefs about and empirical evidence on the bilingual aptitude of children with disabilities, but also signals the importance of providing quality L1 and L2 exposure to support their proficiency. Addressing the latter, we now turn to a body of literature on the quality of the L2 environment for child L2 learners, particularly those with disabilities.

1.2 External IDs: Quality of L2 learning environments

An emerging body of empirical research illuminates that the learning environments of child L2 learners with disabilities in United States' K–12 schools are less optimal for their L2 development (Kangas 2014, 2018; Zehler et al. 2003). Namely, ELs with disabilities often lack access to English language development (ELD) services[1] and more broadly, to support for the L2 proficiency while they are learning academic content. In an ethnographic study, Kangas (2018)

---

1 *English language development* services is a term describing a number of programs used to support students' emerging L2 English proficiency.

found that regardless of their English language proficiency, ELs with disabilities received limited, and at times, no ELD services, as their schedules were arranged to prioritize special education services. Underlying educators' decision to relinquish ELD services were two interrelated beliefs – that learning needs stemming from disability were more consequential than L2 proficiency and that special education services had more "legal teeth" than ELD. Although this study was conducted at two schools, the prevalence of this phenomenon bears out in national-level data. Nearly 15 years prior, Zehler et al. (2003) conducted a national survey of U.S. school leaders, inquiring about service provision for ELs with and without disabilities. The survey results revealed that 16.1% of ELs with disabilities received no ELD services, while 56.2% received less than 10 hours of ELD services each week. Only 27.7% – less than one-third of ELs with disabilities – received 10 or more hours of weekly ELD services. Underservicing of ELs with disabilities for their L2 proficiency remains a pervasive issue even years later. Specifically, in response to ELs with disabilities not receiving ELD services, the U.S. Departments of Justice and Education (2015) issued clarifying guidance on the matter. In the guidance, they identified the elimination of ELD services as one of the most common civil rights violations in the education of EL students and clarified that such a practice constituted a violation of ELs with disabilities' civil rights because it denied them meaningful access to learning.

These findings for ELs with disabilities mirror a larger pattern in the education of ELs in the United States – that L2 learning environments do not support L2 learning and in doing so, operate as an external ID in SLA of child L2 learners. A number of qualitative studies have examined the L2 learning environments of ELs, more generally, finding that ELs were placed in classes that were unlikely to support their L2 development (e.g., Dabach 2014; Harklau 1994; Kanno and Kangas 2014; Valdés 2001). This body of literature, in particular, documented what Valdés (2001) called the "ESL ghetto" (p. 145), that is, learning environments wherein ELs are segregated into specific classes that afford limited exposure to grade-level curriculum, academic discourse input, and interaction in the L2. For instance, Dabach (2014) conducted a qualitative case study of the experiences of ELs in a sheltered program, wherein ELs are grouped together to receive both core academic and ELD instruction. Despite the purpose of the program to support the L2 development of ELs, the ELs in the study had limited opportunity to interact with English proficient peers and were exposed to "watered down" academic content. These qualitative findings comport with Kanno and Kangas' (2014) ethnography of high-school ELs' curricular access. They documented how regardless of their academic performance, ELs were placed in low-level classes wherein efforts to manage students' off-task and disruptive behaviors put academic instruction on hold. With discourse aimed at managing students' behaviors, ELs were afforded scarce opportunity to interact in the L2 and to be exposed to L2 academic discourse. These findings corroborate Harklau's (1994) earlier research on ELs in high school who were placed in lower-level classes that emphasized rote learning, primarily completing multiple choice and fill-in-the blanks as well as locating key vocabulary in abbreviated readings. Such instructional practices that emphasize rote, decontextualized L2 learning contravene findings from task-based language teaching (TBLT) that show engaging child L2 learners in meaningful academic tasks promotes their interaction in the L2 (e.g., García Mayo and Lázaro Ibarrola 2015; Gagné and Park 2013; Mackey and Silver 2005; Pinter 2007). Collectively, these studies, first, illuminate how learning environments may constitute an external ID in the SLA of ELs, as the exposure to the L2 is decidedly poor, and second, underscore the complex interplay between L2 learners' characteristics and their learning environments.

2 Theoretical frame

This study draws upon *deficit thinking* (Valencia 1997) for its theoretical underpinnings. Valencia (1997) conceptualized deficit thinking as a propensity to blame the academic failures of certain student groups on the students themselves or in many cases, on their families and communities. It assumes that the students' challenges – whether academic, social, or behavioral – are the consequences of their own personal deficits. When educators engage in deficit thinking, Valencia further argues, they fail to consider the role of educational environments. In sum, by assuming academic problems lie within the student (or their families and communities), educators do not consider if and how conditions in classrooms and schools could be the causes of the academic problems students experience.

ELs with disabilities are likely to be the recipients of deficit thinking (Kangas 2021). Not only do ELs with disabilities take longer to reach the threshold for L2 English proficiency (Kieffer and Parker 2016; Sahakyan and Ryan 2018; Shin 2020; Slama et al. 2017; Umansky et al. 2017) – even if proficiency in English is conceptualized in schooling in problematic ways (see Flores 2020; MacSwan 2020) – they are also positioned by educators as cognitively and linguistically limited (see Kangas 2021). Germane to this study, we take up deficit thinking as a lens to interrogate the manner in which educators attribute the L2 attainment of ELs with disabilities to the students' alleged internal deficits (i.e., internals IDs) rather than to deficits in the learning contexts (i.e., external IDs).

We also examine how external IDs influence the ability of ELs with disabilities to acquire an L2. To that end, we asked the following research questions:
(1) What are the external IDs in the SLA of ELs with disabilities?
(2) How do these external IDs contribute to internal IDs for ELs with disabilities?
(3) In what ways do these IDs represent deficit thinking?

3 Methodology

The study utilized a multiple case study design (Stake 2006), conducted at two schools in Pennsylvania, United States. As a part of the Ashby District, the Parker and Ashby Schools housed Grades 6 through 8.[2] At both schools, approximately 70% of the students identified as ethnoracial minorities (i.e., 50% Hispanic, 15% African American, 2% Asian, and 3% multiracial) and over 75% of the students were socioeconomically disadvantaged, receiving free or reduced-price lunch. When identifying these two schools as potential sites, we used purposeful selection (Maxwell 2013) on the basis of two criteria. First, we wanted to conduct the study at schools with historically large populations of ELs with disabilities. Second, we aimed to conduct the study in schools wherein stakeholders had an interest in improving the programs and services offered to ELs with disabilities.

Although these criteria were the basis of our selection of Ashby and Parker Schools, in the weeks preceding data collection, the schools were affected by a state-wide policy change relating to reclassification, the process by which ELs are deemed proficient in English and no longer needing ELD services. Specifically, this policy adjusted standards for English proficiency for ELs with disabilities, resulting in the reclassification of approximately 80 ELs with disabilities across the two schools. In short, as a consequence of the policy change, the large population of ELs with disabilities decreased significantly. Of the ELs with disabilities that remained, we recruited 11 to participate in the study. All of the participating ELs with disabilities were identified with LDs in reading, mathematics, and/or written expression; however, five of the 11 also had an additional diagnosis of speech or language impairments and/or attention deficit hyperactivity disorder (Table 1). Nine ELs with disabilities were L1 speakers of Spanish and identified as Latinx, while two were L1 speakers of Urdu and Greek and identified as Asian or multiracial. The socioeconomic status of the

---

[2] Pseudonyms are used for the sites and participating staff and students. Information that could be potentially identifiable purposefully has been made ambiguous.

ELs with disabilities, however, was not provided in student records. In addition to the students, a total of 32 educators, including district- and school-level administrators, teachers (general education, ELD, and special education), and counselors of the focal ELs with disabilities, participated in the study.

Table 1: English learners with disabilities.

Student	Grade	Age in Years	Disability	First Language	English Proficiency Level
Amar	7	12	LD: reading	Punjabi	4.0
Camila	8	13	LD: reading, mathematics, written expression	Spanish	4.1
Dimitrios	7	12	LD: reading, mathematics, written expression; SLI: language disorder	Greek	2.9
Dion	6	10	LD: reading, mathematics, written expression; ADHD; SLI: language disorder	Spanish	P1
Gabriel	6	12	LD: reading	Spanish	4.5
Imani	6	11	LD: reading, mathematics, written expression; SLI: language order	Spanish	3.2
Jud	8	13	LD: reading, written expression	Spanish	2.5
Maria Elena	8	13	LD: reading, mathematics, written expression	Spanish	2.8
Mateo	6	10	LD: reading, mathematics, written expression; ADHD	Spanish	3.8
Miguel	8	13	LD: reading, mathematics, written expression; ADHD	Spanish	3.1
Monica	6	11	LD: reading, mathematics, written expression	Spanish	4.3

Note. English proficiency scores are based on the ACCESS for ELLs 2.0, except for Dion, who took the Alternate ACCESS proficiency assessment for ELs with significant cognitive disabilities. On the ACCESS for ELLs 2.0, the proficiency bands are as follows: Entering (1.0–1.9), Emerging (2.0–2.9), Developing (3.0–3.9), Expanding (4.0–4.9), Bridging (5.0–5.9), and Reaching (6.0). LD: Learning Disability, SLI: Speech or Language Impairment, ADHD: Attention Deficit Hyperactivity Disorder.

3.1 Data collection

This multiple case study included the following ethnographic data sources: classroom observations, student and educator interviews, and school artifacts. During the 74 observations we conducted, the first author shadowed each of the ELs with disabilities for two school days. The observations focused on ELs' learning environments, specifically their academic classes as well as special education and ELD services, with each observation lasting between 45 to 52 minutes. We also conducted 53 semi-structured interviews with the following participants: ELs with disabilities; district and school administrators; and each EL's school counselor, ELD teacher, special education teacher, and one general education teacher. While educators were interviewed once, we conducted interviews with the ELs with disabilities twice – once to inquire about the students' academic histories and to understand their backgrounds and then a second interview to understand the students' perceptions of their L2 proficiency, academic abilities, and educational experiences as well as to probe the occurrences of the classroom observations. We also collected artifacts from each student's ELD records (e.g., L1 backgrounds, English proficiency scores), special education records (e.g., referral dates, evaluation scores, and Individualized Education Programs), as well as demographic information, school enrollment history, class schedules, and academic grades.

3.2 Data analysis

We analyzed the data through a hybrid inductive–deductive coding approach (Fereday and Muir-Cochane 2006), whereby inductive codes in the data were mapped on to broader codes relating to the theoretical framework. Both authors independently conducted a first round of coding, using open codes that emerged from the dataset itself (Saldaña 2021). For the observation data, in particular, open codes focused on the quality of the L2 input, output, and interaction in the learning environment. Specifically, we used the Sheltered Instruction Observation Protocol (SIOP; Echevarría et al. 2016), a framework of evidence-based practices for supporting L2 development during content learning, to inform our codes. Following this, we assessed our intercoder reliability, with the aim of achieving at least 95% agreement for each code, as recommended in the literature (Campbell et al. 2013). Jointly, we conducted a second round of coding, employing axial coding, whereby we grouped initial codes into broader codes (Saldaña 2021) and then connected them to the theoretical framework.

4 Findings

The data analysis indicated that the ELs with disabilities had a history of fluctuating L2 English proficiency over the course of their schooling. Educators at the schools attributed these fluctuations to the students' internal IDs, namely to their disabilities. Yet, the observation data illuminated the ways in which external IDs in the learning environments inhibited the SLA of ELs with disabilities. Ultimately, by focusing on internal IDs as the sole contributor for the variable L2 proficiency of ELs with disabilities and simultaneously ignoring external IDs, we argue educators' mindset resembled deficit thinking.

4.1 Fluctuating L2 proficiency

According to school district records, all of the participating students were identified as ELs in kindergarten and thus, they had been receiving ELD services for six to eight years without reaching standards for English proficiency. Across their schooling, their L2 proficiency, in fact, fluctuated: ELs with disabilities had increasing English proficiency scores from kindergarten through third grade but either plateauing or decreasing scores in subsequent grades (see Table 2). It is worth noting that the English proficiency of ELs in the U.S. is evaluated annually through standardized assessments. The WIDA ACCESS for ELLs 2.0 is a standardized English proficiency assessment utilized in 35 of the 50 states in K-12 schools (WIDA 2021). On the ACCESS for ELLs 2.0, the proficiency bands are as follows: Entering (1.0–1.9), Emerging (2.0–2.9), Developing (3.0–3.9), Expanding (4.0–4.9), Bridging (5.0–5.9), and Reaching (6.0). The district data revealed that in first grade, all ELs with disabilities' English proficiency scores fell between 2.3 to 3.9 based on a 6-point scale. However, five of the ELs with disabilities had a decrease in their WIDA ACCESS scores from first to second grade (range 2.1 to 3.7). With the exception of one student, the WIDA ACCESS scores from all the ELs trended upward from second to third grade – a juncture when seven of the students, in fact, scored a 4.0 or higher. In fourth grade, five of the ELs with disabilities' scores peaked. Of the remaining six students, five achieved their highest WIDA ACCESS score in sixth grade, and just one student in seventh. In the most recent school year, however, seven of the 11 ELs with disabilities' scores dropped, which was likely a result of the change in assessment's format. The English proficiency scores of Monica (Grade 6), Amar (Grade 7), and Miguel (Grade 8) were representative of this broader pattern among participants (see Figure 1). As we will explore next, with this downward, or at best, plateauing L2 proficiency trend, educators attributed the students' internal IDs, primarily their disabilities, as the reason for their inability to meet the standards for English proficiency.

Table 2: Annual English proficiency score by grade.

Student	Grade						
	1	2	3	4	5	6	7
Maria Elena	2.7	2.5	3.3	P2	3.1	3.6	2.8
Miguel	2.8	2.5	4.3	3.7	4.7	4.0	3.1
Camila		3.3			4.4	3.6	4.0
Jud	3.3	3.1	4.0	4.4	4.4	4.0	2.5
Dimitrios	2.9	3.1	3.0	2.8	3.6	2.9	
Amar	2.9	3.2	4.7	3.9	4.4	4.0	
Gabriel	3.7	4.3	4.8	4.0	4.5		
Monica	3.2	3.5	4.9	4.4	4.3		
Imani	2.6	3.2	5.2	3.1	3.2		
Mateo	2.9	3.0	4.8	3.3	3.8		
Dion	2.4	2.1	2.5	P2	P1		

Note. Grey squares denote the students' peak English proficiency score. The solid line indicates the year in which the WIDA ACCESS underwent content and format changes. Camila has missing scores because she moved in and out of the school district. The P1 and P2 scores for Maria Elena and Dion indicate that they took the Alternate ACCESS for ELLs with significant cognitive disabilities.

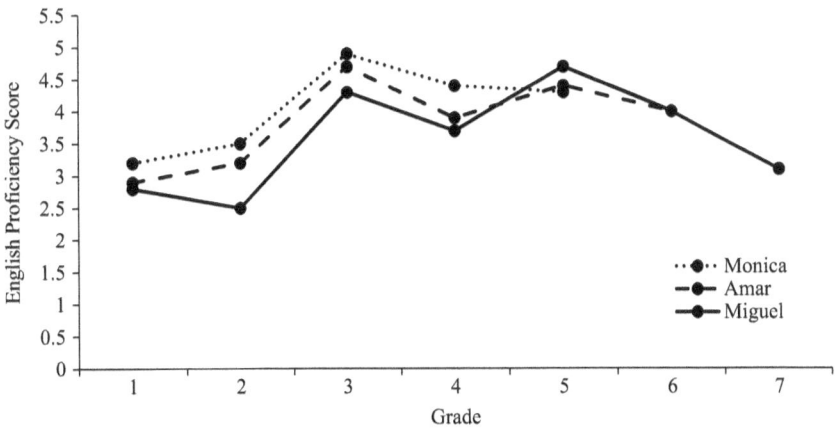

Figure 1: L2 English proficiency trends over time.

4.2 Internal IDs: "The learning disability is gonna be there"

Throughout the study, educators predominantly characterized both the bilingual aptitude of ELs with disabilities as limited, reasoning that the students' disabilities were an internal ID that stunted their L1 and L2 attainment. In terms of L2 attainment, some educators identified the disabilities of ELs as the reason for their fluctuating English proficiency and thus their continued need for ELD services. For instance, Ms. Rider, an eighth-grade special education teacher, explained: "That would also make sense why they aren't making proficiency levels for ESOL,[3] because the learning disability is gonna be there through even their ESOL services" (Kangas 2020: 280). Her special education colleague, Ms. LaGreca also attributed the students' inability to meet the standards for English proficiency to their LDs, ultimately describing them as being caught in a reinforcing cycle wherein their LDs hindered their L2 learning which in turn constrained their ability to learn academic content. Summarizing her perspectives on the role of disability in inhibiting both academic and L2 learning, an eighth-grade counselor, said: "I think kids struggle more with that language development if they have a learning disability."

While some educators cited disability as an inhibitor to L2 proficiency more broadly, others reasoned that the ELs' disabilities constrained their proficiency more narrowly in the domains of reading and writing. Notably, all 11 ELs with disabilities in the study had LDs in reading. For example, Mrs. Kleinfeld, a special education teacher, said this of her students: "Like these kids on my caseload, at least, have a lot of trouble understanding the language when we're reading stories. The figurative language. And that goes back to, once again, their language not being their first language." An ELA teacher at the same school posited that ELs had underdeveloped academic vocabulary, which influenced their L2 writing, in particular. She opined about the ELs with disabilities in her class: "Their writing's going to suffer because of their lack of academic vocabulary or even just like um, the scope of the vocabulary that they can, like, word choice that they can use in writing. So it's limited" (Kangas 2020: 277). Adhering to Cummins' (1979) distinction between Basic Interpersonal Communication Skills (BICS) and Cognitive Academic Language Proficiency (CALP), the same teacher described the ELs with disabilities as being conversationally on par with English-proficient peers yet lacking academic vocabulary. ELD teacher Mr. Salvatino believed the LDs of ELs limited their ability to acquire academic L2 proficiency: "Their ability

---

3 *English for Speakers of Other Languages* (ESOL) was the term the district used for their ELD services.

to speak socially is up here but their ability to use it academically really, really diminishes as we go down and depending upon the situational use of academic language" (Kangas 2020: 277).

Extending beyond L2 English proficiency, some educators at the schools believed ELs with disabilities were so called *semilinguals* (Cummins 1979; Skutnabb-Kangas 1981), a much repudiated construct that describes individuals as lacking proficiency in both the L1 and L2. For example, the Special Education Director for the district said: "They don't have a language proficiency in either language" (Kangas 2020: 277). Likewise, a bilingual counselor, Mrs. Kenz, shared how the ELs' lack of L1 proficiency constrained their L2 proficiency: "Because the [L1] foundation is so weak, it is difficult to build up the English skills." A mathematics teacher elaborated on this perspective in characterizing the ELs with disabilities' foundation language skills as "missing." She explained: "They're missing bits and pieces here and there, so then they get into the higher-level thinking questions in, let's say, fifth, sixth, seventh, eighth grade, they don't have that basic structure" (Kangas 2020: 274).

Several educators attributed this perceived limited L1 proficiency to the students' families, citing that families did not provide ample exposure to the L1 nor emotional stability and support. The Special Education Director, for example, believed the home environments lacked exposure to the L1. She elaborated:

> But because of low language in the home, often, you know, parents are working . . . They've heard a lot less words in Spanish, so they're very low in their own language and then the second language is just like, they're just swimming in language.
>
> (Kangas 2020: 278)

In contrast, an ELD teacher at Parker identified the role parents can play in a child's academic and linguistic outcomes:

> I mean looking at the big picture, like a whole child, because okay, so let's say a student has a disability but has supportive parents at home. That student is not going to have the same outcome as a student who has a disability and a chaotic life at home.

Mr. Barret, a science teacher, similarly attributed student learning needs to a lack of familial support, stating: "You know, there's definitely more need. Socioeconomic need, mental health needs, behavioral needs, um just because a lot of the home supports aren't there." In addition, family supports were connected to one focal EL's work ethic, according to ELD teacher Mr. Salvatino: "His lack of motivation can be attributed to the fact that he's not truly supported at home, educationally."

Across the interview data, educators at the two schools positioned disability as a limiting internal ID for the ELs with disabilities, citing at times that these IDs were compounded by deficits in students' families; specifically, the LDs of the ELs were understood as the reasons for their fluctuating L2 proficiency and their perceived underdeveloped L1 proficiency.

4.3 External IDs: "A product of their own habitat"

While most educators identified internal IDs as limiting ELs' bilingual proficiency, student interview and observation data illuminated the role external IDs, particularly the learning environment played in shaping students' L2 attainment. ELs with disabilities in the two schools were grouped into what the educators in the district referred to as *inclusionary classrooms*, wherein students with disabilities would receive individualized supports for their disabilities while learning academic content. These classrooms were, in fact, dubiously named as they functioned as self-contained special education classrooms, in many instances almost exclusively serving students with disabilities. In fact, the Special Education Director referred to these inclusionary classrooms as a "de facto special ed ESOL class" (Kangas and Cook 2020: 2430). In these inclusionary classrooms, general education teachers and special education teachers worked side by side in supporting students with disabilities' learning. One mathematics teacher described the affordances of these cotaught classrooms: "It is a slightly smaller group and we also have additional support [special education] teachers . . . . This year we have a teacher's assistant that follows our section all day long" (Kangas and Cook 2020: 2437). Mrs. Stapleton, too, described how the inclusionary classrooms provided opportunity for the students to receive differentiated instruction for their academic needs across the school day through adapted lessons.

Despite the supports provided to ELs for their disabilities, the observation data indicated these learning environments were linguistically poor, offering limited opportunity for ELs with disabilities to develop their L2 proficiency. With higher levels of students with disabilities grouped into these classrooms, behavior management was at the forefront of most interactions between teachers and students. Throughout the study, educators minced no words in describing the behaviors in inclusionary classrooms, labeling them as "pretty tough," "appalling," and "combative" (Kangas and Cook 2020: 2434). Observation data illuminated the common behavioral incidents that detracted from academic instruction and rich L2 exposure. Incidents ran the gamut from minor disruptions, such as ongoing chatter and misuse of computers and phones, to more significant interruptions, such as verbal fights and knocking over desks. For instance, during one observation a guest speaker came to Dimitrios' class to share strategies with students on regulating their emotions and avoiding impulsive behavior. The guest speaker discussed a scenario for them to practice applying these self-regulation strategies, stating: "You're hanging out with friends. One of your friends offers you a cigarette. Your crush takes one and looks at you. Will you (a) take a cigarette, (b) say 'no thanks,' or (c) not sure?" The guest speaker's efforts ironically backfire, as described in the fieldnotes:

> Students are amused by this example and shout out different inappropriate responses. Dimitrios quietly raises his hand. So many students are yelling. The teachers asks Mr. Hanes [a paraprofessional] to take a student's crutches because they keep "falling" over as an intentional source of distraction . . . . One student provides a response that elicits "boo's" from the class. "Shhhhhhhh!" Dimitrios attempts to quiet his classmates.

As illustrated, attempts to manage students' behaviors became the primary focus of these classrooms. Some of the focal ELs with disabilities contributed to these disruptive learning environments; Gabriel, for instance, repeatedly "fell" out of his chair and would often rile up classmates with his goofy demeanor. On more than one occasion, focal ELs with disabilities were asked to leave the classroom because of their escalating behaviors. Although some of the behaviors of ELs with disabilities contributed to these learning environments, others, attempted to stay on track. Mateo, an EL with multiple LDs and ADHD, described how his classmates interrupted his learning, stating: "They're really cool. But sometimes they're noisy. But sometimes they're like, 'Shhh, be quiet. Trying to concentrate.'" Another focal student, Monica, admitted that her teachers cannot spend a lot of time on instruction because they dedicate a large portion of class to "correcting chit chat." When asked about her classroom, Imani described her classmates' behaviors as "rude," sharing about an incident where she excused herself from the classroom:

> And then I got frustrated, so I told [classmates] to shut up and then teacher was "Oh, don't say that." And then, um, and I tell her that they keep bothering me and she's not doing anything so I just kinda came out of her classroom.

Other students also worked to stay on task despite the interruptions, but similarly felt frustrated or distracted by classmates' behaviors. Across the study, however, only two educators intimated that the learning environments themselves perpetuated the behavioral issues that sidelined academic content and discussion. Following an observation, one of these educators said: "Unfortunately, the students are a product of their own habitat" (Kangas and Cook 2020: 2435).

The persistent emphasis on behavior management had a rippling effect on quality of the L2 learning environments. With frequent disruptions, teachers were hesitant to incorporate pair- or group-work into learning and thus ELs with disabilities primarily engaged in individual work. Throughout the observations

ELs with disabilities had limited opportunity to interact with and to produce the L2, as they, for example, worked individually on their personal computers – solving mathematics problems, catching up on missing homework, and typing in responses to comprehension questions as they listened to audio passages. The prevalence of independent work was such that during 74 observations of the study, there were only 10 individual instances of ELs with disabilities engaging in pair- or group-work. Using independent work as a strategy for controlling behavior, however, further limited the quality of the L2 environment for ELs with disabilities. One assistant principal recognized that rostering classrooms in this way exacerbated behavioral issues: "You put all those . . . Like all these kids together that need a lot and that they're gonna feed off of each other, y'know." He further explained that teachers apply the following logic to their instructional practices: "Like, well, they're lower section kids, so I can't do that activity. Because, to put them in groups, they're not gonna be able to handle it." A focal student, Maria Elena, was aware that the behaviors in her class resulted in limited opportunity for group work, describing what happens: "Because we pick our friends." She explained further "And that happens and then already it becomes a whole mess" (Kangas and Cook 2020: 2435). With such sparse opportunity interaction in the L2 and the prominence of behavior management discourse, the inclusionary classrooms highlight how external IDs can inhibit L2 attainment for ELs with disabilities.

5 Discussion

The data analysis indicated that collectively the ELs with disabilities had a history of plateauing and in many cases, decreasing L2 English proficiency throughout their years in elementary and middle school. Their L2 learning is reflective of a larger pattern in the United States whereby ELs with disabilities are less likely than their EL peers without disabilities to reach the established standards for English proficiency (Kieffer and Parker 2016; Sahakyan and Ryan 2018; Shin 2020; Slama et al. 2017; Umansky et al. 2017). In the study, educators explained this pattern by pointing to the LDs of ELs, reasoning that the cognitive abilities of the ELs limited both their L1 and L2 attainment. In doing so, they positioned disability ultimately as an internal ID – and one composed of deficits. Yet, the ELs with disabilities were placed in inclusionary classrooms that provided few affordances for acquiring an L2 as both classroom management discourse and individual work prevailed. As their placement in the inclusionary classrooms was a result of their LDs, in this sense, disability operated as an external ID.

These findings, we argue, resemble the contours of deficit thinking (Valencia 1997). In his theorization of deficit thinking, Valencia (1997) argued that the perceived internal deficits of minoritized students and even their families are located as the source for a range of problems, while external contributors, such as those in the classrooms and schools, are ignored. According to the educators at the schools, the fluctuating L2 English proficiency of the ELs with disabilities and their subsequent inability to meet *English proficient* status were a result of the internal cognitive deficits caused by their LDs, or in SLA terms, an internal ID. Recall how some of the educators, in fact, believe these internal deficits originated in the homes of ELs with disabilities, as parents failed to provide the necessary L1 input and even familial support for the children's L1 and L2 attainment. While honing in on explanations innate to the students and their families, educators overlooked external IDs – context-driven reasons for the L2 proficiency of the ELs with disabilities. Observation data revealed, however, the inclusionary classrooms functioned as an "ESL ghetto" (Valdés 2001: 145), as ELs with disabilities were isolated from peers without disabilities in linguistically poor learning environments.

There are several critical lessons that can be drawn from these findings. First, educators' presupposition that LDs were the cause of ELs' bilingual attainment indicates that the limited capacity theory of bilingualism (Paradis et al. 2021) still pervades. Their assumptions of the constraining effects of LDs in acquiring an L2, in particular, signal that improved teacher training on the intersection of L2 learning and disability is exigent. Critically, special education and ELD teachers alike understood the language aptitude of ELs with disabilities as one defined by deficits. Thus, those in teacher training programs – whether in language education or special education – should actively address the common yet unsubstantiated belief that bilingualism will overburden the cognitive abilities of children with disabilities.

Second and relatedly, the findings in many respects serve as a cautionary tale of the ways in which adhering to the limited capacity theory of bilingualism can blind educators to suboptimal conditions for L2 learning and more broadly, to the interplay between internal and external IDs. Scholars, in fact, have called attention to complex interactions between L2 learners' characteristics and their surrounding environments (DeKeyser 2012; Dörnyei 2009; Paradis 2011; Pfenninger 2017; Ushioda 2009). The findings of this study highlight these complexities: ELs with disabilities were placed in particular classrooms because of their learner characteristics – primarily as students with LDs – and these physical environments, in turn, contained conditions that hindered L2 English development. As a consequence, their prolonged L2 proficiency needs became a defining learner characteristic. Given this interplay, examining and improving the linguistic quality of the learning environments of child L2 learners with disabilities will be integral to their L2 proficiency. Teachers and administrators who oversee L2 learner education for their respective schools and districts should conduct systematic classroom observations to evaluate the linguistic quality of the learning environments of child L2 learners with disabilities.

Despite the implications of the study, there are two methodological limitations that constrained our data analysis. First, the school district records did not include information about the socioeconomic status of the focal ELs with disabilities. Second, we did not have access to the racial demographics of all the students in inclusionary classrooms. Thus, in our analysis, we were unable to account for race and socioeconomic status in understanding external IDs in the learning environments of ELs with disabilities. Nevertheless, the study was conducted in the United States K–12 system – which historically organizes learning through labeling and sorting students into classrooms according to their learner characteristics (see Lipsky 2010; Oaks 2005; Valencia 2010) – thus, the findings may be relevant to other western contexts in which similar organizational structures are employed. Yet, additional research on child L2 learners with disabilities is needed to further interrogate the interplay between internal and external IDs particularly in schools contexts. Understanding whether in other schools contexts the learning environments of L2 learners with disabilities similarly structure opportunities for L2 development will be critical for contextualizing their L2 attainment and for countering assumptions about their cognitive capabilities.

Notes

This chapter incorporated elements from the following published journal articles:

Kangas, Sara E. N. 2020. Counternarratives of English learners with disabilities. *Bilingual Research Journal*, **43**(3). 267–285. https://doi.org/10.1080/15235882.2020.1807424.

Kangas, Sara E. N. & Megan Cook. 2020. Academic tracking of English learners with disabilities in middle school. *American Educational Research Journal*, **57**(6). 2415–2449. https://doi.org/10.3102/0002831220915702

References

Bialystok, Ellen. 2001. *Bilingualism in development: Language, literacy and cognition*. Cambridge, United Kingdom: Cambridge University Press.

Block, David. 2003. *The social turn in second language acquisition*. Washington, D.C.: Georgetown University Press.

Campbell, John. L., Charles Quincy, Jordan Osserman & Ove K. Pedersen. 2013. Coding in-depth semistructured interviews: Problems of unitization and intercoder reliability and agreement. *Sociological Methods & Research* **42**(3). 294–320. https://doi.org/10.1177/0049124113500475

Cheatham, G. A. & Juliet E. Hart Barnett. 2017. Overcoming common misunderstandings about students with disabilities who are English language learners. *Intervention in School and Clinic* **53**(1). 58–63. https://doi.org/10.1177/1053451216644819

Cioè-Peña, María. 2020. Raciolinguistics and the education of emergent bilinguals labeled as disabled. *The Urban Review* **53**. 1–27. https://doi.org/10.1007/s11256-020-00581-z

Cummins, James. 1979. Linguistic interdependence and the educational development of bilingual children. *Review of Educational Research* **49**(2). 222–251. https://doi.org/10.3102/00346543049002222

Dabach, Dafney B. 2014. "I am not a shelter!": Stigma and social boundaries in teachers' accounts of students' experience in separate "sheltered" English learner classrooms. *Journal of Education for Students Placed at Risk (JESPAR)* **19**(2). 98–124. https://doi.org/10.1080/10824669.2014.954044

DeKeyser, Robert. 2012. Interactions between individual differences, treatments, and structures in SLA. *Language Learning* **62**(2). 189–200. https://doi.org/10.1111/j.1467-9922.2012.00712.x

Dörnyei, Zoltán. 2009. Individual differences: Interplay of learner characteristics and learning environment. *Language Learning* **59**(1). 230–248. https://doi.org/10.1111/j.1467-9922.2009.00542.x

Dörnyei, Zoltán & Stephen Ryan. 2015. *The psychology of the language learner: Revisited*. New York: Routledge.

Echevarría, Jana, MaryEllen Vogt & Deborah J. Short. 2016. *Making content comprehensible for English learners: The SIOP model*, 5th edn. New York, NY: Pearson.

Ehrman, Madeline. E., Betty Lou Leaver & Rebecca L. Oxford. 2003. A brief overview of individual differences in second language learning. *System* **31**(3). 313–330. https://doi.org/10.1016/S0346-251X(03)00045-9

Fereday, Jennifer & Eimear Muir-Cochrane. 2006. Demonstrating rigor using thematic analysis: A hybrid approach of inductive and deductive coding and theme development. *International Journal of Qualitative Methods* **5**(1). 80–92. https://doi.org/10.1177/160940690600500107

Firth, Alan & Johannes Wagner. 2007. Second/foreign language learning as a social accomplishment: Elaborations on a reconceptualized SLA. *The Modern Language Journal* **91**. 800–819. https://doi.org/10.1111/j.1540-4781.2007.00670.x

Flores, Nelson. 2020. From academic language to language architecture: Challenging raciolinguistic ideologies in research and practice. *Theory into Practice* **59**(1). 22–31. https://doi.org/10.1080/00405841.2019.1665411

Gagné, Nathalie & Susan Parks. 2013. Cooperative learning tasks in a Grade 6 intensive ESL class: Role of scaffolding. *Language Teaching Research* **17**(2). 188–209. https://doi.org/10.1177/1362168812460818

García Mayo, María del Pilar & Amparo Lázaro Ibarrola 2015. Do children negotiate for meaning in task-based interaction? Evidence from CLIL and EFL settings. *System* **54**. 40–54. https://doi.org/10.1016/j.system.2014.12.001

Genesee, Fred. 2015. Myths about early childhood bilingualism. *Canadian Psychology/Psychologie Canadienne* **56**(1). 6–15. https://doi.org/10.1037/a0038599

Gonzalez-Barrero, Ana Maria & Aparna Nadig. 2018. Bilingual children with autism spectrum disorders: The impact of amount of language exposure on vocabulary and morphological skills at school age. *Autism Research* **11**(12). 1667–1678. https://doi.org/10.1002/aur.2023

Gregg, Kevin R. 2006. Taking a social turn for the worse: The language socialization paradigm for second language acquisition. *Second Language Research* **22**(4). 413–442. https://doi.org/10.1191/0267658306sr274oa

Hakuta, Kenji. 1986. *Mirror of language: The debate on bilingualism*. New York, NY: Basic Books.

Harklau, Linda. 1994. ESL versus mainstream classes: Contrasting L2 learning environments. *TESOL Quarterly* **28**(2). 241–272. https://doi.org/10.2307/3587433

Kangas, Sara E. N. 2014. When special education trumps ESL: An investigation of service delivery for ELLs with disabilities. *Critical Inquiry in Language Studies* **11**(4). 273–306. https://doi.org/10.1080/15427587.2014.968070

Kangas, Sara E. N. 2017. "That's where the rubber meets the road": The intersection of special education and bilingual education. *Teachers College Record* **119**(7). 1–36.

Kangas, Sara E. N. 2018. Breaking one law to uphold another: How schools provide services to English learners with disabilities. *TESOL Quarterly* **52**(4). 877–910. https://doi.org/10.1002/tesq.431

Kangas, Sara E. N. 2021. "Is it language or disability?": An ableist and monolingual filter for English learners with disabilities. *TESOL Quarterly* **55**(3). 673–683. https://doi.org/10.1002/tesq.3029

Kanno, Yasuko & Sara E. N. Kangas. 2014. "I'm not going to be, like, for the AP" English language learners' limited access to advanced college-preparatory courses in high school. *American Educational Research Journal* **51**(5). 848–878. https://doi.org/10.3102/0002831214544716

Kay-Raining Bird, Elizabeth, Patricia Cleave, Natacha Trudeau, Elin Thordardottir, Ann Sutton & Amy Thorpe. 2005. The language abilities of bilingual children with Down syndrome. *American Journal of Speech-language Pathology* **14**. 187–199. http://doi.org/10.1044/1058-0360(2005/019)

Kay-Raining Bird, Elizabeth, Erin Lamond & Jeanette Holden. 2012. Survey of bilingualism in autism spectrum disorders. *International Journal of Language & Communication Disorders* **47**(1). 52–64. http://doi.org/10.1111/j.1460-6984.2011.00071.x.

Kay-Raining Bird, Elizabeth, Fred Genesee & Ludo Verhoeven. 2016. Bilingualism in children with developmental disorders: A narrative review. *Journal of Communication Disorders* **63**. 1–14. https://doi.org/10.1016/j.jcomdis.2016.07.003.

Kieffer, Michael J. & Caroline E. Parker. 2016. *Patterns of English learner student reclassification in New York City public schools* (REL 2017–200). Washington, DC: U.S. Department of Education, Institute of Education Sciences, National Center for

Education Evaluation and Regional Assistance, Regional Educational Laboratory Northeast & Islands. http://ies.ed.gov/ncee/edlabs.

Lipsky, Michael 2010. *Street-level bureaucracy: Dilemmas of the individual in public service*, 2nd edn. New York, NY: Russell Sage Foundation.

MacSwan, Jeff. 2020. Academic English as standard language ideology: A renewed research agenda for asset-based language education. *Language Teaching Research* 24(1). 28–36. https://doi.org//107.171/1773/6123612618681881877777540

Maxwell, Joseph A. 2013. *Qualitative research design*, 3rd edn. Thousand Oaks, CA: Sage.

Mackey, Alison & Rita E. Silver. 2005. Interactional tasks and English L2 learning by immigrant children in Singapore. *System* 33(2). 239–260. https://doi.org/10.1016/j.system.2005.01.005

Oakes, Jeannie. 2005. *Keeping track: How schools structure inequality*, 2nd edn. New Haven, CT: Yale University Press.

Oliver, Rhonda & Agurtzane Azkarai. 2017. Review of child second language acquisition: Examining theories and research. *Annual Review of Applied Linguistics* 37. 1–15. https://doi.org/10.1017/S0267190517000058

Paradis, Johanne. 2007. Second language acquisition in childhood. In Erika Hoff & Marilyn Shatz (eds.), *Blackwell handbook of language development*, 387–405. Malden, MA: Blackwell Publishing.

Paradis, Johanne, Fred Genesee & Martha F. Crago. 2021. *Dual language development and disorders: A handbook on bilingualism and second language learning*, 3rd edn. Baltimore, MD: Brookes.

Paradis, Johanne. 2011. Individual differences in child English second language acquisition. *Linguistic Approaches to Bilingualism* 1(3). 213–237. https://doi.org/10.1075/lab.1.201par

Pfenninger, Simone E. 2017. Not so individual after all: An ecological approach to age as an individual difference variable in a classroom. *Studies in Second Language Learning and Teaching* 7(1). 19–46. https://doi.org/10.14746/ssllt.2017.7.1.2

Pinter, Annamaria. 2007. Some benefits of peer–peer interaction: 10-year-old children practising with a communication task. *Language Teaching Research* 11(2). 189–207. https://doi.org/10.1177/1362168807074604

Sahakyan, Narek & Sarah Ryan. 2018. *Long-term English learners across 15 WIDA states: A research brief* (WIDA Research Brief No. RB-2018-1). WIDA at the Wisconsin Center for Education Research.

Saldaña, Johnny. 2021. *The coding manual for qualitative researchers*, 4th edn. Los Angeles, CA: Sage.

Shin, Nami. 2020. Stuck in the middle: Examination of long-term English learners. *International Multilingual Research Journal* 14(3). 181–205. https://doi.org/10.1080/19313152.2019.1681614

Simon-Cereijido, Gabriela & Vera F. Gutiérrez-Clellen. 2013. Bilingual education for all: Latino dual language learners with language disabilities. *International Journal of Bilingual Education and Bilingualism* 17(2). 235–254. doi:10.1080/13670050.2013.866630

Skutnabb-Kangas, Tove. 1981. *Bilingualism or not: The education of minorities*. Clevedon, England: Multilingual Matters.

Slama, Rachel, Ayrin Molefe, Dean Gerdeman, Angelica Herrera, Iliana Brodziak de Los Reyes, Diane August & Linda Cavazos. 2017. Time to Proficiency for Hispanic English Learner Students in Texas. REL 2018-280. *Regional Educational Laboratory Southwest*.

Stake, Robert E. 2006. *Multiple case study analysis*. New York, NY: Guilford Press.

Thomas, Wayne P. & Virginia P. Collier. 2012. *Dual language education for a transformed world*. Albuquerque, NM: Dual Language Education of New Mexico – Fuente Press.

Umansky, Ilana M., Karen D. Thompson & Guadalupe Díaz. 2017. Using an ever-English learner framework to examine disproportionality in special education. *Exceptional Children* **84**(1). 76–96. https://doi.org/10.1177/0014402917707470

U.S. Department of Justice & U.S. Department of Education. 2015. *English learner (EL) dear colleague*. https://www2.ed.gov/about/offices/list/ocr/letters/colleague-el-201501.pdf

Ushioda, Ema. 2009. A person-in-context relational view of emergent motivation, self and identity. In Zoltán Dörnyei & Ema Ushioda (eds.), *Motivation, language identity and the L2 self*, 215–228. Bristol, United Kingdom: Multilingual Matters.

Valdés, Guadalupe. 2001. *Learning and not learning English: Latino students in American schools*. New York, NY: Teachers College Press.

Valencia, Richard R. 1997. *The evolution of deficit thinking: Educational thought and practice*. New York, NY: Routledge.

Valencia, Richard R. 2010. *Dismantling contemporary deficit thinking: Educational thought and practice*. New York, NY: Routledge.

WIDA. 2021. *WIDA Consortium*. https://wida.wisc.edu/memberships/consortium

Zehler, Annette M., Howard L. Fleischman, Paul J. Hopstock, Michelle L. Pendzick & Todd G. Stephenson. 2003. *Descriptive study of services to LEP students and LEP students with disabilities*. Washington, D.C.: Department of Education.

M. J. H. Van Koert, N. L. Leona, J. E. Rispens, J. Tijms,
M. W. Van der Molen, V. H. P. van Daal and P. Snellings

The role of memory in the acquisition of vocabulary and grammar in the first language and in English as a foreign language

Abstract: Previous studies showed that phonological short-term and working memory spans are related to vocabulary and grammar learning in children learning a second language. Typically, short-term storage, as measured by simple span tasks such as non-word repetition, are connected to vocabulary learning. Grammar learning is generally linked to the working memory system. This system is often tested by complex span tasks that require participants to process and store information simultaneously. Yet, few studies have investigated the role of both memory mechanisms in native and foreign vocabulary and grammar learning longitudinally. The current study determines whether phonological short-term and verbal working memory spans contribute differentially to the acquisition of vocabulary and grammar in Dutch as a first language (L1) and in English as a foreign language (EFL). The participants for this study are monolingual Dutch children (N = 138), in grades 4 and 5 (aged 9;0–11;0), learning EFL in the classroom. An L1 and an EFL non-word repetition task were used to measure phonological short-term memory and verbal working memory was measured with a backward digit span task. Receptive vocabulary and production of grammatical knowledge was measured in Dutch and in English, as well as receptive grammar in English. The data indicated that when the same children are longitudinally followed in both L1 and EFL, only past performance is important for L1 vocabulary learning. Phonological short-term memory does not contribute to L1 vocabulary. As expected, working memory span significantly predicts L1 grammar learning. For EFL vocabulary learning, past performance is most important; L1 vocabulary has a smaller but independent role and in line with previous research, phonological short-term memory also has an independent role. For both receptive and productive EFL grammar learning, contrary to expectations, working memory span did not play a role. In contrast, EFL phonological short-term memory had a small but independent role for receptive grammar learning. EFL vocabulary had a similar role for receptive and productive grammar, which was stronger than EFL phonological short-term memory for receptive grammar. However, past performance had the largest role

https://doi.org/10.1515/9783110743043-003

for both types of grammar learning. In sum, when looking at the initial stages of EFL in a formal setting, we only found a role for working memory span in L1 grammar but not in EFL. Phonological short-term memory only had a role in EFL vocabulary and receptive grammar learning, and was language specific. In all, the current data show that in addition to phonological short-term memory, past performance on vocabulary and grammar contributed significantly to vocabulary and grammar learning and that the role of vocabulary and phonological short-term memory and working memory span in grammar learning is language specific.

Keywords: EFL, early second language acquisition, phonological processing, vocabulary, grammar, working memory

1 Introduction

Verbal working memory can be divided into a domain specific short term storage component, also known as the phonological loop, and a domain general component that facilitates both processing and storing verbal information (Baddeley and Hitch 1974; Adams and Gathercole 2000). With regard to language learning most research has focused on the phonological loop, and many studies have also focused on the structure of working memory. The phonological loop represents phonological short-term memory for verbal information and the current study will determine its role in the development of vocabulary and grammar in children. A number of studies have focused on the role of phonological short-term memory in the L1 as a measure of the domain specific short term storage component of verbal working memory. Either studying its effect on vocabulary acquisition (Gathercole et al. 1992), on grammar (Boersma et al. 2018), or on both L1 vocabulary and grammar (Adams and Gathercole 2000). Other studies have focused on phonological short term memory in FL learning, either the effects on vocabulary learning (Cheung 1996; Masoura and Gathercole 2005; Messer et al. 2010), on FL grammar (O'Brien et al. 2006), or on both (Ellis and Sinclair 1996; Paradis 2011). Only few studies (Engel de Abreu and Gathercole 2012) focused on both phonological short-term memory and working memory span, the latter as a measure of the domain general component of verbal working memory. Engel de Abreu and Gathercole (2012) studied only effects on vocabulary, in both L1 and FL. Kormos and Sáfár (2008) studied effects on both vocabulary and grammar, but only in the FL.

In general, working memory span is associated with grammatical proficiency and phonological short-term memory is related to vocabulary knowledge.

However, some studies have also found vocabulary knowledge to be related to working memory span and grammatical proficiency to phonological short-term memory (Archibald and Gathercole 2006; Ellis and Sinclair 1996; Kormos and Sáfár 2008; Martin and Ellis 2012; O'Brien et al. 2006; Paradis 2011; Service and Kohonen 1995). The present study aims to determine whether individual differences in short-term memory and working memory span predict individual differences one year later in both receptive vocabulary knowledge and grammatical proficiency in the first language (L1) and in the initial stages of English as a foreign language (EFL).

1.1 Memory and vocabulary

There are many different ways to measure the span of the phonological loop storage, as it can be quantified by means of serial recall of (non-)words, letters or digits or by non-word repetition (NWR) (Archibald and Gathercole 2006; Crannell and Parrish 1957). Although many studies lump together NWR with other verbal short-term memory tasks (Archibald and Gathercole 2006; Engel de Abreu and Gathercole 2012; Kormos and Sáfár 2008; Paradis 2011; Verhagen and Leseman 2016), there are also studies that argue that they are not identical (O'Brien et al. 2006; Rispens and Baker 2012; Rispens and de Bree 2017). Verbal short-term memory represents phonological processing in the phonological loop. The longer the verbal material is that needs to be retained, the more difficult it is, because the memory traces fade so quickly in the phonological store. Besides, the articulatory rehearsal process is challenged by long verbal material (Baddeley 2003). For example, adults can typically recall a list of seven digits but remembering nine digits is already a more difficult task and retaining fifteen is highly unusual (Crannell and Parrish 1957). Hence, digit span reflects the nature of verbal short-term memory, namely temporary storage. NWR is apart from length of the non-word also susceptible to other factors, such as phonotactic frequency, syllable frequency and wordlikeness, i.e. how much does the non-word look like an existing word (Messer et al. 2010; O'Brien et al. 2006; Rispens and Baker 2012). In fact, Rispens and Baker (2012) found that phonological short-term memory and phonological representations contribute to NWR ability. Thus, there are long-term memory effects that trickle through in NWR (but note that simple span tasks like repetition of existing words are also influenced by long term memory representations, arguably because of chunking, see Jones (2012)). Both digit recall and NWR have been found to be related to vocabulary knowledge (Archibald and Gathercole 2006; Paradis 2011) but their separate contribution to vocabulary knowledge and grammatical performance has – to our knowledge – not been assessed in a sample of young FL learners in an instructed foreign language learning setting. NWR thus measures phonological short-term memory, but as it also depends on phonological processes, it is better described as a task that measures phonological processing, which involves short term memory, but also more long term knowledge.

NWR can be administered in the L1 and/or in the FL. Studies on children learning an FL have shown that they are better at repeating non-words in the language they speak best, underlining the relationship between NWR and language knowledge (Masoura and Gathercole 2005; Messer et al. 2010; Rispens and de Bree 2017). Previous studies that administered NWR in L1 found significant correlations between NWR and FL vocabulary knowledge (Engel de Abreu and Gathercole 2012; Kormos and Sáfár 2008). Prior research that included an NWR in the FL also found significant correlations between NWR and FL vocabulary knowledge (Cheung 1996; Service and Kohonen 1995). Since NWR reflects the storage of long-term phonological representations, it is likely that FL NWR is more tightly related to FL vocabulary than L1 NWR. To our knowledge, only one study, Masoura and Gathercole (2005), investigated the contributions of L1 NWR and FL NWR to FL vocabulary. In that study Greek children aged between 8;6 and 13;7 participated; they were learning English as an FL. The English vocabulary tests consisted of translation assignments, whereby English words had to be translated to Greek and vice versa. Although the focus of the study was on the relative contribution of phonological memory for participants with a large vocabulary and those with a small vocabulary, the correlations between English NWR and the English vocabulary tests are somewhat stronger than those between Greek NWR and English vocabulary tests. The current study aims to compare the relative contributions of L1 and FL NWR to investigate which of the two is a better predictor of FL vocabulary.

Several studies have found that the strength of the relationship between NWR and vocabulary diminishes as the size of the lexicon increases (Cheung 1996; Gathercole et al. 1992; Rispens and Baker 2012). These findings imply that phonological processing is central in the initial stages of vocabulary learning, but when the lexicon reaches a certain threshold, new words seem to be learned on the basis of existing long-term lexical knowledge rather than on the basis of short-term phonological storage. For example, the correlations between L1 NWR and L1 vocabulary knowledge were stronger at age 4 than at age 8 in Gathercole et al.'s (1992) study. Second language acquisition studies found that FL NWR correlated more strongly in learners with low foreign language proficiency than in those with high foreign language proficiency (Cheung 1996; Engel de Abreu and Gathercole 2012; Kormos and Sáfár 2008). The goal of the present study is to investigate the relative contributions of L1 and FL NWR in L1 vocabulary and FL vocabulary. The group of interest are Dutch ten-year-old children learning English as a foreign language. Based on the literature, we expect that FL NWR will contribute to FL vocabulary. However, the literature is less clear on whether L1 NWR also contributes to L1 vocabulary.

1.2 Memory and grammatical performance

Although NWR is typically related to vocabulary acquisition, some studies have also found an influence of NWR on grammatical performance (Archibald and Gathercole 2006; Ellis and Sinclair 1996; Kormos and Sáfár 2008; O'Brien et al. 2006; Paradis 2011; Service and Kohonen 1995). For instance, Service and Kohonen (1995) tested nine-year-old Finnish children by means of an English (as an FL) NWR. Three years later the same children had to complete several tests measuring their knowledge of English, including listening, reading, essay writing and vocabulary. The results showed that NWR was strongly correlated with all of the English tests. Later studies found differences between beginning and more advanced learners. For instance, Kormos and Sáfár (2008) tested Hungarian 16-year-olds on their L1 NWR and working memory span skills and also examined their English (as an FL) grammatical performance. They found that there was a difference between the beginning and the more advanced English language learners: whereas the beginning learners showed no effect of NWR, the more advanced learners did show a correlation between NWR and FL grammar scores. The interpretation of this finding is somewhat complicated, as the grammar scores came from a test which assessed lexical and grammatical knowledge in an integrated manner (Kormos and Sáfár 2008: 268). Kormos and Sáfár assumed that only the lexical retrieval skills differed between the more advanced students and that their grammatical processing skills were similar; this could then explain why an effect of NWR was found in their grammatical performance, as it actually reflected their lexical skills. Another example is the study by O'Brien et al. (2006) who argued that in the initial stages FL learners tend to focus on content words whilst skipping function words. They stated that meaning is more important for beginning FL learners and focusing on meaning consumes most of the working memory space. As FL learners become increasingly more proficient, lexical retrieval becomes easier, making it possible for learners to process words that do not carry meaning, such as function words and grammatical markers. O'Brien et al. (2006) found a relationship between L1 NWR and function words, i.e. grammatical performance, for the more advanced learners, for whom lexical access did not pose any difficulties. Although the present study does not differentiate between beginning and more advanced learners, the contribution of NWR to grammatical performance is assessed.

Grammatical performance is most often linked to the domain general component of working memory (Archibald and Gathercole 2006; Ellis and Sinclair 1996; Martin and Ellis 2012; Verhagen and Leseman 2016). It has been found that working memory-impaired children struggle with parsing and analysing linguistic constructions in their L1 (Marton and Schwartz 2003). Since working memory is linked to noticing and processing new information, it has been argued that working memory is a mechanism to detect new structures in an FL and extract rules from those structures. Grammar is exactly where new structures appear and various studies have found that working memory span influences grammatical performance. For example, Verhagen and Leseman (2016) compared monolingual Dutch children to Dutch-Turkish bilingual children, who had learned Dutch in a naturalistic setting, on their domain general working memory skills in relation to their grammar knowledge in Dutch. Working memory was measured with a backward digit recall task. The grammar task included production of morphologically complex items and sentence repetition. They found no differences between these two groups of 5-year-old children regarding the relationship between working memory and grammar knowledge. For both the monolinguals and the bilinguals, working memory predicted grammar, whereas short-term memory predicted vocabulary and grammar. Verhagen and Leseman (2016) concluded that the same memory mechanisms are employed in L1 and L2 children learning their L2 naturalistically. Another example is a study by Martin and Ellis (2012), who investigated university students implicitly learning an artificial language with intricate morphological rules. They found a robust relationship between vocabulary and grammar scores, suggesting a strong interdependence. They also found that there was a stronger relationship between working memory span and grammar than between short term memory and grammar, implying that the memory mechanisms employed for memorizing items, i.e. vocabulary, are different from abstracting patterns, i.e. grammar. The current study aims to investigate the contribution of working memory span to grammatical performance in both the L1 and in the FL.

Whereas verbal short-term memory and NWR are usually connected with vocabulary learning, working memory span is typically associated with grammar learning. However, the findings of previous studies are inconclusive: both vocabulary and grammar learning can be affected by working memory capacity and NWR skills. The participant's language proficiency level seems to play a role as well. The present study includes verbal short-term memory, NWR and working memory span to determine the effects on L1 vocabulary and grammar and FL vocabulary grammar. Since our study was part of a longitudinal project, all of the predictors were measured a year prior to the outcome measures. To control for past performance, the past value of the outcome variable of interest was also entered into the analyses. Thus we could determine whether the memory measures had any effect on top of past vocabulary and grammatical performance in the L1 and in the FL.

2 The current study

The main research question of the present study was whether phonological short term memory as measured with NWR tasks and domain general working memory as measured with a working memory span task contribute to vocabulary and grammar performance in Dutch (L1) and English as a foreign language (EFL) a year later. We asked two specific research questions:
1. Is the relative contribution of NWR measured in grade 4 taking into account vocabulary performance a year prior significant for vocabulary knowledge measured in grade 5?
2. Is the relative contribution of working memory span measured in grade 4 taking into account grammatical performance a year prior significant for the grammatical performance displayed in grade 5?

We hypothesised that NWR is correlated with and predicts receptive vocabulary knowledge, while working memory span is correlated with and predicts grammatical proficiency. NWR measures the capacity to store verbal information and gives an indication of the strength of long-term phonological representations. In addition, previous research indicated strong connections between phonological processing and FL vocabulary learning. Working memory span measures the ability to process verbal information while it is being stored. It is involved when learners have to notice and process linguistic structures; hence, its importance for grammar learning. Grammar learning is a complex process whereby individual items need to be memorized and the relationships between those items need to be recognized. The first step in the current study was to check whether both predictions were verified for Dutch. The next step was to determine whether these different memory components were differentially employed for English vocabulary learning versus English grammar learning, too.

3 Method

3.1 Participants

Two hundred and ninety-eight grade 4 pupils from seven primary schools in the Randstad area of the Netherlands took part in the first wave of data collection. Two hundred and eight of those were assessed a year later in the 5th grade. Parental permission was obtained for each participant. The study was approved by the Ethical Review Board of the university. The participating schools had different pupil populations regarding social-economic status based on their postal codes, and regarding the number of children with Dutch as an additional language based on the answers the participants gave in the language background questionnaires. These seven schools formed a representative sample of the primary school population in the Netherlands. Four of the seven schools offered English language lessons before grade 4, but no differences on the crucial measures were found between the participants who had received English language lessons and those who had not.[1] In the present study, the data from dyslexic children ($N = 16$) were excluded, as were the data from children who had a mother tongue other than Dutch ($N = 123$). Some pupils did not complete all tasks in this study and those data were excluded too ($N = 7$). Finally, some pupils changed to another school between grade 4 and grade 5 or their permission was withdrawn; therefore, they did not participate in the second round of data collection. Those data were also excluded ($N = 6$). Hence, the total number of participants was 138 pupils. There were 69 male and 69 female participants. The mean age of the participants was 9 years and 10 months in grade 4 and 10 years and 10 months in grade 5.

3.2 Instruments

All tasks were administered on a tablet, rather than the usual paper and pencil set-up (see Procedure).

---

[1] English as a foreign language is a compulsory subject from grade 5 (ages 10–11 years) onwards in the Netherlands (Toorenburg and van Oostdam 2002). However, primary schools may decide to offer English language lessons from an earlier grade onwards. Of the current 138 participants, 99 pupils received English lessons at school and 39 pupils did not in grade 4. All of the participants received English lessons at school in grade 5. No significant differences were found on the tasks in this study between the pupils who had received English lessons at schools and those who had not.

Non-verbal intelligence. The measure of the non-verbal intelligence was the RAVEN Standard Progressive Matrices (RAVEN-NL SPM, Dutch adaptation by Harcourt Assessment 2006). The RAVEN consists of five blocks, each containing 12 items (N_{RAVEN} = 60). Each item consists of a geometric pattern with one piece missing. Participants have to discover the principles, relationships and rules between the patterns and decide which of six given pieces is the missing one. A test-retest reliability of .88 was reported for the test (Raven 2003). This task was used to measure participants' logical reasoning skills. Participants had 30 minutes to complete the test (Hamel and Schmittman 2006), instead of an unlimited test situation.

Verbal short-term memory. The measure of verbal short-term memory was the digit span forwards from the Wechsler Intelligence Scale for Children (WISC-III-NL, Dutch adaptation by Kort et al. 2005). In the digit span forward, lists of increasing length are presented. Two of each length (2–8). Each digit occurs only once in a list. The lists were pre-recorded by a female native speaker of Dutch. Participants were asked to recall the lists in correct serial order. The test started with a list of two digits and had a maximum of eight digits. At each length two lists were presented separately. Testing was finished when a participant failed to recall both lists of the same length correctly. Each correctly recalled list was awarded with one point.

NWR. There were two measures of non-word repetition: L1 non-word repetition and L2 non-word repetition. The Dutch (L1) non-word repetition (Rispens and Baker 2012) consisted of three trials and 22 items. The non-words were based on Dutch phonotactics. Item length varied between three and five syllables. All syllables had to be repeated correctly for a point to be awarded. The non-words were pre-recorded by a female native speaker of Dutch. The English (FL) non-word repetition was from the Comprehensive Test of Phonological Processing – Second Edition (CTOPP-2, Wagner et al. 2013). It consisted of three trials and 18 items. The non-words were based on English phonotactics. Item length varied between one and six syllables. The items increased in difficulty. All syllables had to be repeated correctly for a point to be awarded. The non-words were pre-recorded by a female native speaker of American English.[2]

Working memory span. The measure of working memory span was the digit span backwards from the Wechsler Intelligence Scale for Children (WISC-III-NL, Dutch adaptation by Kort et al. 2005). It is identical to the digit span

---

[2] The non-word repetition tasks were rated by an independent rater after the tests were administered.

forwards, except that the participant is required to recall the sequence of spoken digits in reverse order and that there is a maximum of seven digits. A trial item is given in order to ensure the participant understands the concept of reverse recall.

L1 vocabulary. The measure of L1 vocabulary was the Peabody Picture Vocabulary Test, Third edition (PPVT-III-NL, Dunn and Dunn 1997; Dutch translation by Schlichting 2005). The test provides an estimate of receptive vocabulary for standard Dutch. Participants saw four yellow and blue coloured pictures and heard a sound file containing the target word that was played automatically. The sound file was recorded by a female native speaker of Dutch. Participants had to select the correct picture, out of four pictures, upon hearing the target word. If they did not respond within five seconds, they received a warning message saying *select a picture*. This test was administered in class, all of the participants completed sets 7 up and including 11 in grade 4 ($N_{PPVT-NLgr4}$ = 59) and sets 8 up and including 12 in grade 5 ($N_{PPVT-NLgr5}$ = 59), regardless of how many mistakes they made in a set.[3] These sets were selected, as they were deemed appropriate for these age groups, whereas normally the starting set is adjusted for each individual.

L1 sentence assembly. L1 sentence production was examined by using the task Sentence Assembly from the Clinical Evaluation of Language Fundamentals (CELF-4-NL, Wiig, Semel and Secord 2003; Dutch adaptation by Kort, Schittekatte and Compaan 2010). There were two trial items and 13 exercises ($N_{CELF-ZS}$ = 13). This test was administered to assess the participants' ability to formulate grammatically acceptable and semantically meaningful sentences by manipulating and transforming given words and word groups. This task was used to assess L1 grammar knowledge in previous studies (Justice et al. 2010; Rescorla 2002; Weber-Fox and Neville 1996). Participants saw word groups on the screen of their tablet and had to type in two grammatically correct sentences for each item. If both sentences were correct, the participant received one point for that item. Secondly, since the CELF-manual allowed very few sentences to count as correct, we listed all the grammatically correct and semantically meaningful versions of the sentences and manually judged those to be correct. Typos, punctuation and spelling errors were ignored.

---

3 Originally there were 60 items in sets 7–11 of the PPVT-III-NL and all of these items were administered. However, since one item (*groente* 'vegetable') was also used in the English version of the PPVT, it was excluded from the analysis. That item did not appear in sets 8–12; yet, another item (*globe* 'globe') was also used in the English version of the PPVT. Therefore, it was excluded from the analysis.

FL vocabulary. The measure of English (FL) vocabulary was the Peabody Picture Vocabulary Test, Fourth edition (PPVT-4, Dunn and Dunn 2007). The test measures receptive vocabulary knowledge. Participants were presented with four coloured pictures and heard a sound file containing the target word that was played automatically. The sound file was recorded by a female native speaker of British English. Participants had to select the correct picture, out of four pictures, upon hearing the target word. If they did not respond within five seconds, they received a warning message saying *select a picture.* They could play the sound file up to three times. A difference from standard administration was that all of the participants completed sets 1 up and including 7 in grade 4 ($N_{PPVT\text{-}ENgr4}$ = 61) and sets 2 up and including 8 in grade 5 ($N_{PPVT\text{-}ENgr5}$ = 58), regardless of how many mistakes they made in a set, because the test was administered in class.[4] These sets were selected, as they were deemed appropriate for these age groups.

FL oral comprehension. English (FL) oral grammar comprehension was examined by using the task Sentence Structure from the Clinical Evaluation of Language Fundamentals (CELF-4, Wiig, Semel and Secord 2003). There were three trial items and 26 test sentences ($N_{CELF\text{-}SS}$ = 26). The test was administered to assess the participants' ability to interpret spoken sentences and to select the pictures that illustrate referential meaning of the sentences. This test was used to assess English L1 grammar knowledge in previous studies (Justice et al. 2010; Rescorla 2002; Weber-Fox and Neville 1996). Participants were presented with four coloured pictures and heard a sound file containing the target sentence that was played automatically. The sound file was recorded by a female native speaker of British English. Participants had to select the correct picture, out of four pictures, upon hearing the target sentence.

FL morpho-syntax. Word Structure from the Clinical Evaluation of Language Fundamentals (CELF-4, Wiig, Semel and Secord 2003) was used to examine (English) FL grammar production. It was administered to measure the participants' ability to apply morphological rules to mark inflection and comparison

---

[4] Originally there were 84 items in sets 1–7 and sets 2–8 of the PPVT 4th edition and all of these items were administered. However, since two items (*vegetable* and *globe*) were also used in the Dutch version of the PPVT and since other items were deemed Dutch cognates (*ball, foot, banana, cup, bus, cookie, dancing, lamp, penguin, net, tunnel, envelope, calendar, panda, vest, cactus, uniform, gigantic, group, chef flamingo, hyena, river, timer, vase, harp, bloom, heart*), they were excluded from the analysis. The authors independently rated the cognates and then came to an agreement. Baird, Palacios and Kibler (2016: 448) indicate that "cognates [are] words that are semantically and phonologically or orthographically similar in two languages". In the present study, we considered English and Dutch words to be cognates, when a concept is very close in its pronunciation in the two languages (for example *ball – bal*).

and their ability to select and use appropriate pronouns to refer to people. This test was used to examine English L1 grammar knowledge in previous studies (Justice et al. 2010; Rescorla 2002; Weber-Fox and Neville 1996). There were 32 items in the original test, but we chose to simplify it, on the basis of a pilot study, by reducing the number of items to 12 ($N_{CELF\text{-}WS}$ = 12). There were two trial items. Participants saw the picture on a laptop screen. Then a sound file containing the target sentence was played. The sound file was recorded by a female native speaker of British English. Participants were asked to complete the target sentence in English. All of the instructions were in Dutch.

3.3 Procedure

All of the tests were part of a larger test battery in a three-year longitudinal study into the predictors of English language learning by Dutch primary school pupils. The test battery consisted of class sessions, in which participants worked by themselves in their classrooms, and individual sessions, in which a test administrator tested a participant individually in a separate room. In the larger test battery, there were five class sessions and six individual sessions in grade 4. Three of the class sessions contained Dutch (L1) language tests and the other two included English (FL) language tests. There were four class sessions and six individual sessions in grade 5. Two of the class sessions contained Dutch language tests and the other two included English language tests. Half of the schools did the Dutch language tests first and the other half did the English tests first. The order of the languages was counterbalanced, meaning that the schools that had started with the Dutch language tests in grade 4 began with the English tests in grade 5 and vice versa. During the class sessions, participants carried out the tests by themselves on a tablet; they wore headphones and a short video served as an instruction for each test. Each participant had a tablet (T550 Galaxy Tab A 9.7) to work on. The non-verbal intelligence test, the Dutch and English vocabulary tests, the Dutch sentence assembly and the English oral comprehension test were part of the classical sessions. All the class tests were converted to an online survey (www.qualtrics.com), so that the participants' answers were recorded and stored automatically and digitally. Each class session took about 45–60 minutes to complete. The language background test, the short-term memory tests, the working memory tests and the English (FL) morpho-syntax test were administered individually. Individual sessions took about 30 minutes to complete. The individual sessions were also counterbalanced, meaning that half of the schools started with English and the other half with Dutch and the order was changed in grade 5.

3.4 Data analysis

First, the participants' scores were inspected for outliers and normality. For all the tests, standardized measures for skewness and kurtosis did not exceed the value of 1.3, with the exception of the L1 vocabulary task in grade 4 (skewness = −0.9, kurtosis = 2.1) and the L1 sentence assembly task in grade 4 (skewness = −1.1, kurtosis = 2.6), on which a few participants obtained low scores. There were eight instances where the outliers were greater than three standard deviations below the mean. Because of these outliers, bootstrapping was used as a method to overcome the problems of normal distribution violations in some of the above measures.

The first step was to carry out Pearson r correlation analyses on all the tasks. After significant correlations were found, regression analyses were run. The hierarchical multiple regression analyses were built up step-wise in an identical manner, following theoretical considerations. In this hierarchical regression analysis predictors are entered in separate steps to determine which additional predictors improve the model once predictors in previous steps have been controlled for. The order of the predetermined steps was based on theories of FL learning. An automatic search for the best predictors does not allow for separate steps and therefore does not do justice to theoretical considerations. For example, by entering a past value of the dependent variable first we could control for previous competence in that skill. Also, Dutch primary school children learn their L1 before the FL and previous studies have shown the effect of the L1 on FL aptitude. By entering L1 predictors first we could control for L1 competence and determine the relative contribution of FL predictors. The predictors were only entered into the model when there was a significant ($p < .05$) correlation between the dependent variable and the predictor. First, the autoregressor was entered as a predictor into the model, meaning that a past value, i.e. the value in grade 4, of the variable of interest was used. As a second step, non-verbal intelligence was entered as a predictor into the model, so as to control for intelligence, but only if it correlated significantly with the dependent variable. Then, verbal short-term memory was added (if $p < .05$), as it plays a crucial role in vocabulary learning. The next model always included the L1 NWR but only if it correlated significantly with the dependent variable. To predict L1 grammar, L1 vocabulary was added in the fifth model. The L1 measures were added before the FL measures, because L1 competence is thought to have an effect on FL aptitude. For the FL dependent variables, FL NWR was added in the subsequent model, as this represented the ability to form long-term phonological representations, phonological processing and sublexical skills. Then, FL receptive vocabulary knowledge was added for the FL grammar dependent variables, as it indicated FL lexical knowledge. Finally, in all the analyses, working memory was added in the last model, as it was a measure of the ability to integrate linguistic information. To obtain robust results, all the regression analyses were bootstrapped and the 95% bias corrected and accelerated confidence intervals were reported.

4 Results

The mean scores of the 138 participants on the non-verbal intelligence test, on the memory tasks and on the Dutch (L1) and English (FL) measures are reported in Table 1. The non-verbal intelligence scores fell within the normal range. The verbal short-term memory score and the working memory score were normal for these age groups, as were the scores for NWR in L1 and FL. The mean scores on the L1 and FL vocabulary tests were quite similar in both grades; however, the L1 items were suitable for Dutch native speakers between the ages of 6;6 and 15;11, whereas the FL items were suitable for English native speakers between the ages of 2;6 and 9;0. Hence, the L1 vocabulary items were more

Table 1: The mean, standard deviation, reliability, range and number of items per task.

	Year	M	SD	α	Range	No. of items
Non-verbal intelligence	grade 4	38.5	6.9	.88[a]	22–53	60
Verbal short-term memory	grade 4	7.7	1.4	.85[a]	4–11	16
Working memory	grade 4	4.7	1.4	.85[a]	2–9	14
L1 NWR	grade 4	9.6	3.2	.64[b]	2–17	22
FL NWR	grade 4	5.2	2.2	.49[b]	1–11	18
L1 vocabulary	grade 4	40.0	5.9	.94[a]	13–51	59
L1 sentence assembly	grade 4	8.8	2.5	.70–.94[a]	0–13	13
FL vocabulary	grade 4	37.3	6.8	.80[b]	18–56	61
FL oral comprehension	grade 4	16.2	4.3	.75[b]	5–26	26
FL morpho-syntax	grade 4	3.7	2.8	.78[b]	0–11	12
L1 vocabulary	grade 5	38.1	6.9	.94[a]	14–54	59
L1 sentence assembly	grade 5	10.0	2.1	.70–.94[a]	3–13	13
FL vocabulary	grade 5	37.8	6.8	.82[b]	22–57	58
FL oral comprehension	grade 5	20.0	4.0	.79[b]	8–26	26
FL morpho-syntax	grade 5	6.9	2.8	.76[b]	0–12	12

Note. N = 138.
[a]Reliability values were taken from the manuals of the standardized tests.
[b]Reliability values were calculated on the current group of participants, as the tests were either not standardized or the reliability in the manual was based on native speaker participants.

difficult than the FL items. Furthermore, the vocabulary items that were tested in grade 5 were more difficult than those in grade 4. These two reasons explain why there was little differences between the mean scores on the L1 and FL vocabulary tests in grades 4 and 5. The mean scores for the L1 sentence assembly task in grades 4 and 5 show a difference: on average the participants were able to construct more correct, meaningful sentences in grade 5 than in grade 4. Finally, the participants scored on average around 57–77% correct on all the language measures.

A Pearson r correlation analysis was carried out to determine whether there was a relationship between the language measures and the memory measures. Table 2 reports the Pearson r correlation values for all the cognitive, L1 and FL measures.

Table 2 shows that there was no significant correlation between verbal short-term memory and L1 vocabulary. However, there was a moderate positive correlation between L1 NWR and L1 vocabulary in grades 4 and 5. Table 2 further shows that there was a moderate positive correlation between working memory and L1 sentence assembly meaning that participants who were relatively good at recalling digits in reverse serial order in grade 4, performed relatively well on the Dutch grammar task in grade 5.

With regard to the FL results, Table 2 shows that there was no correlation between verbal short-term memory and FL vocabulary, or working memory and the FL grammar tasks, nevertheless a moderate positive correlation was observed between FL NWR and FL vocabulary in grades 4 and 5. Both of these results indicate that participants who were better at repeating non-words in English in grade 4, also had a larger vocabulary in English in grade 5.

4.1 Memory and L1

Research question 1 asked whether NWR measured in grade 4 predicted L1 receptive vocabulary knowledge measured in grade 5. A hierarchical multiple regression analysis was run on the data including L1 vocabulary-grade 4, non-verbal intelligence and L1 NWR (predictors) and L1 vocabulary-grade 5 (dependent variable). Table 3 shows the output of the model that had the best fit to the data. Table A in the Appendix presents all of the regression models.

As can be seen in Table 2, L1 receptive vocabulary knowledge measured in grade 5 correlated significantly with L1 vocabulary measured in grade 4, non-verbal intelligence and L1 NWR. Hence, these were the predictors entered in the regression models. Model 1 in Table 3 shows that L1 receptive vocabulary

Table 2: Correlation matrix of the cognitive and L1 and FL language measures.

	1.	2.	3.	4.	5.	6.	7.	8.	9.	10.	11.	12.	13.	14.	15.
1. Non-verbal intelligence	–														
2. Verbal short-term memory	.13	–													
3. Working memory	.17*	.22**	–												
4. L1 NWR	.06	.27**	.16	–											
5. FL NWR	.22**	.26**	.08	.31**	–										
6. L1 vocabulary (grade 4)	.23**	.15	.09	.28**	.19*	–									
7. L1 vocabulary (grade 5)	.24**	.16	.10	.29**	.10	.60**	–								
8. L1 sentence assembly (grade 4)	.17*	.31**	.22**	.15	.09	.38**	.13	–							
9. L1 sentence assembly (grade 5)	.30**	.13	.26**	.01	.05	.18*	.09	.28**	–						
10. FL vocabulary (grade 4)	.16	.09	.16	.18*	.18*	.17*	.22**	.12	.17*	–					
11. FL vocabulary (grade 5)	.15	.03	.15	.23**	.28**	.30**	.26**	.18*	.19*	.78**	–				
12. FL oral comprehension (grade 4)	.17*	–.03	.11	.18*	.16	.18*	.20*	.11	.20*	.62**	.58**	–			
13. FL oral comprehension (grade 5)	.19*	.03	.15	.26**	.28**	.29**	.30**	.16	.36**	.64**	.69**	.67**	–		
14. FL morpho-syntax (grade 4)	.13	.05	.09	.32**	.30**	.31**	.31**	.17	.23**	.65**	.68**	.68**	.71**	–	
15. FL morpho-syntax (grade 5)	.23**	.09	.08	.28**	.22**	.28**	.37**	.12	.31**	.68**	.67**	.63**	.73**	.75**	–

Note. N = 138.
* p < .05, ** p < .01.

Table 3: Regression Model 1 of the L1 receptive vocabulary knowledge in grade 5.

	B	SE B	β	p
Model 1				
Constant	10.57 (−1.64, 20.73)	5.85		.103
L1 vocabulary (grade 4)	.69 (0.43, 0.99)	.15	.60	.001

Note. $N = 138$. $R^2 = .36$ for Model 1; $\Delta R^2 = .01$ for Model 2 ($p = .126$); $\Delta R^2 < .02$ for Model 3 ($p = .051$).

measured in grade 4 was a significant predictor of L1 receptive vocabulary knowledge measured in grade 5. In the next steps, non-verbal intelligence and L1 NWR were entered separately. None of these models (see Table A in the Appendix) proved to be a better fit; thus, Model 1 is the model we base our results on. Table 3 presents the output of the model that had the best fit to the data. About 36% of the variance of the performance on the L1 receptive vocabulary task in grade 5 was explained by the performance on the L1 vocabulary task in grade 4.

Research question 2 asked whether working memory span measured in grade 4 predicted L1 grammatical performance measured in grade 5. A hierarchical multiple regression analysis was run on the data including L1 sentence assembly – grade 4, non-verbal intelligence, verbal short-term memory, NWR, L1 vocabulary and working memory span (predictors) and L1 sentence assembly (dependent variable). Table B in the Appendix presents the different models of the predictors of L1 grammatical performance. Table 4 presents the output of the model that had the best fit to the data.

As can be seen in Table 2, L1 sentence assembly measured in grade 5 correlated significantly with L1 sentence assembly measured in grade 4, non-verbal intelligence, L1 vocabulary and working memory span. Hence, these were the predictors entered in the regression models. Working memory span was a significant predictor in Model 4, which can be seen in Table 4. Intelligence also remained a significant predictor although its influence became slightly smaller after including working memory span. When working memory span was added, L1 sentence assembly in grade 4 was no longer a significant predictor. About 17% of the variance of the performance on the L1 sentence assembly task in grade 5 was explained by the scores on L1 sentence assembly in grade 4, intelligence, L1 vocabulary and working memory span.

Table 4: Regression model of predictors measured in grade 4 of L1 sentence assembly measured in grade 5.

	B	SE B	β	p
Model 4				
Constant	4.16 (1.75, 6.86)	1.28		.003
L1 sentence assembly (grade 4)	0.15 (−0.01, 0.35)	0.09	.18	.094
Intelligence	0.07 (0.01, 0.12)	0.03	.23	.016
L1 vocabulary	0.02 (−0.05, 0.08)	0.03	.05	.624
Working memory span	0.26 (0.06, 0.46)	0.10	.18	.011

Note. $N = 138$. $R^2 = .08$ for Model 1; $\Delta R^2 = .07$ for Model 2 ($p = .002$); $\Delta R^2 < .01$ for Model 3 ($p = .636$); $\Delta R^2 = .03$ for Model 4 ($p = .031$).

4.2 Memory and FL

Second, we wanted to determine whether NWR and working memory span were differentially employed for FL (English) vocabulary learning versus English grammar learning. A hierarchical multiple regression analysis was run on the predictors that correlated significantly with the dependent variable. These included FL vocabulary – grade 4, L1 NWR, L1 vocabulary and FL NWR (predictors) and FL vocabulary – grade 5 (dependent variable). As explained in *Data Analysis*, the first model contained the autoregressor and the other predictors were added one by one in each subsequent model. Table C in the Appendix presents the different models of the predictors of FL receptive vocabulary knowledge. Table 5 presents the output of the model that had the best fit to the data.

About 65% of the variance of the performance on the FL receptive vocabulary task was explained by the scores on FL vocabulary in grade 4, L1 NWR, L1 vocabulary and FL NWR, with FL and L1 vocabulary in grade 4 and FL NWR significantly contributing to FL receptive vocabulary.

Research question 2 asked whether working memory measured in grade 4 predicted FL receptive grammatical performance measured in grade 5, taking into account grammatical performance in grade 4. A hierarchical multiple regression analysis was run on the predictors that correlated significantly with the dependent variable. These included FL oral comprehension – grade 4, non-verbal intelligence, L1 NWR, L1 vocabulary, FL NWR and FL vocabulary (predictors) and FL oral

Table 5: Regression model of predictors measured in grade 4 of FL receptive vocabulary knowledge measured in grade 5.

	B	SE B	β	p
Model 4				
Constant	1.42 (−4.24, 7.73)	2.97		.614
FL vocabulary (grade 4)	0.74 (0.64, 0.85)	0.06	.73	.001
L1 NWR	0.07 (−0.13, 0.28)	0.10	.03	.516
L1 vocabulary	0.16 (−0.02, 0.29)	0.08	.14	.039
FL NWR	0.35 (0.04, 0.68)	0.16	.11	.033

Note. $N = 138$. $R^2 = .61$ for Model 1; $\Delta R^2 < .01$ for Model 2 ($p = .071$); $\Delta R^2 = .02$ for Model 3 ($p = .006$); $\Delta R^2 = .01$ for Model 4 ($p = .042$).

comprehension – grade 5 (dependent variable). Table D in the Appendix presents the different models of the predictors of FL receptive grammatical performance. Table 6 presents the output of the model that had the best fit to the data.

About 56% of the variance of the performance on the FL oral comprehension in grade 5 was explained by the scores on FL oral comprehension – grade 4, intelligence, L1 NWR, L1 vocabulary, FL NWR and FL vocabulary, with FL oral comprehension (grade 4), FL NWR and FL vocabulary significantly contributing to FL oral comprehension.

A hierarchical multiple regression analysis was run in order to answer the question whether working memory span measured in grade 4 predicted FL productive grammatical performance measured in grade 5. Predictors that correlated significantly with the dependent variable were included in the model: FL morpho-syntax – grade 4, non-verbal intelligence, L1 NWR, L1 vocabulary, FL NWR and FL vocabulary (predictors) and FL morpho-syntax – grade 5 (dependent variable). Table E in the Appendix presents the different models of the predictors of FL morpho-syntax. Table 7 presents the output of the model that had the best fit to the data.

About 64% of the variance of the performance on the FL morpho-syntax was explained by the scores on FL morpho-syntax – grade 4, intelligence, L1 NWR, L1 vocabulary, FL NWR and FL vocabulary, with FL morpho-syntax in grade 4 and FL vocabulary being significant predictors.

Table 6: Regression model of predictors measured in grade 4 of FL oral comprehension measured in grade 5.

	B	SE B	β	p
Model 6				
Constant	1.32 (−1.85, 4.48)	1.66		.443
FL oral comprehension (grade 4)	0.39 (0.24, 0.55)	0.08	.41	.001
Intelligence	0.01 (−0.06, 0.09)	0.04	.02	.777
L1 NWR	0.08 (−0.09, 0.25)	0.08	.06	.318
L1 vocabulary	0.08 (−0.01, 0.16)	0.04	.12	.057
FL NWR	0.19 (0.00, 0.37)	0.09	.10	.038
FL vocabulary	0.19 (0.09, 0.29)	0.05	.33	.003

Note. $N = 138$. $R^2 = .45$ for Model 1; $\Delta R^2 = .01$ for Model 2 ($p = .192$); $\Delta R^2 = .02$ for Model 3 ($p = .028$); $\Delta R^2 = .02$ for Model 4 ($p = .046$); $\Delta R^2 = .01$ for Model 5 ($p = .070$); $\Delta R^2 = .06$ for Model 6 ($p < .001$).

5 Discussion

The aim of the present study was to determine whether phonological processing and working memory span in Dutch speaking pupils measured one year prior to the language measures predict receptive vocabulary knowledge and grammatical proficiency in Dutch (L1) and English (FL) in the initial stages of formal foreign language learning.

5.1 Memory and L1

It was hypothesised that Dutch receptive vocabulary would be predicted by NWR. Our results showed that Dutch receptive vocabulary knowledge in grade 5 correlated significantly with NWR and intelligence. This is in line with Gathercole et al. (1992), who also reported significant correlations between vocabulary, NWR and intelligence. We found that when Dutch vocabulary knowledge in grade 4 was entered as an autoregressor in the regression model, it proved to be the best predictor of receptive vocabulary knowledge in grade 5. Subsequent

Table 7: Regression model of predictors measured in grade 4 of FL morpho-syntax measured in grade 5.

	B	SE B	β	p
Model 6				
Constant	−2.50	1.68		.135
	(−5.58, 0.99)			
FL morpho-syntax (grade 4)	0.49	0.09	.50	.001
	(0.33, 0.68)			
Intelligence	0.04	0.03	.11	.093
	(−0.01, 0.09)			
L1 NWR	0.05	0.04	.05	.305
	(−0.04, 0.13)			
L1 vocabulary	0.02	0.03	.04	.502
	(−0.03, 0.08)			
FL NWR	−0.04	0.07	−.03	.570
	(−0.19, 0.09)			
FL vocabulary	0.13	0.03	.33	.001
	(0.06, 0.20)			

Note. $N = 138$. $R^2 = .55$ for Model 1; $\Delta R^2 = .02$ for Model 2 ($p = .020$); $\Delta R^2 < .01$ for Model 3 ($p = .479$); $\Delta R^2 < .01$ for Model 4 ($p = .679$); $\Delta R^2 < .01$ for Model 5 ($p = .504$); $\Delta R^2 = .06$ for Model 6 ($p < .001$).

models did not yield a better fit; hence, we found that vocabulary knowledge was the best predictor of future vocabulary knowledge. NWR did not contribute to the present lexical skills on top of the past lexical skills. This seems to be in line with previous findings as L1 phonological processing effects are typically less apparent when the lexicon has reached a certain size (Cheung 1996; Engel de Abreu and Gathercole 2012; Gathercole et al. 1992). The second expectation stated that Dutch grammatical proficiency (measured with sentence assembly) would be predicted by working memory span. Working memory span and intelligence correlated significantly with Dutch grammatical proficiency. The regression models showed that Dutch grammatical performance was predicted by working memory span and intelligence in the current study. Previous studies found a similar relationship between grammatical performance and working memory span (Archibald and Gathercole 2006; Ellis and Sinclair 1996; Martin and Ellis 2012; Verhagen and Leseman 2016). Thus, our first hypothesis was not confirmed, even though significant correlations were observed between NWR and vocabulary, and the second hypothesis was wholly confirmed, showing that in the L1 these memory components contribute differentially to word learning and grammar over a period of one year. These results show that sufficient working memory capacity is important for processing and creating linguistic structures, which is reflected in the performance of our grammatical task. Our longitudinal design shows that the associations between memory and language are long-term as the memory tasks were administered one year prior to the language measures.

5.2 Memory and FL

For English, it was also hypothesised that NWR would predict receptive vocabulary knowledge. Our results showed that English receptive vocabulary knowledge in grade 5 correlated significantly with NWR and with Dutch vocabulary. When English vocabulary knowledge in grade 4 was entered as an autoregressor in the regression model, it predicted English vocabulary knowledge in grade 5 along with English NWR and Dutch vocabulary as predictors. That NWR predicted English vocabulary knowledge is in line with previous research (Cheung 1996; Engel de Abreu and Gathercole 2012; Kormos and Sáfár 2008; Service and Kohonen 1995; Verhagen and Leseman 2016). Verbal short-term memory (measured with the forward digit span in Dutch) did not predict English vocabulary knowledge to the same degree as NWR, meaning that the two measures likely represent different stages during phonological processing. Whereas verbal short-term memory tasks reflect the capacity of the phonological loop (Baddeley 2003), NWR reflects the capacity of the phonological loop as well as the ability to retrieve and manipulate phonological representations stored in the mental lexicon (Rispens and Baker 2012). These phonological representations are the scaffolds of words. It holds that the more often those representations are encountered, the more firmly they are stored in the lexicon and the easier it is to recognise them. Hence, they can be stored more easily in the phonological loop. It also works the other way around: the more vocabulary knowledge there is, the easier it is to extract the representations from that knowledge and to expand the storage of long-term phonological representations. This also explains why verbal short-term memory is a better predictor of vocabulary than NWR in very young children, whose stored vocabulary knowledge containing phonological representations is limited, and why NWR is a better predictor of vocabulary in somewhat older children (Gathercole et al. 1992; Rispens and Baker 2012).

There are differences between the current study and the previous ones. First, our study contained an autoregressor, meaning that we controlled for past English vocabulary knowledge. This was possible since our study was part of a longitudinal project. We found that the pupils' prior English vocabulary knowledge was the only significant predictor and it accounted for a large part of the variance. Second, the current study included both an L1 and a FL NWR, so that the contribution of both NWRs could be compared. When Dutch NWR was added to the model, but English NWR was not yet added, the former significantly predicted English vocabulary knowledge. This is in line with Engel de Abreu and Gathercole (2012), who found that L1 NWR predicted L1 (Luxembourgish) and L2 (German) vocabulary. Interestingly, L1 NWR did not predict L3/FL (French) vocabulary in their study. They suggested that L1 NWR can only predict L2/FL vocabulary when the languages are phonotactically similar, such as German and Luxembourgish, thereby evoking Baddeley (2003) who stated that immediate recall of non-words is better when those non-words are phonotactically similar to the L1. Our results are in line with both Engel de Abreu and Gathercole (2012) and Baddeley (2003), as L1 NWR was related to FL vocabulary yet when FL NWR was taken into account, our results demonstrate that a language specific NWR is a better predictor of FL vocabulary than L1 NWR, because it taps the phonotactics of the target language. This is the case even though FL NWR in our sample was a less reliable measure. This means that beginning learners who have a greater capacity of the phonological loop and who have stored more long-term phonological representations in English, will be better at learning English vocabulary than their peers who have a smaller capacity and who have stored fewer representations. Third, our study included L1 vocabulary knowledge as a predictor, so that the contribution of more general lexical knowledge was taken into account. Previous research established that L1 vocabulary is an indicator of FL aptitude (e.g. Ganschow and Sparks 2001; Skehan and Ducroquet 1988; Sparks, Patton and Ganschow 2012). Our study thus corroborates that finding, as Dutch vocabulary knowledge indeed contributed to the performance of English vocabulary.

Secondly, it was hypothesised that working memory span would predict English grammatical proficiency, for both oral comprehension and morpho-syntax production. The results showed that working memory span did not significantly correlate with English grammatical proficiency. We thus do not have evidence to conclude that working memory span predicts grammatical proficiency in children learning English. Our null results are different from what previous studies obtained (Archibald and Gathercole 2006; Ellis and Sinclair 1996; Martin and Ellis 2012; Verhagen and Leseman 2016). Differences in tasks and methodology may be responsible for the differences in results. For example, the participants in Martin and Ellis' (2012) study were adults learning an artificial language and the participants in the study by Verhagen and Leseman (2016) were five-year-old Dutch monolingual and Dutch-Turkish bilingual children learning Dutch in a naturalistic setting. Our participants' English vocabulary knowledge predicted current English grammatical performance. Hence, it is likely that our participants used different resources than working memory span while they were performing the grammatical tasks. They might very well count on their English vocabulary and their phonological processing skills to retrieve the meaning of the words in the sentences in the oral comprehension task. Indeed, this is what is indicated by the outcome of the regression analysis: English receptive vocabulary and NWR significantly predicted performance on the receptive grammatical task. This could indicate that our participants used a more lexical approach to this task. Of course, it may also be the case that the relation between working memory span and grammar exists in this group, but appears only when working memory span is measured with a different task than the backward digit span.

An influence of NWR on grammatical proficiency has been found before (Archibald and Gathercole 2006; Ellis and Sinclair 1996; Kormos and Sáfár 2008; O'Brien et al. 2006; Paradis 2011; Service and Kohonen 1995). Both Kormos and Sáfár (2008) and O'Brien et al. (2006) suggest that the more advanced learners are also the more proficient ones, meaning that lexical retrieval is easier for them than for the less advanced learners. When less energy can be spent on lexical retrieval, more working memory space is available to process, for example, function words. When function words are processed, Kormos and Sáfár (2008) and O'Brien et al. (2006) found that NWR and grammatical performance were related in more advanced learners. The present study only included beginning learners, but the contribution of NWR to the oral comprehension task could reflect an advantage in grammatical processing. The question is then why we only see a contribution of NWR in the comprehension task and not in the production task. Our participants scored relatively lower on the production task than on the comprehension task (mean percentage correct = 57% vs. mean percentage correct = 77%). It could be that our participants had to pay more attention to lexical retrieval when producing sentences – and, hence, had no working memory space left to focus on grammatical markers – memory space they did have when comprehending sentences. Perhaps the production task was too challenging to see a direct effect of grammatical proficiency. This could be why we only see an effect of past performance on that task and of English vocabulary knowledge when predicting grammatical production.

Besides English receptive vocabulary knowledge for both grammatical tasks and NWR for the oral comprehension task, another significant predictor of our participants' grammatical proficiency was past performance on the tasks. Since past performance contributed significantly, it indicates that besides a lexical approach, these children use grammatical processing to understand these sentences.

6 Conclusion

Past performance on a task is the best predictor for present performance. In addition, we found that L1 phonological processing as measured by a non-word repetition task is correlated with vocabulary in the first language (L1) and vocabulary in a foreign language (FL). However, phonological processing only predicts vocabulary in a foreign language, and only when a language specific FL measure is used. It seems that phonological processing is more important for lexical learning in the initial stages of FL learning than it is for the L1 at a later stage. In the L1 working memory (WM) predicts grammatical proficiency, meaning that children use their WM to hold the information from the grammatical task available so that they can parse the linguistic structures and create meaningful sentences. However, WM does not predict FL grammatical proficiency a year later. Grammatical performance is predicted by past performance on the same task and by FL vocabulary. Only receptive grammatical performance is also predicted by phonological processing, as measured by a language specific non-word repetition task. Whilst beginning learners of an FL seem to activate their grammatical knowledge when faced with a grammatical task, as indicated by the contribution of past grammatical performance, they also seem to use a more lexical approach to these tasks than in their L1.

Appendix

Table A: Linear models of predictors in grade 4 of L1 receptive vocabulary knowledge in grade 5.

	b	SE B	β	p
Model 1				
Constant	10.57	5.85		.103
	(−1.64, 20.73)			
L1 vocabulary (grade 4)	0.69	0.15	.60	.001
	(0.43, 0.99)			
Model 2				
Constant	7.53	5.02		.155
	(−3.03, 16.58)			
L1 vocabulary (grade 4)	0.66	0.15	.57	.001
	(0.42, 0.98)			
Intelligence	0.11	0.09	.11	.236
	(−0.08, 0.27)			

Table A (continued)

	b	SE B	β	p
Model 3				
Constant	6.46 (−3.74, 15.08)	4.78		.201
L1 vocabulary (grade 4)	0.62 (0.35, 0.95)	0.16	.53	.001
Intelligence	0.11 (−0.08, 0.28)	0.09	.11	.237
L1 NWR	0.30 (0.01, 0.59)	0.15	.14	.052

Note. $N = 138$. $R^2 = .36$ for Model 1; $\Delta R^2 = .01$ for Model 2 ($p = .126$); $\Delta R^2 = .02$ for Model 3 ($p = .051$).

Table B: Linear models of predictors in grade 4 of L1 sentence assembly in grade 5.

	b	SE B	β	p
Model 1				
Constant	7.97 (6.08, 9.49)	0.86		.001
L1 sentence assembly (grade 4)	0.23 (0.08, 0.43)	0.09	.28	.013
Model 2				
Constant	5.25 (2.88, 7.58)	1.18		.001
L1 sentence assembly (grade 4)	0.20 (0.05, 0.38)	0.08	.23	.016
Intelligence	0.08 (0.02, 0.13)	0.03	.26	.009
Model 3				
Constant	4.86 (2.37, 7.40)	1.29		.001
L1 sentence assembly (grade 4)	0.19 (0.02, 0.39)	0.09	.22	.048
Intelligence	0.08 (0.02, 0.13)	0.03	.25	.011
L1 vocabulary	0.02 (−0.05, 0.07)	0.03	.04	.646

Table B (continued)

	b	SE B	β	p
Model 4				
Constant	4.16 (1.75, 6.86)	1.28		.003
L1 sentence assembly (grade 4)	0.15 (−0.01, 0.35)	0.09	.18	.094
Intelligence	0.07 (0.01, 0.12)	0.03	.23	.016
L1 vocabulary	0.02 (−0.05, 0.08)	0.03	.05	.624
Working memory span	0.26 (0.06, 0.46)	0.10	.18	.011

Note. $N = 138$. $R^2 = .08$ for Model 1; $\Delta R^2 = .07$ for Model 2 ($p = .002$); $\Delta R^2 < .01$ for Model 3 ($p = .636$); $\Delta R^2 = .03$ for Model 4 ($p = .031$).

Table C: Linear models of predictors measured in grade 4 of FL receptive vocabulary knowledge measured in grade 5.

	B	SE B	β	p
Model 1				
Constant	8.46 (4.19, 12.42)	2.10		.001
FL vocabulary (grade 4)	0.79 (0.68, 0.90)	0.05	.78	.001
Model 2				
Constant	7.12 (2.77, 11.10)	2.11		.002
FL vocabulary (grade 4)	0.77 (0.67, 0.88)	0.05	.77	.001
L1 NWR	0.21 (0.01, 0.41)	0.10	.10	.047
Model 3				
Constant	1.67 (−3.93, 7.89)	2.99		.559
FL vocabulary (grade 4)	0.75 (0.65, 0.86)	0.05	.75	.001
L1 NWR	0.13 (−0.08, 0.33)	0.10	.06	.196

Table C (continued)

	B	SE B	β	p
L1 vocabulary	0.17 (−0.00, 0.30)	0.08	.15	.026
Model 4				
Constant	1.42 (−4.24, 7.73)	2.97		.614
FL vocabulary (grade 4)	0.74 (0.64, 0.85)	0.06	.73	.001
L1 NWR	0.07 (−0.13, 0.28)	0.10	.03	.516
L1 vocabulary	0.16 (−0.02, 0.29)	0.08	.14	.039
FL NWR	0.35 (0.04, 0.68)	0.16	.11	.033

Note. $N = 138$. $R^2 = .61$ for Model 1; $\Delta R^2 < .01$ for Model 2 ($p = .071$); $\Delta R^2 = .02$ for Model 3 ($p = .006$); $\Delta R^2 = .01$ for Model 4 ($p = .042$).

Table D: Linear models of predictors measured in grade 4 of FL oral comprehension measured in grade 5.

	b	SE B	β	p
Model 1				
Constant	9.93 (7.95, 11.88)	1.02		.001
FL oral comprehension (grade 4)	0.63 (0.5, 0.74)	0.06	.67	.001
Model 2				
Constant	8.24 (5.29, 11.23)	1.51		.001
FL oral comprehension (grade 4)	0.61 (0.50, 0.73)	0.06	.65	.001
Intelligence	0.05 (−0.02, 0.12)	0.04	.09	.160
Model 3				
Constant	7.00 (3.77, 9.89)	1.51		.001
FL oral comprehension (grade 4)	0.59 (0.48, 0.71)	0.06	.63	.001

Table D (continued)

	b	SE B	β	p
Intelligence	0.05	0.04	.08	.190
	(−0.02, 0.12)			
L1 NWR	0.18	0.09	.14	.057
	(−0.01, 0.36)			
Model 4				
Constant	4.57	1.67		.008
	(1.24, 7.71)			
FL oral comprehension (grade 4)	0.58	0.06	.62	.001
	(0.46, 0.70)			
Intelligence	0.03	0.04	.05	.405
	(−0.04, 0.11)			
L1 NWR	0.14	0.09	.11	.144
	(−0.05, 0.31)			
L1 vocabulary	0.09	0.05	.13	.044
	(−0.00, 0.18)			
Model 5				
Constant	4.61	1.59		.006
	(1.51, 7.60)			
FL oral comprehension (grade 4)	0.57	0.06	.61	.001
	(0.46, 0.69)			
Intelligence	0.02	0.04	.03	.657
	(−0.05, 0.10)			
L1 NWR	0.10	0.09	.08	.285
	(−0.08, 0.27)			
L1 vocabulary	0.09	0.04	.13	.053
	(−0.01, 0.17)			
FL NWR	0.23	0.10	.12	.027
	(0.03, 0.42)			
Model 6				
Constant	1.32	1.66		.443
	(−1.85, 4.48)			
FL oral comprehension (grade 4)	0.39	0.08	.41	.001
	(0.24, 0.55)			
Intelligence	0.01	0.04	.02	.777
	(−0.06, 0.09)			
L1 NWR	0.08	0.08	.06	.318
	(−0.09, 0.25)			
L1 vocabulary	0.08	0.04	.12	.057
	(−0.01, 0.16)			

Table D (continued)

	b	SE B	β	p
FL NWR	0.19	0.09	.10	.038
	(0.00, 0.37)			
FL vocabulary	0.19	0.05	.33	.003
	(0.09, 0.29)			

Note. $N = 138$. $R^2 = .45$ for Model 1; $\Delta R^2 = .01$ for Model 2 ($p = .192$); $\Delta R^2 = .02$ for Model 3 ($p = .028$); $\Delta R^2 = .02$ for Model 4 ($p = .046$); $\Delta R^2 = .01$ for Model 5 ($p = .070$); $\Delta R^2 = .06$ for Model 6 ($p < .001$).

Table E: Linear models of predictors measured in grade 4 of FL morpho-syntax measured in grade 5.

	b	SE B	β	p
Model 1				
Constant	4.15	0.31		.001
	(3.55, 4.75)			
FL morpho-syntax (grade 4)	0.73	0.06	.75	.001
	(0.61, 0.85)			
Model 2				
Constant	2.15	0.98		.034
	(0.29, 4.10)			
FL morpho-syntax (grade 4)	0.72	0.06	.73	.001
	(0.59, 0.84)			
Intelligence	0.05	0.02	.13	.042
	(0.00, 0.10)			
Model 3				
Constant	1.86	1.05		.075
	(−0.10, 3.91)			
FL morpho-syntax (grade 4)	0.70	0.07	.71	.001
	(0.57, 0.84)			
Intelligence	0.05	0.02	.13	.041
	(0.00, 0.10)			
L1 NWR	0.04	0.05	.04	.446
	(−0.07, 0.12)			
Model 4				
Constant	1.52	1.43		.288
	(−1.27, 4.28)			

Table E (continued)

	b	SE B	β	p
FL morpho-syntax (grade 4)	0.70	0.07	.71	.001
	(0.56, 0.83)			
Intelligence	0.05	0.03	.13	.049
	(−0.00, 0.10)			
L1 NWR	0.03	0.05	.04	.488
	(−0.06, 0.12)			
L1 vocabulary	0.01	0.03	.03	.682
	(−0.04, 0.08)			
Model 5				
Constant	1.55	1.43		.287
	(−1.22, 4.36)			
FL morpho-syntax (grade 4)	0.71	0.07	.72	.001
	(0.57, 0.84)			
Intelligence	0.05	0.03	.14	.042
	(−0.00, 0.10)			
L1 NWR	0.04	0.05	.05	.433
	(−0.06, 0.14)			
L1 vocabulary	0.01	0.03	.03	.667
	(−0.05, 0.08)			
FL NWR	−0.05	0.08	−.04	.507
	(−0.22, 0.11)			
Model 6				
Constant	−2.50	1.68		.135
	(−5.58, 0.99)			
FL morpho-syntax (grade 4)	0.49	0.09	.50	.001
	(0.33, 0.68)			
Intelligence	0.04	0.03	.11	.093
	(−0.01, 0.09)			
L1 NWR	0.05	0.04	.05	.305
	(−0.04, 0.13)			
L1 vocabulary	0.02	0.03	.04	.502
	(−0.03, 0.08)			
FL NWR	−0.04	0.07	−.03	.570
	(−0.19, 0.09)			
FL vocabulary	0.13	0.03	.33	.001
	(0.06, 0.20)			

Note. $N = 138$. $R^2 = .55$ for Model 1; $\Delta R^2 = .02$ for Model 2 ($p = .020$); $\Delta R^2 < .01$ for Model 3 ($p = .479$); $\Delta R^2 < .01$ for Model 4 ($p = .679$); $\Delta R^2 < .01$ for Model 5 ($p = .504$); $\Delta R^2 = .06$ for Model 6 ($p < .001$).

References

Adams, A.-M., & Gathercole, S.E. 2000. Limitations in working memory: Implications for language development. *International Journal of Language & Communication Disorders* 35(1). 95–116. https://doi.org/10.1080/136828200247278

Archibald, L.M.D., & Gathercole, S.E. 2006. Research report. Short-term and working memory in specific language impairment. *International Journal of Language & Communication Disorders* 41(6). 675–693. https://doi.org/10.1080/13682820500442602

Baddeley, A.D. 2003. Working memory: Looking back and looking forward. *Nature* 4(10). 829–839. https://doi.org/10.1038/nrn1201

Baddeley, A.D., & Hitch, G. 1974. Working memory. In G. Bower (ed.), *The psychology of learning and motivation: Advances in research and theory*, 47–89. New York: Academic Press.

Baird, A.S., Palacios, N., & Kibler, A. 2016. The cognate and false cognate knowledge of young emergent bilinguals. *Language Learning* 66(2). 448–470. https://doi.org/10.1111/lang.12160

Boersma, T., Baker, A., Rispens, J., & Weerman, W. 2018. The effects of phonological skills and vocabulary on morphophonological processing. *First Language* 38(2). 147–174. https://doi.org/10.1177/0142723717725430

Cheung, H. 1996. Nonword span as a unique predictor of second-language vocabulary learning. *Developmental Psychology* 32(5). 867–873.

Crannell, C.W., & Parrish, J.M. 1957. A comparison of immediate memory span for digits, letters, and words. *The Journal of Psychology* 44. 319–327.

Dunn, L.M., & Dunn, D.M. 2007. *Peabody picture vocabulary test*, 4th edn. New York: Pearson.

Ellis, N.C., & Sinclair, S.G. 1996. Working memory in acquisition of vocabulary and syntax: Putting language in good order. *The Quarterly Journal of Experimental Psychology Section A* 49(1). 234–250. https://doi.org/10.1080/713755604

Engel de Abreu, P.M.J., & Gathercole, S.E. 2012. Executive and phonological processes in second-language acquisition. *Journal of Educational Psychology* 104(4). 974–986. https://doi.org/10.1037/a0028390

Ganschow, L., & Sparks, R. 2001. Learning difficulties and foreign language learning: A review of research and instruction. *Language Teaching* 34(2). 79–98. https://doi.org/10.1017/S0261444800015895

Gathercole, S.E., Willis, C.S., Emslie, H., & Baddeley, A.D. 1992. Phonological memory and vocabulary development during the early school years: A longitudinal study. *Developmental Psychology* 28(5). 887–898.

Hamel, R., & Schmittmann, V.D. 2006. The 20-minute version as a predictor of the Raven advanced progressive matrices test. *Educational and Psychological Measurement* 66(6). 1039–1046. https://doi.org/10.1177/0013164406288169

Jones, G. 2012. Why chunking should be considered as an explanation for developmental change before short-term memory capacity and processing speed. *Frontiers in Psychology* 3. 167.

Justice, L.M., McGinty, A.S., Cabell, S.Q., Kilday, C.R., Knighton, K., & Huffman, G. 2010. Language and literacy curriculum supplement for preschoolers who are academically at risk: a feasibility study. *Language, Speech, and Hearing Services in Schools* 141, 161–178. https://doi.org/10.1044/0161-1461(2009/08-0058)

Kormos, J., & Sáfár, A. 2008. Phonological short-term memory, working memory and foreign language performance in intensive language learning. *Bilingualism: Language and Cognition* **11**(2). 261–271. https://doi.org/10.1017/S1366728908003416

Kort, W., Schittekatte, M., Bosmans, M., Compaan, E.L., Dekker, P.H., Vermeir G., & Verhaeghe, P. 2005. *Wechsler Intelligence Scale for Children III (WISC-III-NL)*. Amsterdam: Harcourt Test Publisher.

Kort, W., Schittekatte, M., & Compaan, E. 2010. *CELF-4-NL | Test voor diagnose en evaluatie van taalproblemen (Nederlandse bewerking)*. Amsterdam: Pearson.

Martin, I.K., & Ellis, N.C. 2012. The roles of phonological short-term memory and working memory in L2 grammar and vocabulary learning. *Studies in Second Language Acquisition* **34**(3). 379–413. https://doi.org/10.1017/S0272263112000125

Marton, K., & Schwartz, R.G. 2003. Working memory capacity and language processes in children with specific language impairment. *Journal of Speech, Language, and Hearing Research* **46**(5). 1138–1153. https://doi.org/10.1044/1092-4388

Masoura, E.V., & Gathercole, S.E. 2005. Contrasting contributions of phonological short-term memory and long-term knowledge to vocabulary learning in a foreign language. *Memory* **13**(3–4). 422–429. https://doi.org/10.1080/09658210344000323

Messer, M.H., Leseman, P.P.M., Boom, J., & Maya, A.Y. 2010. Phonotactic probability effect in nonword recall and its relationship with vocabulary in monolingual and bilingual preschoolers. *Journal of Experimental Child Psychology* **105**(4). 306–323. https://doi.org/10.1016/j.jecp.2009.12.006

O'Brien, I., Segalowitz, N., Collentine, J., & Freed, B. 2006. Phonological memory and lexical, narrative, and grammatical skills in second language oral production by adult learners. *Applied Psycholinguistics* **27**(3). 377–402. https://doi.org/10.1017/S0142716406060322

Oostdam, R., & van Toorenburg, H. 2002. 'Leuk is not enough': Het vraagstuk van de positionering van Engels in het basisonderwijs en de aansluiting met het voortgezet onderwijs. *Levende Talen Tijdschrift* **3**(4). 3–18. https://levendetalen.nl/publicaties/tijdschrift/

Paradis, J. 2011. Individual differences in child English second language acquisition: Comparing child-internal and child-external factors. *Linguistic Approaches to Bilingualism* **1**(3). 213–237. https://doi.org/10.1075/lab.1.3.01par

Raven, J., Raven, J.C., & Court, J.H. 2003. *Manual for Raven's progressive matrices and vocabulary scales*. San Antonio, TX: Harcourt Assessment.

Rescorla, L. 2002. Language and reading outcomes to age 9 in late-talking toddlers. *Journal of Speech, Language, and Hearing Research* 45, 360–371. https://doi.org/10.1044/1092-4388(2002/028)

Rispens, J., & Baker, A. 2012. Nonword repetition: The relative contributions of phonological short-term memory and phonological representations in children with language and reading impairment. *Journal of Speech, Language, and Hearing Research* **55**(3). 683–694. https://doi.org/10.1044/1092-4388

Rispens, J., & de Bree, E. 2017. Past tense production in children with SLI and bilingual children: The influence of vocabulary and non-word repetition. In E. Blom, L. Cornips, & J. Schaeffer (eds.), *Cross-linguistic influence in bilingualism: In honor of Aafke Hulk*, 259–277. Amsterdam: John Benjamins Publishing Company.

Schlichting, L. 2005. *Peabody Picture Vocabulary Test-III NL*. Amsterdam: Harcourt Test Publisher.

Service, E., & Kohonen, V. 1995. Is the relation between phonological memory and foreign language learning accounted for by vocabulary acquisition? *Applied Psycholinguistics* **16**(2). 155–172. https://doi.org/10.1017/S0142716400007062

Skehan, P., & Ducroquet, L. 1988. A comparison of first and foreign language ability. ESOL Department, Institute of Education, London University: Working Documents. No. 8.

Sparks, R., Patton, J., & Ganschow, L. 2012. Profiles of more and less successful L2 learners: A cluster analysis study. *Learning and Individual Differences* **22**(4). 463–472. https://doi.org/10.1016/j.lindif.2012.03.009

Verhagen, J., & Leseman, P. 2016. How do verbal short-term memory and working memory relate to the acquisition of vocabulary and grammar? A comparison between first and second language learners. *Journal of Experimental Child Psychology* **141**. 65–82. https://doi.org/10.1016/j.jecp.2015.06.015

Wagner, R., Torgesen, J., Rashotte, C., & Pearson, N.A. 2013. *Comprehensive Test of Phonological Processing*, 2nd edn. New York: Pearson.

Weber-Fox, C.M., & Neville, H.J. 1996. Maturational constraints on functional specializations for language processing: ERP and behavioral evidence in bilingual speakers. *Journal of Cognitive Neuroscience* **8**(3), 231–256. https://doi.org/10.1162/jocn.1996.8.3.231

Wiig, E.H., Semel, E., & Secord, W.A. 2003. *Clinical Evaluation of Language Fundamentals*, 4th edn. San Antonio, TX: Pearson/PsychCorp.

Ferran Gesa and Maria del Mar Suárez

Individual differences and young learners' L2 vocabulary development: The case of language aptitude and exposure to subtitled TV series

Abstract: Individual differences have been shown to influence language development (Skehan 1989) and vocabulary learning (Dóczi and Kormos 2016) to a great extent. Among them, language aptitude has been found to be a good L2 proficiency predictor, even if it is said to have a low predictive validity for vocabulary learning (Li 2016). Research has also shown that extensive television viewing may be beneficial for vocabulary learning at beginner levels (Gesa 2019). However, there is virtually no research exploring the mediating role of language aptitude in the learning of L2 vocabulary through multimodal input.

This chapter aims at filling the existing gap by exposing Grade 6 Catalan / Spanish EFL learners aged 11–12 (N=40) to L1 subtitled TV series for an academic term. Participants were pooled from two intact classes, which were randomly allocated to the experimental or control group. Weekly, both groups were pre-taught a set of Target Words (TWs) and completed two active learning vocabulary tasks. However, only those in the experimental group additionally watched a total of eight episodes of a TV series where the TWs appeared. In order to be able to compute for lexical gains, all learners took a pre- and a posttest, assessing TW form and meaning recall, at the beginning and at the end of the term. Language aptitude was measured using the multicomponential Modern Language Aptitude Test – Elementary in Catalan (Suárez 2010).

Statistical analyses do not yield significant differences between experimental conditions, but descriptive statistics suggest that those exposed to subtitled TV series learn more vocabulary than learners who just received formal instruction. Moreover, language aptitude is revealed to impact word form learning. Conclusions are drawn in relation to how type of exposure (TV series and explicit vocabulary teaching) and some language aptitude components mediate vocabulary learning through multimodal input.

Keywords: extensive viewing, language aptitude, multimodal input, vocabulary learning

1 Video viewing and foreign language vocabulary learning

This chapter presents a research study on vocabulary learning in a formal English as a Foreign Language (EFL) context using unabridged, authentic audiovisual materials, particularly, a TV series in English subtitled in First Language (L1) Spanish and it also explores the role that language aptitude plays in the process.

While watching TV series and movies subtitled in the L1 or in the Foreign Language (FL) is nowadays highly promoted (Teng 2021), it is yet to be seen how effective this practice can be, particularly among young learners. TV series or movies as such are not devised as EFL teaching materials, yet their multimodal nature has been found to be especially effective in FL learning (Vanderplank 2016), in the light of the theoretical framework provided by the Dual Coding Theory (Paivio 1986, 2007) and the Cognitive Theory of Multimedia Learning (Mayer 2002, 2009). Following this theoretical perspective, standard subtitling (i.e., the presentation of Second Language (L2) audio and L1 subtitles) helps input to become more comprehensible (Danan 2004) and is said to facilitate the establishment of the form-meaning link between the L2 word presented in an aural form and its L1 translation (Talaván 2012). Such subtitling technique has proved to be especially advantageous for low-level learners as it allows them to access authentic materials they would not be able to follow without the support provided by their native language (Koolstra and Beentjes 1999). From all areas of language acquisition, subtitled television viewing is thought to be specifically beneficial for vocabulary acquisition (Peters and Webb 2018; Rodgers and Webb 2020) and audiovisual comprehension (Rodgers and Webb 2017). When it comes to vocabulary learning, the main focus of the present study, watching subtitled TV series has been shown to be effective since, among other reasons, television viewing provides learners with a great deal of lexical repetition, so necessary in vocabulary intake (Rott 1999; Waring and Takaki 2003), and accumulation of background knowledge (Webb and Rodgers 2009), more than when exposed to other sources of language input like extensive reading (Cobb 2007).

Benefits have mainly been reported with adult learners exposed to short clips or unrelated TV programmes (e.g., Montero Perez 2019; Peters and Webb 2018; Sydorenko 2010). However, the few studies available on extensive viewing (Webb 2015) have shown that it is beneficial in a variety of contexts and following different approaches. For instance, Rodgers and Webb (2020) found that Japanese university learners benefited from watching several episodes of a

TV series lasting more than seven hours and that this led to more vocabulary gains than no video viewing in meaning recognition tests. On a different line, Pujadas and Muñoz (2019) exposed high-school learners to subtitled TV series during one academic year and found that those that were pre-taught the target vocabulary recalled more items than those that incidentally acquired them. However, no significant differences were observed between having been exposed to L1 or L2 subtitles. In contrast, Frumuselu et al. (2015) reported that advanced English majors learned more colloquial vocabulary when exposed to L2 subtitles rather than L1 after having watched thirteen episodes of a TV series over seven weeks. Last, it seems that extensive viewing is also mediated by participants' proficiency level (Gesa and Miralpeix 2022; Suárez and Gesa 2019), with more advanced learners outperforming beginners.

It is precisely at this latter proficiency level where research is even scarcer. To the authors' knowledge, there is no study to date that has looked into the effects of extensive viewing on young learners at the outset of their FL learning endeavour. However, there are some studies with shorter videos and following a less experimental approach, which have shown that informal at-home TV viewing has a positive effect on word identification (Rice et al. 1990) and translation tests (Kuppens 2010). In more (quasi-)experimental studies, subtitles are said to be beneficial for children's FL vocabulary development (Koolstra and Beentjes 1999; Teng 2019) although opposite results have also been reported (Galimberti and Miralpeix 2018).

The next section will discuss language aptitude, one of the Individual Differences (ID) that research has shown can mediate learners' vocabulary learning (Lee 2020), even though it is yet to be seen how it can impact vocabulary learning from audiovisual input.

2 Aptitude as a predictor of foreign language learning

Language aptitude has traditionally been defined as a set of cognitive abilities that are 'predictive of how well, relative to other individuals, an individual can learn a foreign language in a given amount of time and under given conditions' (Carroll and Sapon 2002: 23). Aptitude tests validations make use of standardized proficiency tests or objective criterion variables, but they have not been widely used in experimental research. Also, while aptitude is believed to be a multicomponent construct, there being specific tests to measure the aptitude to learn vocabulary, for instance, in language learning aptitude studies, the scores used to define the role of aptitude tend to be the total score (the sum of the parts of aptitude tests), regardless of what each part or subtest measures. Aptitude tests aim to measure the diverse abilities needed to learn languages although these aptitudes may not necessarily correspond to one subtest only. Also, one subtest might tap into more than one ability. Consequently, the aptitude to specifically learn vocabulary has not been researched in depth, and even less the role of aptitude in vocabulary learning through extensive television viewing.

According to Carroll (1981), language aptitude consists of four main constructs. First, phonemic coding ability, that is, the ability to identify and memorize new sound strings. In the second place, grammatical sensitivity, which is the ability to understand the grammatical function of words within a sentence. Thirdly, and though not directly measured by any Modern Language Aptitude Test (MLAT) subtest, we find the inductive language learning ability, which, according to the reconceptualization defined by Skehan (1991), is the ability to infer grammatical rules from language samples. Finally, the last construct would be rote memory, the ability to memorize through semantic associations or sound-symbol correspondences.

One of the most widely used aptitude tests to date is the MLAT validated by Carroll and Sapon (1959), to be taken by adult populations. This test was the starting point for the creation of the MLAT-E (the Modern Language Aptitude Test-Elementary) for children and pre-adolescents between 9 and 13 years of age (Carroll and Sapon 1967).

The MLAT-E was adapted to the Spanish language by Stansfield and Reed (2005), who called it the MLAT-ES, and later on Suárez (2010) adapted and validated the Catalan version of this test, named MLAT-EC. The latter, as its predecessors, has four parts. The first one, *"Paraules ocultes"* (Hidden words) is believed to tap into vocabulary learning as well as decoding abilities. The second part *"Paraules que es corresponen"* (Matching words) would measure grammatical sensitivity. The ability of hearing and distinguishing speech sounds is measured by Part three, *"Paraules que rimen"* (Finding rhymes). Part four, where test takers are expected to learn the invented name for word numbers and combinations, would measure rote memory, auditory comprehension and, naturally, the ability to learn new words, namely, numbers.

One way to measure the role of aptitude in the different facets of language learning is through correlational studies checking the correspondence between the construct and the test that is supposed to measure the ability to master that construct. Certainly, in more complex research study designs, such as this one, other more complex kinds of statistical analyses such as General Linear Models (GLM), which consider several types of variables simultaneously, might be run so as to further define the role of aptitude in relation to other variables, such as the type of input exposure learners receive. Regarding vocabulary learning, no study so far has shed light on the role of aptitude using any of the versions of the MLAT-E, although it has been used to study the correspondence between lexical diversity in written production, with inconclusive results (Kormos and Trebits 2012; Suárez 2014).

Using the LLAMA test (Meara 2005a), another aptitude test tapping into the four constructs mentioned above, the role of language aptitude in vocabulary learning through captioned multimodal material has been explored in older populations, that is, secondary and higher education learners, who received an extended exposure to L2-subtitled multimodal materials (Suárez, Gesa, and Miralpeix 2017; Suárez and Gesa 2019). These authors found that the power of aptitude was overridden by that of proficiency in both secondary and higher education students, regardless of the type of exposure they had received. Also, while aptitude was a significant factor for Target Word (TW) meaning learning, it had no influence on the learning of TW forms for either of the types of exposure. It is yet to be determined, though, if aptitude plays a similar role in younger populations using aptitude tests other than LLAMA. It should nevertheless be born in mind that the LLAMA test, devised for young adult and older populations, has not undergone a proper validation process as such. Therefore, the results found to date regarding vocabulary learning through multimodal input using the LLAMA test might be different to those one might find in younger populations whose aptitude is measured by means of a validated aptitude test as is the MLAT-E and its versions in languages other than English.

3 Aims and research questions

As previously expounded, research into the influence of aptitude on vocabulary learning through extended TV exposure has proven that it has little to no power in higher education and secondary education populations as compared to other factors like general proficiency (Suárez and Gesa 2019). It remains unknown, however, whether language aptitude and exposure to L1-subtitled TV series will play a role or not in younger populations. This study, therefore, seeks to explore the role of aptitude and multimodal input exposure in primary education students.

Our two working research questions are:
1. In beginner EFL learners, does additional extended exposure to subtitled TV series lead to greater vocabulary learning than formal instruction alone?
2. Is aptitude relevant in the process of FL vocabulary learning in such conditions?

We hypothesize that those participants that additionally watched the episodes of the TV series will outperform their peers who were only taught the target vocabulary in an explicit way. Similarly, we consider that those with a higher language learning aptitude will learn more TWs.

4 Methodology

4.1 Participants

To address these research questions, 40 Catalan / Spanish EFL learners participated in the study, after having excluded some for whom data could not be collected in full. They belonged to two intact classes with a different number of students in each: twenty-two of them were allocated in the Experimental Group (EG) while 18 were placed in the Control Group (CG). Their level of English ranged between the A1-A2 according to the Common European Framework of Reference for Languages after having received about 900 hours of formal instruction, so they are considered to be beginners, as further shown by their vocabulary size (1,530 words), measured using X_Lex (Meara 2005b), a computerised yes/no receptive vocabulary test that taps into the 1K–5K word range. Moreover, independent-samples t-tests showed that there were no differences in terms of vocabulary size between the EG and CG ($t(38)=-.059$, $p=.953$). All participants were studying Grade 6 (the last year of primary school following the Catalan education system), which means their age range was 11–12. All of them attended a semi-private school in Barcelona's metropolitan area.

4.2 Design and instruments

The TV series chosen for this study was *The Suite Life of Zack and Cody* (Kallis et al. 2005). Eight episodes from the first season were selected based on their content (they had to be interesting enough to hook students), the amount of testable vocabulary, and priority was given to successive episodes (Webb and

Rodgers 2009). Each episode lasted 21 minutes approximately, which makes a total of 2 hours 51 minutes of multimodal exposure. The participants watched the TV series in the original version subtitled in Spanish. A corpus analysis of the eight episodes that were shown to students revealed that 95% lexical coverage, deemed to be enough for the understanding of television programmes (Webb and Rodgers 2009), was reached at the 3K level, while 98% coverage, considered to be the ideal coverage level (Hu and Nation 2000), was reached at the 6K level. These figures justify the idea that episodes were shown with Spanish subtitles, since participants' vocabulary size (average: 1,530 words) was below the coverage levels.

From each of the eight episodes, five TWs were selected, so participants were tested on a total of forty TWs. These were selected on the basis of their frequency of occurrence in the episodes (more frequent words were given priority over others) and in general corpora (1K and 2K were avoided whenever possible since there were higher chances of participants being familiar with them, although some had to be included as a result of a lack of low-frequency testeable vocabulary), their cognateness (cognates between English and Catalan / Spanish were not considered, since research has shown they are much easier to learn than non-cognates –Otwinowska 2016), and their concreteness (concrete words were prioritised over abstract words, since the former tend to be easier to learn rather than the latter –De Groot and Keijzer 2000). Overall, much care was taken to select TWs that researchers thought were considered to be unknown to participants (see Table A1 in Appendix for the list of TWs and their characteristics).

The study followed a pre-test / post-test design lasting one academic term. At the beginning of the term, all students took the vocabulary pre-test, containing all the TWs the students were assessed on ($N=40$). It was a form and meaning recall test since participants were instructed to listen to an audio file in which each TW form was read aloud twice, then write the English forms of such words and provide the Catalan / Spanish translation if known. Afterwards, the participants in the EG saw eight episodes of the TV series, one every week, each containing five TWs, whereas the CG followed the regular course activities and was only exposed to the TWs through the vocabulary learning activities (see below). At the end of the intervention (i.e., after having viewed the eight episodes), both groups took the vocabulary post-test, which was identical to the pre-test (see Figure 1 for an example of the pre- and post-test).

A continuación escucharás veinte palabras en inglés. Escríbelas en inglés y tradúcelas al castellano o catalán. Si de alguna palabra conoces más de un significado, escríbelo. Escucharás cada palabra un total de dos veces.

Palabras

	Inglés	Castellano – Catalán
1		
2		
3		
4		
5		

Figure 1: Example of the pre- and post-test.

At the beginning of each of the eight sessions the experiment was divided into, both conditions completed a vocabulary pre-task. It consisted of a varied set of active learning exercises in which the TWs were the object of study, since they were essential to solve the task. There were different types of tasks so as not to make them too repetitive: for instance, matching the TWs with their pictorial representation, fill-in-the-gaps, crosswords or word-searches. As participants were at the beginning of their FL learning journey, care was taken to include easier rather than more challenging activities (e.g., cloze tests). Hence, vocabulary was taught explicitly and participants were given the opportunity to clarify all their doubts regarding the target vocabulary. At the end of each session, both groups again took a vocabulary post-task which resembled a form recall and meaning recognition exercise, since learners were asked to listen to another audio file in which TW forms were read aloud twice, write them down in English and select the best Spanish translation out of six possibilities (see Figure 2 for an example). This post-task was mainly included to confirm that immediate recalling of the TWs was high; since this was the case (participants knew on average 51% of the TW forms and meanings), such results will not be included in the present analysis.

"Footloser"

Escucharás cinco palabras en inglés. Cada palabra se va a repetir dos veces. Di qué significan estas palabras (opción a, b, c. . .). Si no sabes qué quiere decir alguna palabra, elige la opción (f) 'No lo sé'.

1) _____
a) Intacto
b) Jurado
c) Tío
d) Tobillo
e) Codo
f) No lo sé

2) _____
a) Caja
b) Hambriento
c) Sediento
d) Primeramente
e) Magia
f) No lo sé

3) _____
a) Deber
b) Obligar
c) Reír
d) Extraño
e) Arco
f) No lo sé

4) _____
a) Retener
b) Acontecimiento
c) Concurso
d) Protestar
e) Talento
f) No lo sé

5) _____
a) Hacer daño
b) Corazón
c) Criticar
d) Masaje
e) Aire
f) No lo sé

Figure 2: Example of a vocabulary post-task.

The aptitude test used was the Catalan version of the MLAT-E. In the first part of the test, "Hidden Words", the participants had to guess which word was disguised in a misspelled word and relate it with its corresponding synonym or definition. In the second part, "Matching Words", the learners had to infer the function of the word in capitals in a sentence and to relate it with the word performing the same syntactic function in the sentence below. In the third part, "Rhyming Words", the students had to find the word that rhymes with the sample one. Finally, in part four, "Number Learning", the participants had to learn numbers 1, 2, and 3, and their corresponding tens (10, 20 and 30). Then they were dictated 25 numbers which could be any of these six numbers, in a combination or as they were.

4.3 Analysis

In order to answer the first research question, that is, if the extended exposure to a subtitled TV series led to significant vocabulary learning, the relative gains formula (Horst, Cobb, and Meara 1998; Rodgers 2013) was applied (see Figure 3). This formula takes into account the number of words already known in the pre-test and it is considered to be a more fine-grained measure of vocabulary learning.

$$\text{Relative gains for participants} = \frac{N \text{ of TWs learned}}{N \text{ of items tested} - N \text{ of TWs known}} \times 100$$

Figure 3: Relative gains formula.

In this formula 'learned' refers to the number of forms or meanings that were answered incorrectly on the pre-test and correctly on the post-test; and 'known' refers to the number of forms or meanings which were answered correctly on both the pre- and the post-test. The 'N of items tested' was always 40.

To calculate whether there was an improvement in the number of word forms and meanings learned during the term, Wilcoxon signed-rank tests were run with pre- and post-test scores as variables. Next, in order to answer research question 1, relative gains for form and meaning were compared across conditions running an independent samples t-test or a Mann-Whitney U-test, depending on the normality of the data.

The scores of the MLAT-EC were calculated using the model of the MLAT-ES, that is, considering the raw score of each subtest and adding the score of all subtests to obtain the total score, although the percentages for each part were used for further analysis. The aptitude test scores were compared across conditions bearing in mind the normality of the data and, therefore, running an independent samples t-test or a Mann-Whitney U-test accordingly.

To study the effect of aptitude on the vocabulary learning gains, GLMs were run in SPSS for each experimental condition (EG vs. CG), using the Generalised Linear Mixed Model interface. The MLAT-EC total score and its parts were entered as fixed effects, while interactions were not included in the model since the four MLAT-EC subtests are supposed to measure different constructs. Form and meaning were kept as separate constructs since they tap into different aspects of lexical knowledge (Nation 2013).

5 Results

The results show that both groups learned significantly when comparing the pre- and the post-test, as shown by the results of the Wilcoxon signed-rank tests (EG – TW form: $Z = -4.013$, $p = .000$, TW meaning: $Z = -3.829$, $p = .000$; CG – TW form: $Z = -3.728$, $p = .000$, TW meaning: $Z = -3.421$, $p = .001$). However, the Mann-Whitney U-test and the independent samples t-test do not reveal any significant difference in either word form or meaning learning between the EG and the CG (see Table 1).

Table 1: Relative gains by EG and CG for word form and word meaning.

Relative gains (in %)	EG		CG		EG vs. CG
	M	SD	M	SD	
Form	20.82	10.75	18.39	10.42	$t(38) = .721$, $p = .475$
Meaning	10.33	8.35	10.80	10.62	$U = 194$, $z = -.109$, $p = .913$

The second research question addressed how language learning aptitude mediated vocabulary learning through explicit vocabulary learning tasks and also when participants were additionally exposed to subtitled TV series. No significant differences were found in aptitude levels when comparing the EG and CG after running a Mann-Whitney U-test (see Table 2), which allowed for further comparisons between them.

Table 2: MLAT-EC descriptive results for both EG and CG.

MLAT – EC (in %)	EG		CG		p
	M	SD	M	SD	
Part 1	77.88	15.65	75.56	17.90	.798
Part 2	62.12	23.89	75	22.02	.058
Part 3	75.96	21.13	83.92	9.88	.352
Part 4	75.63	26.92	73.33	25.78	.619
TOTAL	72.98	17.94	77.55	12.82	.600

Table 3 shows the results regarding the influence of aptitude (both parts and total scores) on vocabulary gains. The significant values appear in bold. The results show that all the MLAT-EC parts believed to be related to vocabulary learning were relevant for form in the EG except for part 3, while only part 1 was related to TW form gains in the CG. In both conditions the overall aptitude score proves to be significant. Regarding TW meaning, though, only part 4 seems to be relevant in the EG while in the CG it is part 1 the one related to TW meaning gains.

Table 3: GLMs with aptitude test as a fixed effect comparing EG vs CG.

	Form			Meaning		
	F	df1, df2	p	F	df1, df2	p
EG						
Part 1	5.696	1, 20	.027	2.116	1, 20	.161
Part 2	6.912	1, 20	.016	1.071	1, 20	.313
Part 3	3.978	1, 20	.060	2.573	1, 20	.124
Part 4	9.120	1, 20	.007	4.368	1, 20	.050
Total score	10.332	1, 20	.004	3.609	1, 20	.072
CG						
Part 1	10.036	1, 16	.006	5.661	1, 16	.030
Part 2	2.703	1, 16	.120	2.835	1, 16	.112
Part 3	4.019	1, 16	.062	3.442	1, 16	.083
Part 4	2.619	1, 16	.125	1.962	1, 16	.180
Total score	10.556	1, 16	.005	7.759	1, 16	.013

When considering the total aptitude score, it seems to be relevant for TW form gains for both the EG ($F(1, 20)=10.332$, $p=.004$) and the CG ($F(1, 16)=10.556$, $p=.005$). For TW meaning, however, the total score is only relevant in the CG ($F(1, 16)=7.759$, $p=.013$) but not in the EG ($F(1, 20)=3.609$, $p=.072$). In different words, the overall aptitude score is shown to be relevant consistently for the CG in both TW form and meaning but not for the EG, where it only appears to be statistically significant in TW form gains.

6 Discussion

Regarding the first research question, the EG obtained larger gains than the CG in word form learning, though not significantly, that is, additional exposure to L1-subtitled TV series was not determinant in vocabulary learning. It seems true, then, that explicit vocabulary instruction accounted for most part of the results, despite the fact that the EG had more exposure to the target vocabulary than the CG. Grade 6 participants mainly benefited from being taught the TWs at the beginning of each session and being able to clarify the doubts they had. This explicit teaching, quite common at these stages of learning and in an FL context, was a familiar activity to students and they could certainly allocate the attention resources needed to learn the words, in contrast to what may have happened with the viewing of the episodes, quite a novel activity for many of the participants. Moreover, as most of the pre-tasks contained a pictorial representation of the TWs, it could have been easier for students to learn the meaning of the target vocabulary (Stahl and Nagy 2006); precisely, this could partially explain why the CG obtained higher relative gains in word meaning learning. However, we can also conclude that exposure to TV series was not detrimental to learning, since there were no significant differences in favour of the CG. This same reason leads us to think that the additional exposure to TV series that the EG had could have been useful to consolidate the vocabulary knowledge learned through the pre-task, but it did not contribute to learning new vocabulary other than the one partially learned at the beginning of each session. More multimodal input exposure may have been needed for these differences to be found. In a way, learners in the EG were exposed to less than three hours of TV series input, which, even though it is not negligible in FL settings, is not much if compared to the exposure they could have had in an immersion context. If the study had been more prolonged in time (for instance, one academic year instead of a term), we may have been able to grasp more of the benefits that are presupposed to extensive viewing.

Such results also lead us to conclude that the Dual Coding Theory (Paivio 1986), according to which verbal and non-verbal information presented simultaneously may activate the verbal and imagery cognitive subsystems, which in turn might lead to a greater depth of processing and better recall, and the Cognitive Theory of Multimedia Learning (Mayer 2009), which defends that learners learn more deeply from a multimedia explanation than from a verbal one, could be applied, at least partially, to vocabulary learning in the context of this study. In the EG, the participants could benefit from three different types of input (text, sound and image) while the CG was mainly exposed to written input related to the TWs. In addition, multimodality did not have a negative influence on vocabulary learning, as the CG did not significantly obtain better results than the EG. This might be due to the fact that subtitles in the participants' L1 made it easier to understand the input but were not helpful in word form learning either. Finally, it should be highlighted that the potential benefits from TV viewing do not seem to be exclusive to older populations, as previous studies with a similar design have shown (e.g., Suárez and Gesa 2019).

Nevertheless, it should be pointed out that the increase in vocabulary was not very large, as the EG only learned 6.88% of the words they did not know before the experiment. However, there might have been learning gains in vocabulary partially known before the intervention and that, unfortunately, could not be detected as such. It is also remarkable that the pre- and the post-test administered were rather challenging for beginner participants. Consequently, the gains in vocabulary learning may have been shown to be higher if tested using a word recognition test rather than a recall test, for instance. Finally, it should be pointed out that vocabulary learning is a very slow process, which needs a greater deal of repetition and recycling than that received by the EG, and that the TWs should have been encountered a higher number of times so that more of them could be learned (Pigada and Schmitt 2006; Waring and Takaki 2003).

The two groups participating in this study did not differ significantly as far as their aptitude is concerned although Part 2 of the MLAT-EC was not far from differing significantly [M (EG)= 62.12 versus M (CG)= 75.00, p=.058], which might have favored the EG up to a certain extent. However, as far as aptitude is concerned, the Matthew effect (Stanovich 1986) is found rather consistently. That is, the more overall aptitude, the more learning, as shown in the GLMs. This is not the case for the individual parts of the aptitude tests, where no consistent pattern is found. Most of the significant relations between aptitude and gains are to be found mainly regarding form in both the EG and in the CG, although only up to an extent in the latter. Meaning, in contrast, is only related with aptitude in one case (part 1 in the CG). This further confirms that the aptitude score that seems to work best when it comes to relating aptitude with language learning is the total score (Li 2016), as it happened in a previous study (Gesa and Suárez 2020), where bilateral Spearman-rank correlations were run between all the parts and the total score of the MLAT-EC and vocabulary learning gains, assuming there would be some sort of positive relation at least between parts 1, 4 and, up to a certain extent, part 3, as these are the parts believed to tap into vocabulary learning ability. The expected results were found consistently for the EG, but not for the CG, for which part 4 was not relevant either for form or meaning. However, the total score was the one correlating most consistently and strongly across conditions, in both form and meaning gains.

This leads us to question whether correlations, while being the statistical analysis most widely used to relate aptitude test parts with another variable, might also be misleading or not the most refined or appropriate measure to determine the effects of aptitude on vocabulary learning specifically. Reprising the Matthew effect reasoning, it would rather be that a larger overall L2 proficiency, which correlates with a higher aptitude, facilitates vocabulary learning and it overrides the potential predictive power that language aptitude may have (Suárez and Gesa 2019).

Focusing on meaning learning, this variable is the one that was related to aptitude the least consistently in both groups (Gesa and Suárez 2020). Aptitude does seem to have an influence on meaning learning for the CG ($p = .013$) but not for the EG ($p=.072$). Actually, from the results of the GLMs, it is clear that aptitude loses its power in the learning of meaning by the EG. This phenomenon could be explained by external factors as are the type and amount of exposure to the TWs. The participants of both the EG and the CG can recognize the word forms, but meaning was more challenging to learn, despite the pre-tasks with some clarifying images and the actual visual representations found in the TV series. To start with, the participants in this study were not able to use these words in a meaningful context. That would also explain the secondary role that part 1 "Hidden Words" seems to play in the CG, as this part consists in deciphering a written word and relating it, passively, to its synonym or definition, which would not exactly prove the consolidation of word learning, while Part 4 would, and it actually does for form and meaning in the EG. In this latter part, the test-taker memorizes a series of single and compound numbers and then forms combinations of these, which implies further elaboration on the memorized terms.

It should also be taken into account that both groups experienced the learning of the TWs in their first stages. Both the activities and the pre- and post-tests aimed at scribbling down the TW forms together with their meanings, but they did not have to use those TWs in any meaningful or elaborate context. Consequently, it cannot be affirmed that they got to learn the TWs fully (in order to know a word fully, they should have mastered all its meaning – and not just the one shown in the TV series –, its collocations, grammatical functions, etc.), while aptitude tests are supposed to measure vocabulary learning in a more global way. Also, the CG had mostly a formal kind of exposure to the TWs, while the EG did have further contact with them, but the translation of those words occurred in the participants' L1. This means that while the EG actually learned some TWs, though only a few of the potential words they could have learned, they probably had to allocate their aptitude in other learning activities involved in handling those words, as it could be discerning which word matched the Spanish translations they were reading or trying to segment them from the L2 speech string in which they appeared. Consequently, it seems that the type of exposure was not so influential in learning the form of the TWs but it was in meaning learning for those whose exposure to the TWs was in a more traditional form, where aptitude has proven to be more relevant to date. In contrast, the EG was facing a new kind of learning activity for them (that is, watching a TV series in its original version subtitled in the participants' L1) which could have meant an excess of difficulty or novelty in terms of language learning success and rate. It remains to be seen, however, what would have happened if these students had had a lower aptitude than needed to handle this new learning context, as then this type of exposure could have even been detrimental for them due to the cognitive overload it would have implied.

7 Pedagogical implications and conclusions

This study has several pedagogical implications as far as the use of extensive TV viewing in the classroom is concerned. It seems that, in early FL learning, extended TV viewing with subtitles in the L1 is not detrimental to vocabulary learning, but it is not much more powerful than a more traditional approach to FL vocabulary learning, as no significant differences were found at this stage between the EG and the CG. That said, it needs to be born in mind that the authentic audiovisual materials used in this and similar studies should be adapted to the learners' level and these should be provided with sufficient tools and resources (e.g., subtitles, active learning tasks) to be able to follow the storyline and learn from the input (Webb 2015). What is more, it is important that such classroom interventions are sustained in time, since we have seen that, after eight viewing sessions, little benefits are seen. Hence, the benefits of single-viewing sessions could well be indiscernible.

Knowing our students' strengths and weaknesses from the administration of a language aptitude test may also be useful, though not determinant if subtitled TV viewing is to be used in the classroom, as the GLMs proved that aptitude was not so relevant in meaning learning for the EG, probably due to the divergence in the language of administration (L1 subtitles, FL audio). Consequently, aptitude might be more determinant in contexts where the FL is the only language available in the input or in more advanced stages of vocabulary learning.

This study is not without limitations, either, among which we could mention a reduced number of participants, or the lack of an additional group exposed to the TV series episodes without subtitles, which would have been useful to evaluate the extent to which textual support was necessary for learning the TWs. However, given the limited proficiency of the participants, it was not deemed ecologically valid since learning gains derived from the intervention would have been minimal. Moreover, the inclusion of the post-task affected the learning process as a whole, as participants could see it as an immediate post-test and make an extra effort to remember the words. Yet, the two conditions underwent the same process, so the effects of the processing of the TWs should logically be the same for both the EG and the CG. Finally, learners should have been exposed to larger amounts of multimodal input, with an intervention lasting one academic year or with TV series longer than 20 minutes, for more differences to be seen. However, as the study was set in a classroom context, this was not possible as we were very much constrained by the school policies and regulations.

Further research could cover these limitations by increasing the number of participants as well as comparing what happens at different proficiency levels, extending even more the overall amount of exposure, or experimenting with different types of intensity of exposure (e.g., massed vs. spaced repetition of the TWs shown in the TV series, or analyzing the outcomes of intensive vs. extensive viewing). Moreover, looking into the effects of purely incidental vocabulary learning without any kind of task containing the TWs would also be very informative.

Overall, this study puts into question some analytical and theoretical principles used to date, such as the mere and extended use of correlations to determine the role of aptitude or multimodal input theories in early stages of FL learning. Besides, in contrast with other studies, it is longitudinal and includes large quantities of multimodal input, given the FL classroom context in which the study was conducted. It is also contextualized within a whole and coherent pedagogical intervention with materials designed on purpose for their use in the FL classroom, and focuses on young learners who happen to be in their early FL learning stage, and who are, therefore, an under-researched population.

Appendix

Table A1: Characteristics of the TWs on which participants were tested.

TW	Frequency			Part of speech	Concreteness (Mean)	Cognateness (Y / N)
	Episode (N times)	Term (N times)	COCA (Freq. band)			
Admirer	9	9	2k	N	2.93	N
Ankle	3	3	4k	N	4.81	N
To apologize	2	2	3k	V	2.63	N
Awesome	2	4	6k	Adj.	1.83	N
Badge	2	2	5k	N	4.93	N
Ballroom	3	6	Off-list	N	4.70	N
Beauty mark[a]	2	2	1k	N	4.21	N
Burden	4	4	3k	N	2.63	N
Concierge	3	3	12k	N	3.89	Y

Table A1 (continued)

TW	Frequency			Part of speech	Concreteness (Mean)	Cognateness (Y / N)
	Episode (N times)	Term (N times)	COCA (Freq. band)			
Contest	7	9	3k	N	3.52	N
Counter	2	4	2k	N	4.17	N
Cute	5	11	6k	Adj.	2.76	N
Date	5	17	1k	N	3.90	N
To ditch	5	5	5k	V	4.50	N
Dweeb	4	4	20k	N	2.77	N
Goat	2	2	4k	N	5	N
Grounded	5	6	1k	Adj.	2.07	N
To hurt	6	11	1k	V	3.61	N
Lame	5	8	7k	Adj.	2.52	N
Lifeguard	4	4	Off-list	N	4.47	N
Lipstick	2	2	Off-list	N	4.90	N
Lobby	6	10	3k	N	4.70	N
To owe	2	3	2k	V	2.07	N
Pageant	11	11	7k	N	4.00	N
Prize	2	2	2k	N	4.45	N
Prom	23	23	9k	N	3.72	N
Review	4	5	3k	N	2.81	N
Slumber party[a]	2	2	9k	N	3.89	N
Step	4	6	1k	N	4.54	N
Sweet	4	16	1k	Adj.	4	N
Terrific	2	2	5k	Adj.	2.07	N
Thirsty	3	3	1k	Adj.	3.86	N
Tux	3	3	Off-list	N	4.96	N
Vase	4	5	5k	N	5	N
Vent	6	6	5k	N	4.56	Y
Wedding	9	9	1k	N	3.92	N
Weenies	4	4	17k	N	4.22	N
To work out[a]	3	3	1k	V	3.48	N
Wrestler	3	3	5k	N	4.42	N
To yell	4	5	2k	V	3.86	N

[a]In the case of compound nouns and phrasal verbs, only the concreteness mean of the lexical verb (for phrasal verbs) or the less frequent word (for compound nouns) is reported.

References

Carroll, John B. 1981. Twenty-five years of research on foreign language aptitude. In Karl Conrad Diller (ed.), *Individual differences and universals in language learning aptitude*, 83–117. Rowley: Newbury House.
Carroll, John B. & Stanley Sapon. 1959. *Modern Language Aptitude Test*. New York: Psychological Corporation.
Carroll, John B. & Stanley Sapon. 1967. *Modern Language Aptitude Test-Elementary*. New York: Psychological Corporation.
Carroll John B. & Stanley Sapon. 2002. *Manual for the MLAT*. Bethesda: Second Language Testing, Inc.
Cobb, Tom. 2007. Computing the vocabulary demands of L2 reading. *Language, Learning & Technology* 11(3). 38–63.
Danan, Martine. 2004. Captioning and subtitling: Undervalued language learning strategies. *Meta: Journal Des Traducteurs* 49(1). 67–77.
De Groot, Annette M. B. & Rineke Keijzer. 2000. What is hard to learn is easy to forget: The roles of word concreteness, cognate status, and word frequency in foreign-language vocabulary learning and forgetting. *Language Learning* 50(1). 1–56.
Dóczi, Brigitta & Judit Kormos. 2016. *Longitudinal developments in vocabulary knowledge and lexical organization*. Oxford: Oxford University Press.
Frumuselu, Anca Daniela, Sven De Maeyer, Vincent Donche & Maria del Mar Gutiérrez Colon Plana. 2015. Television series inside the EFL classroom: Bridging the gap between teaching and learning informal language through subtitles. *Linguistics and Education* 32(B). 107–117.
Galimberti, Valeria & Imma Miralpeix. 2018. Multimodal input for Italian beginner learners of English. A study on comprehension and vocabulary learning from undubbed TV series. In Carmel Mary Coonan, Ada Bier & Elena Ballarin (eds.), *La didattica delle lingue nel nuovo millennio. Le sfide dell'internazionalizzazione*, 615–626. Venice: Edizioni Ca'Foscari.
Gesa, Ferran. 2019. *L1 / L2 subtitled TV series and EFL learning: A study on vocabulary acquisition and content comprehension at different proficiency levels*. Barcelona: Universitat de Barcelona.
Gesa, Ferran & Imma Miralpeix. 2022. Effects of watching subtitled TV series on foreign language vocabulary learning: does learners' proficiency level matter? In Christiane Lütge (ed.), *Foreign Language Learning in the Digital Age: Theory and Pedagogy for Developing Literacies*, 159–173. London: Routledge.
Gesa, Ferran & Maria del Mar Suárez. 2020. Efectos de la aptitud y la modalidad de input en el aprendizaje de vocabulario a través de series de televisión subtituladas. *E-SEDLL* 3. 185–198.
Horst, Marlise, Tom Cobb & Paul M. Meara. 1998. Beyond a clockwork orange: Acquiring second language vocabulary through reading. *Reading in a Foreign Language* 11(2). 207–223.
Hu, Marcella & I. S. Paul Nation. 2000. Unknown vocabulary density and reading comprehension. *Reading in a Foreign Language* 13(1). 403–430.
Kallis, Danny, Irene Dreayer, Pamela Eells O'Connell & Jim Geoghan. 2005. *The Suite Life of Zack and Cody* [Television series]. Burbank: Disney Channel.

Koolstra, Cees M. & Johannes W. J. Beentjes. 1999. Children's vocabulary acquisition in a foreign language through watching subtitled television programs at home. *Educational technology research and development* 47(1). 51–60.

Kormos, Judit & Anna Trebits. 2012. The role of task complexity, modality and aptitude in narrative task performance. *Language Learning* 62(2). 439–472.

Kuppens, An H. 2010. Incidental foreign language acquisition from media exposure. *Learning, Media and Technology* 35(1). 65–85.

Lee, Sunjung. 2020. Examining the roles of aptitude, motivation, strategy use, language processing experience, and gender in the development of the breadth and depth of EFL learners' vocabulary knowledge. *SAGE Open* 10(4). 1–15,

Li, Shaofeng. 2016. The construct validity of language aptitude. *Studies in Second Language Acquisition* 38. 801–842.

Mayer, Richard E. 2002. Cognitive theory and the design of multimedia instruction: An example of the two-way street between cognition and instruction. *New Directions for Teaching and Learning* 89(1). 55–71.

Mayer, Richard E. 2009. *Multimedia learning*. Cambridge: Cambridge University Press.

Meara, Paul M. 2005a. *LLAMA Language Aptitude Tests: The Manual*. Swansea: Lognostics.

Meara, Paul M. 2005b. X_Lex: the Swansea vocabulary levels test (version 2.05) [Computer software]. Swansea: Centre for Applied Language Studies.

Montero Perez, Maribel. 2019. Pre-learning vocabulary before viewing captioned video: an eye-tracking study. *The Language Learning Journal* 47(4). 460–478.

Nation, I. S. Paul. 2013 [2001]. *Learning vocabulary in another language*, 2nd edn. Cambridge: Cambridge University Press.

Otwinowska, Agnieszka. 2016. *Cognate vocabulary in language acquisition and use: Attitudes awareness, activation*. Bristol: Multilingual Matters.

Paivio, Allan. 1986. *Mental representations: A dual coding approach*. Oxford: Oxford University Press.

Paivio, Allan. 2007. *Mind and its evolution: A dual coding theoretical approach*. Mahwah: Lawrence Erlbaum Associates.

Peters, Elke & Stuart Webb. 2018. Incidental vocabulary acquisition through viewing L2 television and factors that affect learning. *Studies in Second Language Acquisition* 40(3). 551–577.

Pigada, Maria & Norbert Schmitt. 2006. Vocabulary acquisition from extensive reading: A case study. *Reading in a Foreign Language* 18(1). 1–28.

Pujadas, Geòrgia & Carmen Muñoz. 2019. Extensive viewing of captioned and subtitled TV series: a study of L2 vocabulary learning by adolescents. *The Language Learning Journal* 47(4). 479–496.

Rice, Mabel L., Aletha C. Huston, Rosemarie Truglio & John Wright. 1990. Words from "Sesame Street": Learning vocabulary while viewing. *Developmental Psychology* 26(3). 421–428.

Rodgers, Michael P. H. 2013. *English language learning through viewing television: An investigation of comprehension, incidental vocabulary acquisition, lexical coverage, attitudes, and captions*. Wellington: Victoria University of Wellington.

Rodgers, Michael P. H. & Stuart Webb. 2017. The effects of captions on EFL learners' comprehension of English-language television programs. *CALICO Journal* 34(1). 20–38.

Rodgers, Michael P. H. & Stuart Webb. 2020. Incidental vocabulary learning through viewing television. *ITL – International Journal of Applied Linguistics* 171(2). 191–220.

Rott, Susanne. 1999. The effect of exposure frequency on intermediate language learners' incidental vocabulary acquisition and retention through reading. *Studies in Second Language Acquisition* 21(4). 589–619.

Skehan, Peter. 1989. *Individual differences in second language learning*. London: Edward Arnold.

Skehan, Peter. 1991. Individual differences in second language learning. *Studies in Second Language Acquisition* 13(2). 275–298.

Stahl, Steven A. & William E. Nagy. 2006. *Teaching Word Meanings*. Mahwah: Lawrence Erlbaum Associates.

Stanovich, Keith E. 1986. Matthew effects in reading: Some consequences of individual differences in the acquisition of literacy. *Reading Research Quarterly* 21(4). 360–407.

Stansfield, Charles, & Daniel J. Reed. 2005. *Modern Language Aptitude Test-Elementary: Spanish Version. Manual*. Rockville: Second Language Testing Foundation.

Suárez, Maria del Mar. 2010. *Language aptitude in young learners: The Modern Language Aptitude Test in Spanish and Catalan*. Barcelona: Universitat de Barcelona.

Suárez, Maria del Mar. 2014. The concurrent prediction of writing performance in young learners. Paper presented at the 17th AILA World Congress of Applied Linguistics, Brisbane, 10–15 August, 2014.

Suárez, Maria del Mar & Ferran Gesa. 2019. Learning vocabulary with the support of sustained exposure to captioned video: do proficiency and aptitude make a difference? *The Language Learning Journal* 47(4). 497–517.

Suárez, Maria del Mar, Ferran Gesa & Imma Miralpeix. 2017. Vocabulary acquisition through captioned TV series. Are there any aptitude and proficiency effects? Paper presented at the 18th AILA World Congress of Applied Linguistics, Rio de Janeiro, 23–28 July, 2017.

Sydorenko, Tetyana. 2010. Modality of input and vocabulary acquisition. *Language Learning & Technology* 14(2). 50–73.

Talaván, Noa. 2012. Justificación teórico-práctica del uso de los subtítulos en la enseñanza-aprendizaje de lenguas extranjeras. *TRANS: Revista de Traductología* 16. 23–37.

Teng, Mark Feng. 2019. Incidental vocabulary learning for primary school students. The effects of L2 caption type and word exposure frequency. *The Australian Educational Researcher* 46(1). 113–136.

Teng, Mark Feng. 2021. *Language learning through captioned videos. Incidental vocabulary acquisition*. New York: Routledge.

Vanderplank, Robert. 2016. *Captioned media in foreign language learning and teaching: Subtitles for the deaf and hard-of-hearing as tools for language learning*. London: Palgrave Macmillan.

Waring, Rob & Misako Takaki. 2003. At what rate do learners learn and retain new vocabulary from reading a graded reader? *Reading in a Foreign Language* 15(2). 130–163.

Webb, Stuart. 2015. Extensive viewing: Language learning through watching television. In David Nunan & Jack C. Richards (eds.), *Language learning beyond the classroom*, 159–168. London: Routledge.

Webb, Stuart & Michael P. H. Rodgers. 2009. Vocabulary demands of television programs. *Language Learning* 59(2). 335–366.

Vanessa De Wilde and June Eyckmans
'In love with English': A mixed-methods investigation of Flemish children's spontaneous engagement with out-of-school exposure

Abstract: Recent research on EFL in Flanders has shown that Flemish children already possess a significant knowledge of English before they have received English classes in school. Their English skills are heavily influenced by their exposure to English, more specifically by their engagement in multimodal language activities such as using the internet and gaming (De Wilde et al. 2020a). The questionnaire data of the aforementioned large-scale research project also revealed that many children claim to use English spontaneously, even in situations where there is no communicative necessity to do so (for instance, when playing with their Dutch speaking peers).

In this chapter, an emic perspective is taken in order to investigate when and why Flemish children who have not yet received any formal instruction in English engage in spontaneous English language use. Through a questionnaire a group of 43 children between 10 and 12 years old were asked to log the average time they spent daily on several activities in English (i.e. watching television, listening to music, reading, gaming, using the Internet, YouTube and/or social media, and speaking). On the basis of the information gathered in the questionnaires four focus group discussions were organized in which the children were probed to share when they use English productively in their daily lives. The data from the questionnaire were analysed quantitatively. The focus group discussions were transcribed and analysed in a qualitative manner. The analysis of the discussions revealed five main situations in which children engage in English: on holiday with other tourists, new foreign friends, locals and/or hotel staff; at home with their mother, father, siblings and/or to themselves; at school with friends; online while gaming, chatting, texting or posting comments on social media; when singing along with songs. The reasons for using English seem to be hard to articulate for children. They frequently mention that English is 'fun', that it sounds 'more original', 'better', 'cooler' and 'tougher' than their mother tongue (Dutch). It is also clear from the data that even at such young age, children are aware of the value of English in today's world.

Keywords: young learners, out-of-school exposure, speaking, motivation

In large parts of the world English is considered the lingua franca. This is certainly the case in large parts of Europe where English is omnipresent in people's daily lives and where there is often a large amount of exposure to the language through different kinds of media (e.g. television and social media), advertising and even education (e.g. content and language integrated learning (CLIL) in primary and secondary schools and English as a medium of instruction (EMI) in higher education). Researchers have observed that the position of English in some of these European countries is changing from a foreign to a second language (de Bot 2014). As English seems to be ubiquitous in these countries, young learners are already exposed to English at a young age.

Below, we will look into (mainly quantitative) studies which have investigated the role of out-of-school exposure in language learning and we will show the need for an emic perspective on L2 learning through out-of-school exposure. This perspective is highlighted in the current study. Before laying out the aims and research questions of our study, we will also describe the context in which the study took place.

1 L2 English learning through out-of-school exposure

In the past decade researchers have turned their attention to the context described above and have started investigating language learning through out-of-school exposure. Researchers have consistently found that out-of-school exposure to English contributes to L2 learning. In a study with learners from seven European countries which investigated the role of exposure, parents and cognate linguistic distance in young learners' L2 comprehension, Lindgren and Muñoz (2013) found that the strongest predictor of the scores on a reading and listening test was cognate linguistic distance, followed closely by out-of-school exposure. The researchers found that watching subtitled English television was the strongest predictor of test scores, followed by listening to English music and gaming in English, which had a smaller but still a significant impact on the learners' listening and reading skills. Other studies have also clearly demonstrated the positive impact of playing English video games on L2 English learning in young learners (Hannibal Jensen 2017; Sylvén and Sundqvist 2012). Furthermore, several studies have shown that L2 English language learning through out-of-school exposure takes place prior to classroom instruction (De Wilde et al. 2020a; Kuppens 2010; Jóhannsdóttir 2018; Lefever 2010; Muñoz et al. 2018; Puimège and Peters 2019). All these studies have shown that out-of-school exposure contributes to L2 English language learning, but it is less clear which types of out-of-school exposure are most beneficial for language learning as the studies have generated mixed results. De Wilde et al. (2020a) found that the learning gains were largest when children engaged in the following activities: using social media in English, gaming in English and speaking English. The authors suggest that engagement with types of exposure which involve an element of production leads to more language learning. In a study by the same authors (De Wilde et al. 2022) it is suggested that the level of engagement with the language in the different activities (such as watching television, listening to music or gaming) might also explain the differences in results between the studies. A child listening to music for example, could just like the melody and sing along without paying attention to the meaning or could look up the lyrics online and/or check the meaning of certain words in the song. This might result in different learning gains. As all these studies are mainly quantitative in nature, it is hard to pinpoint what exactly is going on in children's minds during these activities.

Only few studies have adopted a qualitative approach when investigating young learners' engagement with out-of-school exposure. Piirainen-Marsh (2011) and Turgit and Irgin (2009) looked into the benefits of online gaming for L2 English learning. Piiranen-Marsh (2011) used a conversation analytic methodology to investigate how gaming could contribute to L2 English learning. She found that the written and spoken dialogue offered in games was a useful resource for gamers when constructing their own utterances. Furthermore, computer games often offer opportunities for participants to interact. The study found that gamers interact with virtual others and thus practice turn-sharing. Turgit and Irgin (2009) investigated L2 English learning in ten 10-to-14-year-old learners while they were gaming in an internet café. The authors point to the benefits of gaming for vocabulary learning. Hannibal Jensen (2019) qualitatively investigated L2 English learning in the wild in 7-to-11-year-old Danish children, who had all already received (a limited amount of) formal English instruction. The author looked into the children's motives for using English during activities 'in the wild' and investigated how children engaged with English. She found that many learners had positive sentiments toward English and felt that English content was more interesting than Danish content. Furthermore, the learners indicated that in using English they became part of a larger 'community of practice' (Lave and Wenger 1991) e.g. groups playing certain games, often in English. The learners in the study also explicitly mentioned the use of strategies to understand the context such as looking up words through Google translate, inferencing, or looking for similarities with Danish. Other learners, however, mentioned that they were not particularly motivated to learn English but that it was a necessary tool to be able to engage in the desired activities.

In this study, we will complement quantitative data collection with a qualitative, emic approach to provide a thick description of children's motives to engage with English in extramural contexts prior to the start of formal classroom instruction. Emic research centers around insider perspectives. It is premised on the idea that behaviour is motivated by the meanings people attribute to situations themselves. Therefore, only people themselves can reveal the motivations and meanings of their actions and experiences (Pavlenko 2002; Punch 2005). We will use focus group discussions to gather insights into the reasons why children seek out contact with English, whether there is a specific purpose to their engagement and how they go about the engagement (i.e. what they do exactly in their dealings with the English language).

2 Context of the study

The current study took place in Flanders, the Dutch-speaking part of Belgium, where the language of instruction is Dutch. Contrary to many other European countries, formal English lessons in Flanders only start in secondary school (when children are 12 to 13 years old).

Belgium has three official languages: Dutch (which is spoken in the northern half of the country), French (which is spoken in the southern half) and German (which is spoken in a small region close to the German border). The capital region Brussels is bilingual (French – Dutch). The Flemish government has decreed that the first foreign language to be taught in schools is French. French classes typically start in the penultimate year of primary school, when children are 10 years old. Since 2017, schools are encouraged to introduce French, English or German through 'language-related activities' (such as singing a song) as early as the first year of primary school and they are allowed to teach French, English or German from the third year onwards (when children are 8 years old). However, most Flemish schools still follow the old legislation and only teach French in the last two years of primary school.

Even though formal English instruction starts relatively late, English is very much present in society in Flanders (e.g. through advertising and the media) and children have many opportunities to engage with English before the start of formal classroom instruction.

3 Aims and research questions

In this study we aim to look into the role of out-of-school exposure to English in Flemish children's daily lives prior to formal instruction. We will look into the amount of out-of-school exposure to English and will further investigate the contexts in which children encounter English and their motivations for using English.

The research questions thus are:
1. How much time do Flemish 10–12-year-old children engage in activities which involve English (prior to formal instruction)?
2. In which contexts do Flemish 10–12-year-old children engage with English?
3. What are Flemish 10–12-year-old children's motivations for using English?

Based on what was found in previous studies (De Wilde et al. 2020a; Puimège and Peters 2019), we hypothesize that most Flemish 10–12-year-old children encounter English on a daily basis through different types of media. Activities which have proven popular in this age group are watching television with subtitles in the home language, listening to English music, gaming in English and using social media in English. Reading in English has not been shown a regular activity in these studies.

A qualitative study by Hannibal Jensen (2019) has shown that children are motivated to use English because it is an appealing language and they think English has a positive status. Children also claim it is important to learn/use English because it includes them in a desired community e.g. a group playing a certain videogame. This study was done with young learners in an early instruction context. In the current study we wish to investigate whether the same motivations are present with young learners growing up in a similar cultural context but prior to the start of formal instruction.

4 Method

4.1 Participants

The participants in this study were 43 children who attended primary school in Flanders, where the language of instruction is Dutch. None of the children had received formal English lessons prior to the study. About 75% of the children only spoke Dutch at home (n = 33) and 25% of the children reported that they spoke at least one other language with one of their parents (n = 11). One of the children was raised in English and this participant's results were therefore left out of the analyses. The other languages that children spoke with their parents were Arabic, Czech, French, German, Japanese, Persian, Romanian, Russian and Turkish. The sample consisted of 24 boys and 19 girls who were between 10 and 12 years old. The children came from two intact classes of two primary schools in Flanders. One group consisted of children who were in the last year of primary school (20 pupils, 13 boys and 7 girls); the other group consisted of 2 subgroups, one group of children who were in the fifth year of primary school (10 pupils, 6 girls and 4 boys) and the other attending the sixth and final year of primary school (14 pupils, 6 girls and 8 boys). As children from these subgroups formed one class group and had one teacher, they were both included in the study. 34 children who participated in the study were in the sixth and last year of primary school and 10 children were in the fifth year.

4.2 Instruments and procedure

4.2.1 Questionnaire

The children filled in a questionnaire which inquired about their out-of-school exposure to English. The children were asked how much time they spent daily on watching English television with subtitles in the home language, listening to English music, reading in English, gaming in English, using social media in English and speaking English. Other questions gauged whether and in which situations the children spoke English and probed their attitude towards English. In the questionnaire they were also asked about the language(s) they spoke with friends and family. The questionnaire was adapted from De Wilde et al. (2020a) and can be found in Appendix A. The children filled in the questionnaire in the classroom. A researcher was present to answer questions about the questionnaire if necessary.

4.2.2 Focus group discussions

In order to gain more insight in the nature of the children's encounters with English four focus group discussions were conducted after the children had filled in the questionnaire. The list with questions that guided the focus group discussions can be found in Appendix B. All focus groups were held in Dutch, the language of instruction. Focus groups are considered valuable to gain insight in children's experiences. Care was taken to take the children's cognitive, linguistic, social and psychological development into account (Gibson 2012). As recommended by Sinner et al. (2013), three of the four focus groups consisted of 10 participants. One group was slightly larger and consisted of 14 participants. This was done because in one school the class group of 24 pupils was split up by age, resulting in a group of 10 fifth form pupils and a group of 14 sixth form pupils. It was decided to respect this division according to age in the focus groups. The focus groups lasted between 15 and 25 minutes, which is certainly an appropriate duration for this age group. Sinner et al. (2013) mention the importance of creating a relaxed and trusting atmosphere between researcher and children. Therefore, the children were approached in an encouraging manner. They were allowed to share all their ideas and experiences. When the discussion went off-topic, the participants were not interrupted but instead the moderator tried to direct the conversation back towards the topic. The children's teachers were not present during the focus groups. The focus groups took place in a corner of the classroom which was usually used for activities such as singing, reading stories, etc. The children sat in a circle during the focus group. The focus groups were filmed. All parents and children gave their consent to participate.

4.2.3 Analysis

The data of the questionnaire were analysed in a quantitative manner. We calculated descriptive statistics and correlations between the different types of exposure. In order to investigate differences in exposure between different age and gender groups, we used Kruskal Wallis and Wilcoxon Rank Sum tests respectively. The focus group discussions were transcribed and the transcriptions were imported in NVivo. All contexts in which children engage with English were identified and so were the motivations to use English.

5 Results and discussion

5.1 Quantitative analysis

In order to be able to answer the first research question, the children filled in a questionnaire asking about the amount of out-of-school exposure to English. Daily exposure to six types of activities was investigated: watching English television with subtitles in the home language, listening to English music, reading in English, gaming in English, using social media in English and speaking

English. The children were asked to indicate how much time they spent on these activities each day. They could choose between 'I don't do this', 'less than 30 minutes', '30 minutes to 1 hour', '1 hour to 1 hour and 30 minutes', '1 hour and 30 minutes to 2 hours' and 'more than two hours'. For our analyses, these answers were given a score from 0 (I don't do this.) to 5 (more than 2 hours). The results of the questionnaire can be found in Table 1 and Figure 1.

Table 1: How much exposure do children have to English per day? (n = 43).

	0 min	0–30 min	30 min–1 h	1 h–1 h 30 min	1 h 30 min–2 h	>2 hours
English spoken TV subtitles home language	11	7	15	4	2	4
Listening to English music	1	7	13	8	3	11
Reading in English	38	5	0	0	0	0
Playing English games	15	2	8	3	4	11
Using social media in English	18	4	6	6	6	3
Speaking English	20	18	1	0	2	2

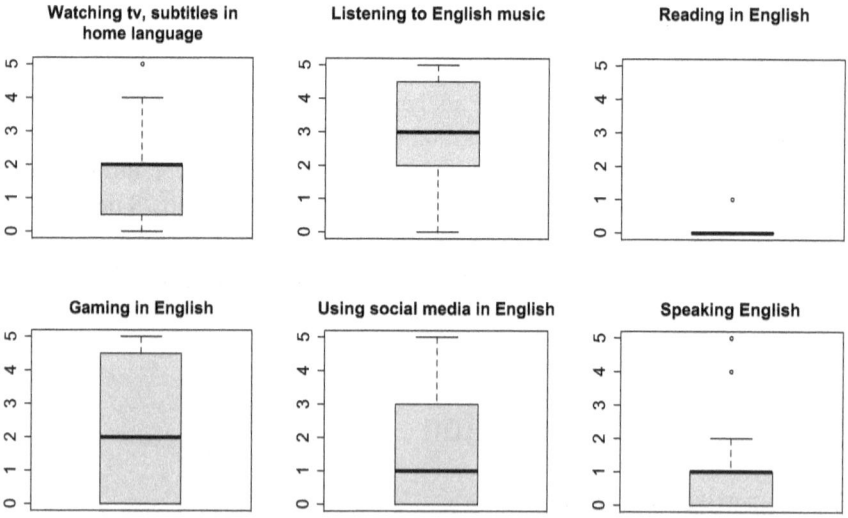

Figure 1: Boxplots illustrating the different types of out-of-school exposure to English per day (n = 43).

Five of the six activities were done by more than half of the participants each day. The only activity which was very uncommon was reading in English. 38 of the 43 participants reported that they never do this, and the remaining five participants reported they did this less than 30 minutes per day. This is in line with previous research on out-of-school exposure in this age group which has shown that reading in English is not a popular out-of-school activity (De Wilde et al. 2020a). There could be different reasons for this. Maybe reading is not popular at this age or maybe the children's L2 English proficiency is too low to be able to read in the foreign language.

The other activities were quite popular with the participants in our study. Nearly all participants (n = 42) reported that they listened to English music every day and about 25% of the children did this for more than two hours. About 75% of the children daily watched subtitled television and 60% of the children reported they gamed in English every day. A quarter of the children mentioned that they gamed over two hours each day. Using social media in English and speaking English were slightly less common but still over 50% of the children claimed they did this every day. These results are also in line with what has been found in previous research (De Wilde et al. 2020a; Jóhannsdóttir 2018; Peters et al. 2019: Puimège and Peters 2019). The boxplots in Figures 2 and 3 show the different types of out-of-school exposure split up by age and gender. Kruskal Wallis tests showed that none of the differences in exposure observed between the different age groups were significant (cf. Appendix C, Table 1). It is hard to interpret these results however, as most children were 11 years old (n = 28), 10 children were 10 years old and only 5 children were 12 years old. Age is not central in this study. If it had been, we would have needed a larger and more balanced research sample. In order to investigate possible differences in exposure between boys and girls, we performed Wilcoxon Rank Sum tests with Bonferroni correction for six comparisons. The results showed that boys spent significantly more time gaming and using social media with a large effect size. Comparison between boys and girls for the other types of exposure proved non-significant (cf. Appendix C, Table 2). The fact that boys are more frequent gamers than girls is in line with results from previous research (Hannibal Jensen 2017; Puimège and Peters 2019; Sylvèn and Sundqvist 2012). Hannibal Jensen (2017) also found that boys were more engaged in YouTube watching than girls. Boys often do this to watch gaming tutorials (Hannibal Jensen 2019).

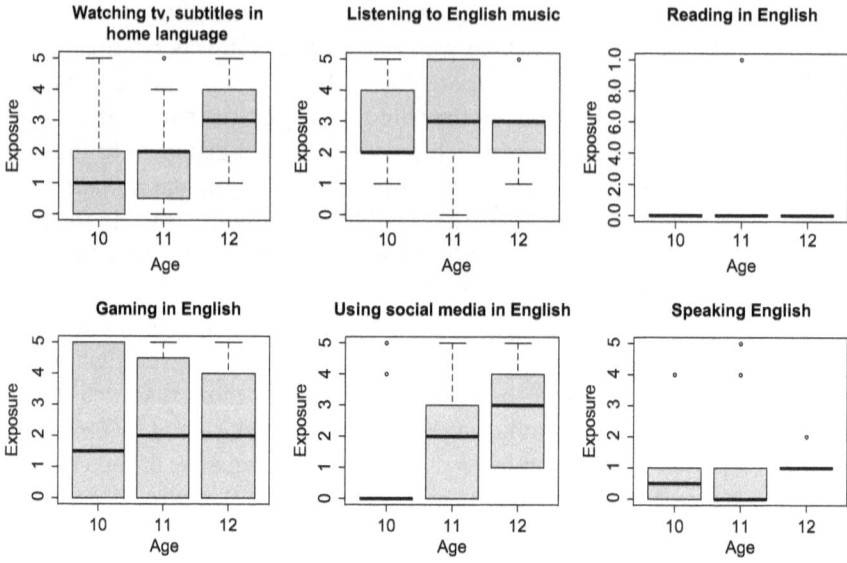

Figure 2: Boxplots illustrating the different types of out-of-school exposure to English per day split up by age (10 years old, n = 10; 11 years old, n = 28, 12 years old, n = 5).

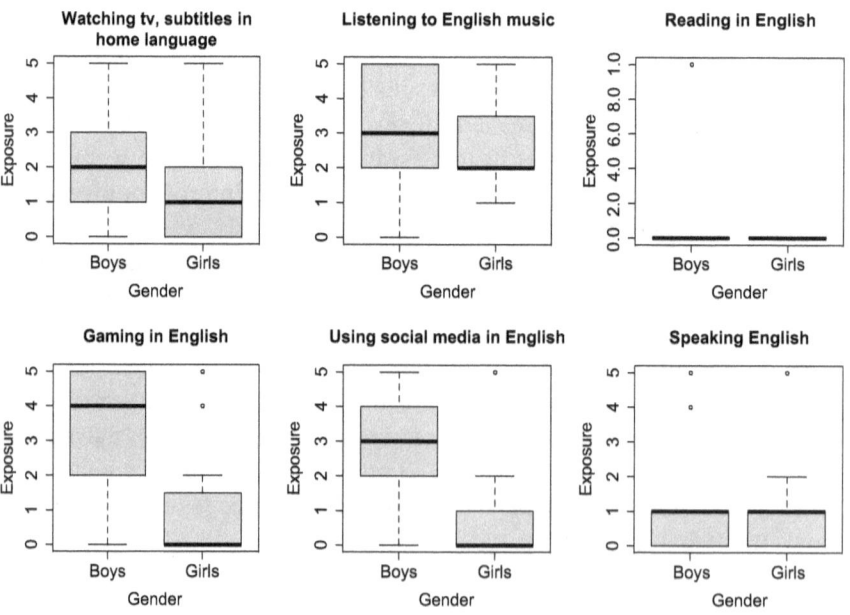

Figure 3: Boxplots illustrating the different types of out-of-school exposure to English per day split up by gender (boys, n = 24; 11 girls, n = 19).

When looking at the correlations between the different types of activities (see Table 2) the correlations between gaming and using social media and gaming and speaking are shown to be highly significant. Again, this is similar to what was found in previous research (De Wilde et al. 2020a) and it could be explained by the fact that frequent gamers often play multiplayer games in which they use (audio)chat (Sylvèn and Sundqvist 2012) or the fact that these frequent gamers sometimes watch gaming videos/tutorials on YouTube (cf. supra).

Table 2: Summary of correlations (Pearson's r) between the different types of exposure.

	1	2	3	4	5	6
1. English spoken tv subtitles home language	1	.24	.20	.32*	.36*	.16
2. Listening to English music		1	.12	.26	.16	.33*
3. Reading English books			1	.20	.23	-.08
4. Playing English Games				1	.65***	.45**
5. Using social media in English					1	.31*
6. Speaking English						1

***p <. 001, **p <. 01, *p < .05.

In the questionnaire we also asked learners in which contexts they use English. 20 children reported they use English when they are on holiday. Other children mentioned they used English while gaming (n=5) or using social media (n=1). Many children reported they use English with their family (n=19) or with their friends (n=12), even though they shared at least one other language (Dutch) with their family and friends and English was not the home language for any of the children in the study. Finally, two children reported they spoke English when talking to themselves.

5.2 Qualitative analysis

The results from the quantitative analysis are in line with what was found in previous research. In the focus group discussions we aimed to get a more detailed view on learners' actual engagement and activities during their exposure to English in the contexts mentioned in the questionnaire. We distilled insights into the contexts in which children used English (RQ2). In order to be able to do this, we imported the transcriptions of the focus group discussions in NVivo. Extracts which mentioned contexts in which English was spoken or motivations for speaking English were highlighted and assigned to one of the two main groups 'contexts' or 'motivations'.

We identified several broad contexts in which children engaged with English: on holiday, at home, at school and with friends/during hobbies. These categories are largely similar to the ones we were able to establish in the questionnaire. All excerpts have been translated from Dutch into English by the authors. The children also mentioned several motivations for using English. Both contexts and motivations will be discussed below using excerpts from the focus group discussions.

The context 'on holiday' was mentioned frequently in the questionnaire but only four times in the focus groups. In two instances, the children commented on how they engage with English in this context.

> Learner 1.2: On holiday. So I was on holiday in Portugal and euh there was one girl who was older than me and she was very good at English and we went to the pool together and then she said 'jump'.
> Researcher: So while making friends on holiday?
> Learner 1.1: I went to Turkey and we went to a hotel for a few days and there I spoke a lot of English with my friends.
> Researcher: A lot of English?
> Learner 1.1: Yes, someone needs to understand us, so yes.
>
> Learner 4.8: On holiday or somewhere else where people talk to you or something, they speak English and you keep on hearing it and then you remember it.

These excerpts show that children use English as a lingua franca when they are on holiday. This type of English use can be expected as the communication cannot take place in the L1. This might explain why this context was mentioned more frequently in the questionnaire than in the focus group discussions as it is a context where the use of English is to be expected and the experiences are similar across learners so they do not feel the need to discuss this elaborately. They probably consider this to be self-evident.

Other contexts that children mentioned were 'at home' (21 references), 'at school' (6 references) and with friends / during hobbies (4 references). In all these situations we can expect that the children share another language (often their L1) with the person they are listening or talking to but still they decide to use English in some situations. At home, children seem to use or pick up English in two contexts, with older siblings and with their parents (see examples below).

> L1.7: My brother often plays those videogames like gta and then he says, when he is shooting he says, euh, 'fuck you motherfucker' or something or 'bitch' and such and one time I was playing with my dolls and they were fighting and they said 'fuck you bitch'.

> L2.3: With my older brother, when he has homework, he needs to check and I have to tell him whether it is right or wrong.
>
> L3.5: Yes, with my mom as well, when I ask something, I sometimes ask it in English.
> Researcher: Yes? And what does she say? Does she like it when you do that?
> L3.5: She, euh, answers my question in English or in Dutch.
>
> L4.9: When my dad speaks, I use English.
> Researcher: Because your dad speaks English or just to practice?
> L4.9: To practice

Some children also referred to the school context. They mentioned using English on the playground during breaks, one child mentioned a short classroom activity during kindergarten where the teacher taught the children how to count in English. Other children mentioned they use English with their friends. The examples are similar to the references that were made to siblings described above (L1.7, L2.3). The children mentioned activities where they use English when playing with older children.

Apart from these broad contexts, there were also many references to the children's engagement with different media. Most of the references were made to online media such as gaming and using social media (32 references) but also singing (16 references) and watching television (6 references) were discussed. When discussing gaming and using social media, several participants mentioned use of English in the (audio) chat during gaming and using English when texting on social media, which confirms the hypothesis we made above based on the quantitative data. Apart from that, children enthusiastically mentioned the names of a lot of different games, social media and YouTube channels they know and use.

> L1.9: When I play gta or another game online and when I put on the phone euh headphone, I speak English.
> L1.7: I play with XX and euh, you often see they speak English in the chat so that lingers a bit.
> L2.4: Euhm, on WhatsApp we write things like 'I love you bae',[1] that's with an 'a' and an 'e' in English.
> L3.2: Like in the chat we all use English words in Messenger chat.

Some children also explicitly mentioned they learned English from songs and subtitled television. An example of each can be found below.

---

[1] African American Vernacular English pronunciation of 'babe' (www.urbandictionary.com).

> Researcher: And where did you learn the sentence?
> L1.10: It's from a song.
> Researcher: From a song.
> L1.10: (starts singing) 'I believe I can fly'.
>
> L1.4: Yes, we have Netflix and there are a lot of nice English films
> L1.2: Yes!
> L1.4: And then most of the times you hear the word and you see where the subtitles are and then you immediately know what it means.

During the focus group discussions, we also asked the participants about their motivations for learning or wanting to learn English. In the analysis of the focus groups, we distinguished several categories. The first motivation seemed to be practical. The children pointed out that they felt English was all around them and thus they felt knowledge of English was necessary to communicate. We identified 16 references in the focus group in which this motivation was mentioned. Sometimes, knowing English was contrasted with knowing French, which is a foreign language they learn in school. French was considered less valuable by some of the participants. A few illustrations can be found below.

> Researcher: So why is English so much fun.
> L2.3: Because almost everyone can speak the language.
> L2.8: Yes, it's a world language.
>
> L3.2: It's a language everyone knows, yes almost everyone knows it and if you know it well, you can do more, you can do more things with it.
>
> L2.3: English is more important than, than
> L2.14: French!
> Researcher: Ok, and why do you think that?
> L2.3: Because everyone knows it.
> L2.4: Euh, English is a world language and French is a language spoken in our country.
> Researcher: French is spoken in our country? But people in France also speak French?
> L2.4: Yes, but for example that we speak English, so in France you can also speak English, but you cannot use French everywhere. In England you speak English but then also in many other countries and for French it's only here.

Learners often also mentioned affective reasons for wanting to use and learn English. They thought English was fun (12 references), beautiful or cool (11 references) and was also very useful when cursing (8 references). Again, a few participants contrasted their feelings towards English with their feelings towards French. Furthermore, children also discussed how some English accents are considered 'cooler' than others.

L1.1: More fun! Yes, that's it!
L1.10: More fun than French!
Researcher: Yes, and why is it more fun than French?
L1.10: Because French is a lot harder. You don't automatically learn it.

L4.6: But yes, I already know a lot of English and it continues to be, I have done this since a very long time, I play in English, euh speak and still, yes, still I think it is a fun language.

Researcher: But why do you say 'I don't know' and not 'ik weet het niet (= Dutch: I don't know)'
L1.4: It sounds much more beautiful.
L1.10: Much more beautiful than French.

L1.7: It' a supercool language!
L1.10: Yes, I think it's fun.
L1.7: I love English.
Researcher: You love English.
L1.7: I'm in love with English!

L1.10: Yes, most of the time we curse in English.

L3.2: Yes, that one, Canada is a bit, is actually a bit English.
L3.7: Yes! That's some kind of fancy English I think.
Researcher: Fancy English? Like euh, from England?
L3.2: No no! In America, euh in England, Britain! There they speak good English.
Researcher: Yes, there they speak good English.
L3.5: Yes, he has such a cool accent.

The results from the focus group analysis align with the participants' answers on the question in the questionnaire about their attitude towards English. 40 participants reported they had a positive attitude towards the language, two participants had a negative attitude and one participant did not answer this question.

Some children experienced English to be an easy language and contrasted it with learning French, which they considered to be harder. In one of the focus groups, it was explicitly mentioned by the children that English is easier than French because it is a Germanic language and thus linguistically more similar to Dutch than French. The excerpts below show that children this age are already aware of the advantage they have when learning a language with a lot of similarities to their L1, an advantage which has been demonstrated in several studies (De Wilde et al. 2020b, Lindgren and Muñoz 2013; Muñoz et al. 2018; Van der Slik 2010).

> L2.3: It is more like Dutch.
> Researcher: Do you think it is more like Dutch?
> L2.3: Yes.
> L2.7 + L2.8: No.
> L2.13: I think it is just easier.
>
> Researcher: Why do you think English is so much easier than French?
> L2.2: Because English is more like Dutch and in French there are many many accents.
> Researcher: Accents, yes.
> L2.10: Because it is a Germanic language!

Some learners mentioned they had no real reason for using English. They claimed that it is something that happens without their control or intention (5 references).

> L1.6: I really have no idea why I use English.
> Researcher: No idea.
> L1.8: Me neither.
> Researcher: Nothing?
> L1.2: Just sometimes
> L1.1: Once in a while
> L1.4: It just happens.

Finally, some participants indicated that around them people seemed to use English as a secret language (two references in the focus groups), which could also be a motivation for wanting to learn English.

> L1.1: One time my brother's friend euh came to our house and euh when we were eating they were speaking Dutch and I was not supposed to know what they said so then they spoke English.

Similarly as in Hannibal Jensen's study (2019), the children assign positive emotions to their use of English and these positive emotions surpass the notion of practicality (being able to communicate with people when on holiday). It is also clear that even children of this young age are "digital consumers" (Mascheroni and Ólafsson 2014) and are consequently acutely aware of the fact that knowledge of English allows them to participate in the world of social media. Although quite a few children assessed the utility of English and set it off against their esteem of the utility of French, the children did not emphasize specific learning goals as such. Rather, they gave evidence of using English in various activities that revolve around play and communication.

6 Conclusion

In this study we have adopted a quantitative as well as a qualitative approach to investigate Flemish children's extramural engagement with English. The quantitative data were assembled by means of a survey and they have furnished important information about what kind of L2 English activities young learners engage in, how intense this engagement is and how regular the interaction with the foreign language is. Of the six activities that were probed, five were exercised by more than half of the children every day (watching English television with subtitles in the home language, listening to English music, gaming in English, using social media in English and speaking English). Only reading in English was hardly ever done.

The quantitative analysis confirmed previous research on engagement with out-of-school exposure which is important for the qualitative element in this study. This was added to corroborate the quantitative findings and to provide richer, more detailed information about when and why children opt to use English, something we could only speculate on thus far. While previous research has demonstrated that extramural engagement of children of this early age showed reading, writing, and talking to be negligible activities (cf. Lindgren and Muñoz 2013), the qualitative results of this study allow us to conclude that Flemish children's spontaneous engagement with English also involves speaking. The children in this study claim to use English for play and communication with Dutch-speaking friends and family. In fact, more than half of the children report to speak English on a daily basis with people with whom they share a mother tongue and a few children testified to speaking English to themselves when they are alone. The different findings in our study compared to the study by Lindgren and Muñoz (2013) could have several reasons. In our study, all children live in a context where English is easily accessible. Furthermore, since there are many similarities between English and Dutch, the step to try and speak (some) English might be quite small. In the study by Lindgren and Muñoz (2013) children come from seven different contexts, some of which might be less inviting (fewer exposure, more linguistically distant). This hypothesis would have to be investigated in future research. Another difference between the studies is that in Lindgren and Muñoz (2013) parents filled in the questionnaire whereas in our study children completed the questionnaire and participated in the focus group discussions. Parents might not always be aware of exactly how often and in which situations their children speak English.

As far as motivation goes, the Flemish children in this study, who had not received any formal instruction of English, bring forward similar reasons to use English as the Danish children who had already received formal instruction in the study by Hannibal Jensen (2019). They use English because it is an appealing language and they think it has a positive status. The Flemish children are aware of the potential of knowing English for their school career but this does not seem to be the primary reason for their engagement with the language. They seem to find it entertaining to use English at home, with friends and when engaging with their hobbies. The motivational factor of activities that are chosen because of their entertainment value is not to be underestimated. The idea that language users' or language learners' positive perception of a language leads to learning affordances has been established before (van Lier 2000, 2004): how you relate to a language can have a considerable impact on learning since it instigates interaction with the language environment. However, we did not gather performance data from the children and hence we can make no statements to the relation between the children's attitudes and their level of proficiency.

Similarly, we cannot make any inferences about the relation between the amount of extramural engagement and the children's knowledge of English from this study. From previous research with very young learners (below the age of eight) we know that the amount of engagement in extramural activities has not always led to learning effects (Unsworth et al. 2015; Hannibal Jensen 2017). Studies with older children (10–12 years old) however, have shown that out-of-school exposure explains about 20% of the variance in children's overall L2 English proficiency (e.g. De Wilde et al. 2020a).

Finally, the emic perspective that was taken in this study has benefits as well as limitations. The information that is gathered through the focus group discussions has added ecological validity and texture to the quantitative findings, but one can never rule out the social desirability bias that is typical of interview situations (i.e. the children's wish to cater to the expectations of the experimenter or of the other children in the group).

Appendices

Appendix A: Questionnaire

School: _____
Class : _____ Number : _____
Name : _____
Date of birth : _____
I am _____ years old. I am a boy/girl (circle the answer that applies).

General information:

1. Which language(s) do you speak at home (with your mother, father, brothers or sisters)?
   _____

2. Which language do you usually speak with your friends?
   _____

How much contact do you have with the English language?

1. Tick the box. How many hours/minutes do you do the activities in the list **per day**:

In **ENGLISH**	I don't do this.	Less than 30 minutes	30 minutes– 1 hour	1 hour– 1 hour 30 minutes	1 hour 30 minutes– 2 hours	More than 2 hours
Watch TV with subtitles in the home language						
Listen to English music						
Read English books, magazines, comics						
Gaming in English						
Youtube, use of social media in English						
Speak English						

2. Do you think English is a fun language? Yes / No
3. Do you sometimes speak English? Yes / No

If yes, where, when, with whom?
a. On holiday? Yes / No　　　　　　　　　With whom? _____
b. At home? Yes / No　　　　　　　　　　With whom? _____
c. In a sports club/youth movement? Yes/No　With whom? _____
c. In other situations? Yes / No　　　　　　In which situations? _____
　　　　　　　　　　　　　　　　　　　　With whom? _____

Appendix B: Guiding questions for the focus group discussions

- I read in the questionnaires that you sometimes speak English amongst yourselves or with friends. Can you tell me when / why / in which situations you do this?
- Do you sometimes call out English words when you are playing a game?
- Which ones?
- Where did you pick up these words? In school? TV? Gaming?...
- Why do you use English words?
- Is it fun?
- Is it a habit? Something everyone does?
- Would you like to improve at speaking English?
- How would you like to improve speaking English?
- What can you do to improve?
- Do you think it is hard or does it happen without any effort?
- In school you don't learn English but French? Do you sometimes use French on the playground or at any other moment (except in class)?
- Why do/don't you do this?
- Is there anything you would like to add about the subject?

Appendix C: Supplementary tables

Table 1: Results of Kruskal Wallis tests for different types of exposure and age.

	Kruskal Wallis chi-squared	p
Watching tv, subtitles in home language	4.3989	.111
Listening to English music	0.0564	.972
Reading in English	2.9605	.228
Gaming in English	0.1178	.943
Using social media in English	5.438	.066
Speaking in English	3.8494	.146

Table 2: Results of Wilcoxon rank-sum tests and effect size for different types of exposure and gender.

	Boys Median	Girls Median	Cliff's delta	p
Watching tv, subtitles in home language	2	1	.40	.124
Listening to English music	3	2	.10	n.s.
Reading in English	0	0	.21	.231
Gaming in English	4	0	.72	<.001***
Using social media in English	3	0	.64	.001**
Speaking in English	1	1	.03	n.s.

** p < .01, *** p < .001 (after Bonferroni correction for 6 comparisons).

References

de Bot, K. 2014. The effectiveness of early foreign language learning in the Netherlands. *Studies in Second Language Learning and Teaching 3*. 409–418.

De Wilde, V., Brysbaert, M., & Eyckmans, J. 2020a. Learning English through out-of-school exposure. Which levels of language proficiency are attained and which types of input are important? *Bilingualism: Language and Cognition* 23(1). 171–185.

De Wilde, V., Brysbaert, M., & Eyckmans, J. 2020b. Learning English Through Out-of-School Exposure: How Do Word-Related Variables and Proficiency Influence Receptive Vocabulary Learning? *Language Learning* 70(2). 349–381.

De Wilde, V, Brysbaert, M., & Eyckmans, J. 2022. Formal versus informal L2 learning: How do individual differences and word-related variables influence French and English L2 vocabulary learning in Dutch-speaking children? *Studies in Second Language Acquisition* 44(1). 87–111.

Gibson, J. 2012. Interviews and Focus Groups With Children: Methods That Match Children's Developing Competencies. *Journal of Family Theory & Review* 4(2). 148–159.

Hannibal Jensen, S. 2017. Gaming as an English Language Learning Resource among Young Children in Denmark. *CALICO Journal* 34(1). 1–19.

Hannibal Jensen, S. 2019. Language learning in the wild: A young user perspective. *Language Learning and Technology* 23(1). 72–86.

Johannsdóttir, Á. 2018. English exposure and vocabulary proficiency at the onset of English instruction. In Arnbjörnsdóttir, B., & Ingvarsdóttir, H. (Eds.), *Language Development across the Life Span. The Impact of English on Education and Work in Iceland*. Switzerland: Springer.

Kuppens, A. H. 2010. Incidental foreign language acquisition from media exposure. *Learning, Media and Technology* 35(1). 65–85.

Lave, J., & Wenger, E. 1991. *Situated learning: Legitimate peripheral participation*.Cambridge: Cambridge university press.

Lefever, S. 2010. *English skills of young learners in Iceland: "I started talking English when I was 4 years old. It just bang . . . just fall into me."*. Menntakvika Conference, Reijkjavik, Iceland.
Lindgren, E., & Muñoz, C. 2013. The influence of exposure, parents, and linguistic distance on young European learners' foreign language comprehension. *International Journal of Multilingualism* 10(1). 105–129.
Mascheroni, G., & Ólafsson, K. 2014. *Net children go mobile: Risks and opportunities*.Milan: Educatt.
Muñoz, C., Cadierno, T., & Casas, I. 2018. Different Starting Points for English Language Learning: A Comparative Study of Danish and Spanish Young Learners. *Language Learning* 68. 1076–1109.
Pavlenko, A. 2002. Poststructuralists approaches to the study of social factors in L2. In V. Cook (Ed.), *Portraits of the L2 User*, 277–302. Clevedon, UK: Multilingual Matters.
Peters, E., Noreillie, A. S., Heylen, K., Bulté, B., & Desmet, P. 2019. The impact of instruction and out-of-school exposure to foreign language input on learners' vocabulary knowledge in two languages. *Language Learning* 69(3). 747–782.
Piirainen-Marsh, A. 2011. Enacting interactional competence in gaming activities: Coproducing talk with virtual others. In J. K. Hall, J. Hellermann, & S. Pekarek Doehler (Eds.), *L2 interactional competence and development*, 19–44. Bristol: Multilingual Matters.
Puimège, E., & Peters, E. 2019. Learners' English Vocabulary Knowledge Prior to Formal Instruction: The Role of Learner-Related and Word-Related Variables. *Language Learning* 69(4). 943–977.
Punch, K.F. 2005. *Introduction to social research* [2nd edition]. Thousand Oaks, CA:Sage.
Sinner, P., Prochazka, F., Paus-Hasebrink, I., & Farrugia, L. 2013. FAQ 34: What are some good approaches to conducting focus. In K. Ólafsson, S. Livingstone, & L. Haddon (Eds.), *How to research children and online technologies? Frequently asked questions and best practice*, 87–90. London: EU Kids Online, LSE.
Sylvén, L. K., & Sundqvist, P. 2012. Gaming as extramural English L2 learning and L2 proficiency among young learners. *ReCALL* 24(03). 302–321.
Turgut, Y., & İrgin, P. 2009. Young learners' language learning via computer games. *Procedia – Social and Behavioral Sciences* 1(1). 760–764.
Unsworth, S., Persson, L., Prins, T., & De Bot, K. (2015). An investigation of factors affecting early foreign language learning in the Netherlands. *Applied Linguistics, 36*(5), 527–548. https://doi.org/10.1093/applin/amt052
Van der Slik, F. W. P. 2010. Acquisition of Dutch as a Second Language. *Studies in Second Language Acquisition* 32(03). 401–432.
van Lier, L. 2000. 'From Input to Affordance: Social-interactive Learning from an Ecological Perspective', in J. Lantolf (Ed.), *Sociocultural Theory and Second Language Learning*. Oxford: Oxford University Press.
van Lier, L. 2004. *The Ecology and Semiotics of Language Learning: a Sociocultural Perspective*. Dordrecht: Kluwer Academic Publishers.

Claire Goriot and Roeland van Hout
The relation between out-of-school exposure to English and English vocabulary development in Dutch primary school pupils

Abstract: The aim of this study was to investigate how often Dutch pupils from early-English and mainstream primary schools were exposed to English outside of school, and whether this exposure was positively related to their English vocabulary development. Parents of 263 primary school pupils aged 4 to 12 filled in a questionnaire about out-of-school exposure to English. Children performed the Peabody Picture Vocabulary test in English and Dutch to assess their vocabulary knowledge in both languages. It was found that pupils in the upper grades were more exposed to English than pupils in the lower grades. Pupils in the lower grades were also exposed to different activities than pupils in the upper grades. They engaged more in educational activities in English, whereas older pupils engaged more in gaming, subtitled activities and activities in English in which no subtitles were used and they had to listen actively. For younger pupils, educational activities in English, subtitled activities, and active listening activities were positively related to their English vocabulary. For older pupils, subtitled activities, active listening, gaming in English, and listening to English songs were positively related to English knowledge. These relations remained when taking Dutch vocabulary knowledge into account, and did not differ between pupils from early-English and mainstream schools. These results show that individual differences in out-of-school exposure to English are positively related to differences in English vocabulary knowledge, but that the extent of exposure and the kind of English activities pupils engage in, differ between older and younger pupils.

Keywords: out-of-school exposure to English, primary school, English as a foreign language, informal language learning, early English education

1 Introduction

In many primary schools in Europe, pupils are learning English as a foreign language. Generally, pupils start in one of the higher grades of primary school, although starting in the lower grades is becoming more common nowadays

(Enever et al. 2011). At the same time, pupils are exposed to English outside the formal setting of the school. Many of their everyday activities, such as listening to the radio or playing videogames, are (partly) in English. Research has shown that children do acquire the English language by engaging in such activities, even when not being exposed yet to English in a formal setting (De Wilde et al. 2020). In this chapter, we investigate the type and amount of out-of-school exposure to English and the relation with English vocabulary development of Dutch pupils across lower and upper primary school grades.

In the Netherlands, children may start as young as four years old with learning English in so-called early-English schools, but mainstream school practices start around the age of eleven. In both early-English and mainstream schools, children get about 45 minutes of English lessons per week, while all other lessons are in Dutch (Jenniskens et al. 2017; Thijs et al. 2011). The main difference between the two types of education thus is that, at the end of primary school, early-English pupils have been exposed to formal English education for a much longer time (i.e., eight years) than mainstream pupils (i.e., two years).

It has been shown that early-English education benefit pupils' knowledge of English, but it should be noted that differences between those two groups of pupils are usually small (Dutch Inspectorate of Education 2019), and sometimes even absent (Goriot et al. 2020, 2021b), whereas individual mainstream pupils occasionally outperform pupils from early-English schools (de Graaff 2015). Previous studies showed, for example, that early-English pupils have a larger English vocabulary than mainstream pupils (Goriot et al. 2021a; Lobo 2013; Unsworth et al. 2015). Even when taking the development of their first language into account, early-English pupils have more balanced lexicons than mainstream pupils, meaning that their English vocabulary development is more in line with their Dutch vocabulary development (Goriot et al. 2018). Early-English pupils also have more knowledge of English grammar (Unsworth et al. 2015), and have better reading and listening skills in English (de Graaff 2015) than pupils from mainstream schools.

The question is what other factors may contribute to pupils' English language knowledge, and could help to account for the (lack of) differences between the pupils of early-English and mainstream schools. One of the factors that is found to enhance pupils' knowledge of English, is pupils' engagement in informal English activities, outside of the school context. Especially for older primary school pupils, it has been shown that pupils engage in English activities in their spare time and that these leisure activities show a positive relation with pupils' knowledge of English.

Puimège and Peters (2019) investigated Flemish 10- to 12-year-old pupils' English vocabulary knowledge prior to formal English instruction. It was found that 12- and 11-year-old children were more frequently exposed to English than 10-year-old pupils. Informal (passive) exposure to English, as for example through listening to English songs, was positively related to pupils' passive vocabulary in English. More active exposure through gaming and video streaming was positively related to pupils' active English vocabulary (Puimège and Peters 2019). Another study with 10- to 12-year-old Flemish pupils yielded similar results: social media use in English, playing English computer games, and speaking in English was positively related to pupils' passive English vocabulary. Listening to English songs, however, showed a negative relation with vocabulary, and watching English television with subtitles and listening to English music was not related to pupils' English language development (De Wilde et al. 2020).

Whereas the previous studies investigated English knowledge prior to formal instruction, Muñoz, Cadierno, and Casas (2018) investigated differences in English knowledge between a group of children that had started English education and a group that did not. They examined English vocabulary and grammar knowledge of 7- and 9-year-old Spanish and Danish children. Spanish children had started formal instruction of English in preschool, but Danish children had just had 10 to 12 hours of English instruction in total. Still, the Danish children's vocabulary knowledge of English was comparable to that of the Spanish children's. One of the factors that contributed to the children's English vocabulary and grammar score, was their exposure to films in English. The Danish children's more frequent exposure to films in English may have provided them with opportunities for learning English implicitly (Muñoz et al. 2018).

De Graaff (2015) examined the English language knowledge of Dutch 11-year-old primary school pupils who attended either a mainstream school and had thus just started English education, and early-English pupils who had been receiving English lessons for multiple years. It was found that pupils who had more exposure to English outside school, performed better on English language tests for reading, writing, use of English, and spelling than pupils with less exposure to English in their spare time. This difference was the same for mainstream as for early-English pupils (de Graaff 2015). The results are similar to those found in recent Dutch national research: early-English and mainstream pupils are exposed to English outside school to a similar extent. The amount of exposure was positively related to pupils' listening, reading, and vocabulary performance in English (Dutch Inspectorate of Education 2019). These results are also in line with research on Swedish children from the same age: it was shown that children's exposure to English games was positively related to their English vocabulary knowledge (Sylvén and Sundqvist 2012).

Another Dutch study investigated ten-year-old primary school pupils' English vocabulary knowledge in relation to out-of-school exposure. More specifically, the authors looked at four types of exposure: 'Entertaining Media' (such as watching English films), 'Family' (speaking English at home, for example), 'Friends' (as for example speaking English with peers), and 'Formal Reading' (e.g. reading books in English). Pupils were directly asked to indicate how often they engaged in these activities. It was found that both for pupils in mainstream schools and pupils in early-English schools there was a positive relation between exposure to English outside the classroom through Family and Entertaining Media, and English vocabulary development. For mainstream pupils this was a direct relation. For early-English pupils, however, this relation was fully mediated by pupils' linguistic self-confidence. The authors hypothesized that early-English pupils receive more feedback on their English, especially from peers and teachers, than mainstream pupils, and therefore they may evaluate their knowledge of English more explicitly than mainstream pupils (Leona et al. 2021).

Less data are available for younger primary school pupils' exposure to English outside the school environment. In the Netherlands, one study investigated the relation between 4 to 6 year-old pupils' out-of-school exposure and skills in English, next to the influence of weekly exposure to English at school and teachers' English proficiency (Unsworth et al. 2015). No relation was found between out-of-school exposure to English and pupils' English vocabulary or grammar development. The authors provided two possible explanations for not finding an effect of out-of-school exposure. The first is that only 67% of the parents filled in the questionnaire. The second is that children were young and hardly had exposure to English outside of school.

To summarise, it is known that Dutch-speaking pupils develop their English vocabulary during primary school, regardless of whether they have been exposed to English or not, although early-English pupils' vocabularies may develop faster than mainstream pupils' (Goriot et al. 2021a; Unsworth et al. 2015). The fact is, however, that Dutch pupils live in a society in which English is omnipresent. Many advertisements are in English, and television shows are subtitled rather than dubbed. In addition to this rather passive kind of exposure to English, pupils may also deliberately engage in activities in English, such as playing English videogames. In this study, we first investigate whether Dutch primary school pupils in both the lower and the upper grades are exposed to activities in English, and if so, to what kind of activities they are exposed. Our first research question was to what extent primary school pupils of different ages are exposed to English outside of school, and what kind of activities they engage in. We expected that the majority of Dutch pupils would have at least some exposure to English, given the prominence of that language in Dutch society, but that substantial individual differences would exist because of children's home situation and the availability of media and digital facilities.

Our second research question was whether out-of-school exposure to English would differ between pupils of different grades. Since, in general, younger pupils are less exposed to television and play video games less often than older pupils (Anderson et al. 2008), we expected that older pupils have more exposure to English through different activities than younger pupils.

The third and final research question was whether there is a positive relation between individual differences in out-of-school exposure to English and English vocabulary knowledge, both for pupils in the lower and in the higher grades of primary school. We have cross-sectional data, meaning that we have to carefully interpret a simultaneous increase of exposure and vocabulary knowledge over grades. For that reason, we made a distinction between the lower and the higher grades to answer the research question. Although we expected to find evidence within these two clusters of a positive relation between out-of-school exposure to English and vocabulary knowledge in English, the outcome may be more likely for pupils in the upper grades as they possibly benefit more from exposure as proficiency increases. Another effect might be that early-English pupils engage more in English activities outside school than mainstream pupils, since early-English pupils are exposed to English at school, too. We therefore investigated whether the answers to the research questions would differ for pupils from early-English and mainstream schools, although we realize that de Graaff (2015) did not find differences between early-English and mainstream pupils.

This study will provide insight in how often Dutch primary school pupils engage in activities in English in their spare time, and in what kind of activities they engage in. Whereas previous studies (de Graaff 2015; Leona et al. 2021) focused on older primary school pupils' out-of-school exposure to English, this study will also shed light on younger pupils' exposure to English outside the school environment. The results of this study contribute to the knowledge about how pupils' English vocabulary development develops along primary school, and which factors contribute to that vocabulary development.

2 Method

2.1 Participants

Participants were 572 primary school pupils (288 boys) between 4 and 12 years old from 19 schools that were located in the middle, the south or the west of the

Netherlands. Nine schools were early-English schools and ten were mainstream schools. Mainstream schools were matched as much as possible on early-English schools in terms of denomination, educational vision, and pupil population. Pupils were in grade 1 or 2 (kindergarten), 3, 5 or 8 (final grade) of primary school. Of these pupils 52.3% attended an early-English school, and had thus received English lessons from the start of primary school. The other pupils attended mainstream schools and did not receive English lessons until the penultimate grade (grade 7). All children had Dutch as their mother tongue and spoke Dutch with their parents. Parents received a questionnaire about demographic factors and their child's out-of-school exposure to English. The response rate was approximately 46% (n = 263 pupils; n = 125 boys). Table 1 shows the number of pupils per grade for early-English and mainstream schools, as well as their mean age in months. Data on age was missing for five pupils, all from control schools. An ANOVA with Grade, Type of Education, and the interaction between Grade and Type of Education showed no significant interaction effect, but there was a significant main effect of Type of Education ($F(1,248) = 4.39, p = .039$). Early-English pupils were slightly younger than mainstream pupils.

Table 1: Number of pupils per grade and mean age for mainstream and early-English schools.

	Mainstream		Early-English	
	n	$M_{\text{age in moths}}$ (SD)	n	$M_{\text{age in moths}}$ (SD)
Grade 1	46	58.35 (4.69)	57	56.82 (3.62)
Grade 2	25	71.60 (3.78)	18	68.56 (4.05)
Grade 3	21	82.16 (3.48)	22	80.00 (4.05)
Grade 5	23	108.48 (8.38)	23	108.26 (5.93)
Grade 8	16	144.06 (5.43)	12	143.83 (6.18)
Total	131	84.60 (29.28)	132	79.16 (28.03)

2.2 Materials

Vocabulary. Pupils' English vocabulary knowledge was examined with the Peabody Picture Vocabulary Test (PPVT-4), in which children are orally presented with an English word and have to choose the correct meaning out of four visually presented alternatives (Dunn & Dunn 2007). In addition, we measured pupils' vocabulary knowledge in Dutch. We used the Dutch version of the PPVT (Dunn et al. 2005).

The English PPVT consists of 228 items, the Dutch of 204 items. In both versions items are grouped in sets of 12. Children start with an age-appropriate set, and are presented with easier or more difficult sets depending on their performance. In the English version, testing stops if a child makes 8 or more errors in one set. For the Dutch version, testing stops with 9 or more errors in one set. The final score is computed as the number of the highest performed item, minus the number of errors. We used the raw scores instead of the norm score since the PPVT is originally developed for native speakers of English (Dunn & Dunn 2007), and their norm scores do not apply for second language learners. To be consistent, we used raw scores for the Dutch version, too.

Language balance. Since it is likely that individual variation does not only exist in children's English vocabulary knowledge but also in their knowledge of Dutch vocabulary (i.e., their first language), and knowledge of Dutch and English are related to each other (Goriot et al. 2018), we included a measure of lexical balance. To calculate lexical balance, we divided children's proportion correct on the PPVT-4 by their proportion correct on the PPVT in Dutch, and took the natural logarithm out of that score (see Goriot et al. 2018). A score of 0 means participants have perfectly balanced lexicons. A negative score means they are more proficient in Dutch than in English, and for those with a positive score it is the other way around.

Out-of-school contact with English. A questionnaire that has been used in previous research (Unsworth et al. 2015) to investigate Dutch kindergartners' out-of-school exposure to English was complemented with additional questions tailored to older pupils' English activities. The final questionnaire consisted of 14 activities. Parents were asked to indicate how often their child engaged in a specific activity, and for how many hours per week. An example is: *How often does your child 'rehearses what he/she learned at school with respect to English'*. Parents could choose between *'never'*, *'once a month'*, *'weekly'*, and *'daily'*, and could indicate the number of hours per week their child spends on this activity. The full questionnaire is displayed in Appendix A.

2.3 Procedure

Questionnaires were used in three different studies to gather information on pupils' exposure to English out of school (Goriot et al. 2018, 2020, 2021a). In each of the three studies, children of different grades performed different language-related and cognitive tasks at their schools. These tasks always included the PPVT in English and Dutch. Those tests were always examined in different sessions, with the PPVT in English always being in the first session. Sessions lasted between 20 and 30 minutes. Parents were asked to fill in the questionnaire on out-of-school exposure to English. They completed either a paper or an online version, depending on the schools' preferences. Parents of all pupils gave informed consent for participation.

3 Results

First, we investigated children's exposure to English activities outside the school environment. We explored both the time children spent on English activities, and the kind of activities they were involved in. Figure 1 shows the division of out-of-school exposure to English in hours per week for pupils of different grades and types of education.[1]

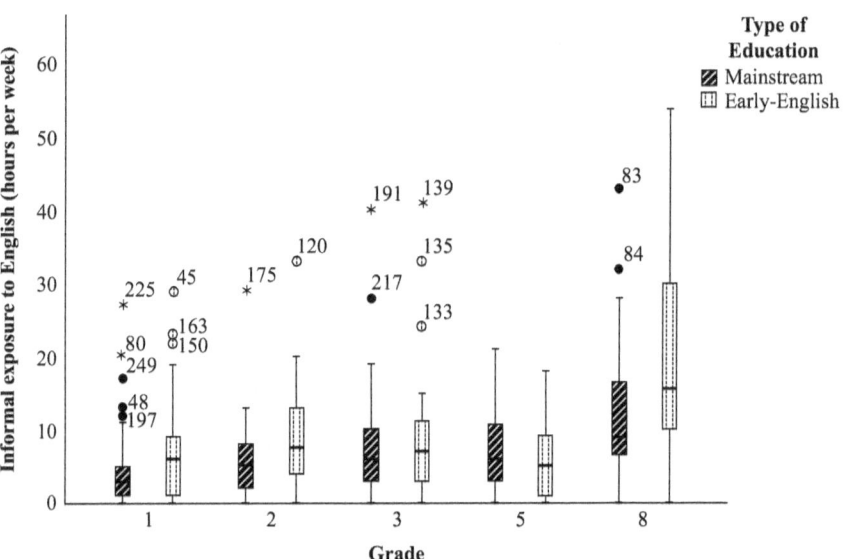

Figure 1: Division of out-of-school exposure to English in hours per week per grade and type of education.

Table 2 shows the average total amount of informal exposure to English per week, English vocabulary score, Dutch vocabulary score, and lexical balance score, for

---

[1] The most striking outlier is pupil number 251, who spends 102 hours per week on English activities. Closer inspection of the data learns that this pupil spends 8 to 10 hours per week on 11 out of the 14 activities mentioned in the questionnaire. As this is timewise almost impossible, data of this pupil were removed from the analysis.

pupils in the different grades. Pupils in the highest grade have on average the most hours of exposure, the highest vocabulary scores, and the most balanced lexicons. It is noteworthy to mention that 35 participants did not have any informal exposure to English according to their parents. This was mostly ($n = 17$) the case for first-grade pupils, but also parents of pupils in other grades reported no exposure to English. Part of these participants ($n = 11$ out of 35) came from a protestant religious background, and had no or limited access to television or computers at home. For other participants, the lack of informal exposure to English remains speculative, but may have to do with lack of access to media, or with lack of interest. It is also noteworthy that some pupils' exposure to English is very high. Even parents of some very young pupils report exposure rates as high as 33 hours per week. An ANOVA with Grade, Type of Education, and the Interaction between the two as independent variables and Total amount of exposure as dependent variables showed a significant effect of Grade ($F(4,252) = 11.00$, $p < .001$). School Type ($F(1,252) = 3.15$) and the interaction effect between Grade and School Type ($F(4,252) = 1.21$) were not significant ($p > .05$). Tukey post-hoc tests revealed that pupils in Grade 8 had more exposure to English than pupils in the lower grades. The same analysis but with English vocabulary as dependent variable showed a non-significant effect of the interaction between Grade and Type of Education ($F(1,252) = 2,18$, $p = .072$), a main effect of Type of Education ($F(1, 252) = 17.22$, $p < .001$), and a main effect of Grade ($F(4, 252) = 165.12$, $p < .001$). In general, early-English pupils obtained significantly higher English vocabulary scores than mainstream pupils. Tukey post hoc tests revealed that pupils' English vocabulary scores significantly differed per grade, with pupils in the higher grades having higher English vocabulary scores than pupils in the lower grades, except for the difference between grade-two and grade-three pupils that was not significant.

Based on children's activities, five types of activities were computed based on the similarity between these activities. The first one, called '*Games*', consists of the sum of 'English sport (computer) games', 'English computer games', and 'English (board) games'. The second factor '*Educative activities*', consists of activities with an educational character, namely: 'Dutch tv with English words (like Dora)', 'English tv for Dutch kindergartners (like Muzzy)', 'English tv for English kindergartners (like Peppa Pig)', and 'rehearsing what was learnt at school'. The third factor '*Subtitles*', consists of 'English tv with subtitles', and 'English films with subtitles'. The fourth one, '*Active listening*', consists of 'English tv without subtitles', 'English films without subtitles', 'English stories', and 'English talks'. Finally, there is '*Songs*', solely consisting of 'English songs'. Figures 2a to e show the average time spent on each of the five types of activities, for children from different grades and different types of education. These figures show that pupils

Table 2: Average hours of informal exposure to English, English and Dutch vocabulary scores, and lexical balance score.

	Mainstream					Early-English				
Grade	1	2	3	5	8	1	2	3	5	8
N	46	25	21	23	15	57	18	22	23	12
Informal exposure to English; $M_{hours\ per\ week}$ (SD)	4.78 (5.60)	6.20 (6.05)	9.10 (9.90)	7.26 (5.56)	13.60 (11.98)	6.40 (6.53)	9.22 (8.36)	9.95 (10.23)	6.00 (5.16)	20.50 (15.41)
Min.-Max.	0–27	0–29	0–40	0–21	0.43	0–29	0–33	0–41	0–18	0–54
English vocabulary, M_{score} (SD)	15.67 (11.54)	23.24 (14.40)	31.62 (17.10)	50.83 (19.79)	97.93 (39.98)	19.91 (11.01)	32.83 (10.12)	40.59 (16.33)	52.39 (14.13)	121.83 (25.23)
Dutch vocabulary, M_{score} (SD)	72.74 (12.40)	87.12 (7.49)	95.05 (9.60)	111.39 (7.12)	132.07 (13.91)	72.16 (11.76)	86.33 (9.14)	96.05 (8.23)	112.17 (7.21)	138.33 (6.95)
Lexical balance, M_{score} (SD)	−1.86 (0.65)	−1.68 (0.81)	−1.36 (0.57)	−0.97 (0.41)	−0.48 (0.34)	−1.57 (0.62)	−1.12 (0.31)	−1.04 (0.34)	−0.90 (0.29)	−0.26 (0.16)

in the lower grades engage in different English activities than pupils in the upper grades, and that some activities are more popular than others.

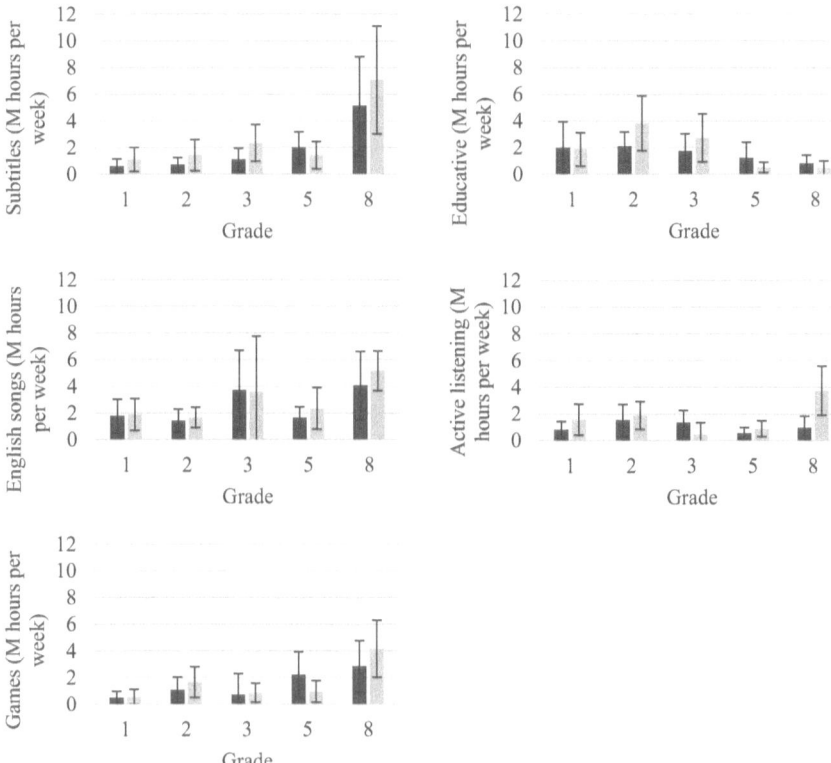

Figure 2: (a–e) Differences in English activities between pupils from different grades and school types (dark grey for mainstream, light grey for early English).

To investigate whether time spent on activities in English differed between younger and older children, ANOVAs with Grade, School Type and the interaction between Grade and School Type as independent variables and the different activities (Games, Subtitles, Active Listening, Education, Songs) as dependent variables were conducted. Table 3 shows the outcomes. For all activities, there are mainly differences between Grades. Pupils in the higher grades (usually those from grade 8) spend more time on English activities than pupils in the lower grades. There are two exceptions to this general outcome. The first one is time spent on 'Education'. Grade 2 pupils spend significantly more time on Educational activities in English than pupils from grades 5 and 8. The second one is Active Listening. For this type, we again observed an effect of grade such that pupils in the higher grades spend more time on active listening in English than younger pupils. In addition, there is also an effect of School Type: Early-English pupils spend more time on active listening than mainstream pupils. The interaction between Grade and School Type was nearly significant ($p = .052$).

Table 3: Relation between grade, school type, and English activities.

	.Games	Education	Subtitles	Active listening	Songs
Grade	$F(4,252) = 9.45, p < .001$	$F(4,252) = 4.91, p = .004$	$F(4,252) = 16.36, p < .001$	$F(4,252) = 2.88, p = .023$	$F(4,252) = 4.59, p = .001$
School Type	$F(4,252) = 0.16, p > .05$	$F(4,252) = 0.56, p > .05$	$F(4,252) = 2.87, p > .05$	$F(4,252) = 8.89, p = .003$	$F(4,252) = 0.40, p > .05$
Grade*School Type	$F(4,252) = 2.02, p > .05$	$F(4,252) = 1.37, p > .05$	$F(4,252) = 0.91, p > .05$	$F(4,252) = 2.38, p = .052$	$F(4,252) = 0.16, p > .05$
Post hoc (Tukey)	5 > 1 8 > 1, 2, 3, 5	2 > 5,8	8 > 1, 2, 3, 5	8 > 5 Early English > mainstream	3 > 1 8 > 1,2,5

Finally, to investigate whether individual differences in out-of-school exposure to English activities are related to individual differences in pupils' vocabulary, regression analyses were conducted. Because time and type of out-of-school activities differed between pupils from the lower and the upper grades, we analysed those groups separately. The lower primary school grades (1, 2, and 3) were analysed together, and the upper grades (5 and 8) were analysed together.

We performed linear models in R (version 3.6.2), with activity type (Games, Educative activities, Subtitles, Active Listening or Songs), Grade, Type of Education and the interaction between the two as independent variables and English vocabulary as dependent variable. We also added the interaction between Type of Education and Activity, but as this interaction was never significant, we decided to report the most parsimonious model. The results are shown in Table 4 For pupils in the lower grades, there were still positive relations between Educative activities, subtitles and active listening. The main effects of Grade and Type of Education were also significant. Tukey post hoc analyses showed that pupils in grade 3 performed better on the English vocabulary test than pupils in grade 2, who in turn performed better than pupils in grade 1. Pupils from early-English school had better knowledge of English vocabulary than pupils from mainstream schools. The interaction between Grade and Type of Education was never significant.

Table 4: Relation between English activities, grade, type of education and English vocabulary for pupils in the lower and upper grades.

		English vocabulary	
		Lower grades	Upper grades
Games		$F(1,182) = 2.74, p > .05$	$F(1,68) = 16.50, p = .001$
Grade		$F(2, 182) = 29.63, p < .001$	$F(1, 68) = 76.56, p < .001$
Type of education		$F(1,182) = 11.71, p = .001$	$F(1,68) = 3.11, p > .05$
Grade * Type of education		$F(2, 182) = 0.09, p > .05$	$F(1, 68) = 2.48, p > .05$
		$R^2 = .270$	$R^2 = .568$
Educative activities		$F(1,182) = 5.88, p = .016$	$F(1,68) = 1.46, p > .05$
Grade		$F(2, 182) = 30.33, p < .001$	$F(1, 68) = 87.67, p < .001$
Type of education		$F(1,182) = 10.75, p = .001$	$F(1, 68) = 2.51, p > .05$
Grade * Type of education		$F(2, 182) = .66, p > .05$	$F(1, 68) = 3.47, p > .05$
		$R^2 = .279$	$R^2 = .559$
Subtitles		$F(1,182) = 11.55, p = .001$	$F(1,68) = 18.28, p < .001$
Grade		$F(2, 182) = 27.48, p < .001$	$F(1, 68) = 70.80, p < .001$
Type of education		$F(1,182) = 9.55, p = .002$	$F(1,68) = 2.71, p > .05$
Grade * Type of education		$F(2, 182) = 0.78, p > .05$	$F(1, 68) = 3.17, p > .05$
		$R^2 = .276$	$R^2 = .558$
Active listening		$F(1,182) = 6.84, p = .001$	$F(1,68) = 25.03, p < .001$
Grade		$F(2, 182) = 30.76, p < .001$	$F(1, 68) = 68.31, p < .001$
Type of education		$F(1,182) = 10.16, p = .002$	$F(1,68) = 1.29, p > .05$
Grade * Type of education		$F(2, 182) = 1.07, p > .05$	$F(1, 68) = 2.14, p > .05$
		$R^2 = .284$	$R^2 = .563$
Songs		$F(1,182) = 0.16, p > .05$	$F(1,68) = 10.53, p = .001$
Grade		$F(2, 182) = 31.41, p < .001$	$F(1, 68) = 78.78, p < .001$
Type of education		$F(1,182) = 11.82, p = .001$	$F(1,68) = 2.91, p > .05$
Grade * Type of education		$F(2, 182) = 0.87, p > .05$	$F(1, 68) = 3.44, p > .05$
		$R^2 = .273$	$R^2 = .559$
Post hoc analyses	Grade:	3 > 2 > 1	8 > 5
	Type of education	Early-English > Mainstream	–

For pupils in the upper grades, we found significant and positive relations between Gaming, Subtitles, Active listening and Songs and English Vocabulary. The interaction between Grade and Type of Education was never significant, nor was the main effect of Type of Education. There was always a significant effect of Grade, and Tukey post-hoc analyses showed that grade 8 pupils had better English vocabulary knowledge than grade 5 pupils.

Thereafter, we performed the same analyses but now with Lexical Balance as the dependent variable, to take pupils' vocabulary knowledge in Dutch as well as the relation between their Dutch and English vocabularies into account. Again, we tested whether there were significant interaction effects between Type of Education and Activity, but none of these interactions was significant and we reported the more parsimonious model.

These analyses resulted in largely similar results as for the previous analyses. The only exception is the effect of Grade for the lower-grade pupils, as Tukey post-hoc analyses showed that first-grade pupils' English vocabulary knowledge was still lower than that of second- and third-grade pupils when controlling for their Dutch vocabulary knowledge, but second- and third-grade pupils' knowledge of English was no longer significantly different (see Table 5).

Table 5: Relation between English activities, grade, type of education and lexical balance for pupils in the lower and upper grades.

	Balance	
	Lower grades (1,2,3)	Upper grades (5, 8)
Games	$F(1,182) = 2.30, p > .05$	$F(1,68) = 11.91, p = .001$
Grade	$F(2, 182) = 10.67, p < .001$	$F(1, 68) = 40.38, p < .001$
Type of education	$F(1,182) = 17.29, p < .001$	$F(1,68) = 2.89, p > .05$
Grade * Type of education	$F(2, 182) = 0.64, p > .05$	$F(1, 68) = 0.48, p > .05$
	$R^2 = .162$	$R^2 = .418$
Educative activities	$F(1,182) = 5.64, p = .02$	$F(1,68) = 3.17, p > .05$
Grade	$F(2, 182) = 11.18, p < .001$	$F(1, 68) = 47.63, p < .001$
Type of education	$F(1,182) = 16.05, p < .001$	$F(1,68) = 1.93, p > .05$
Grade * Type of education	$F(2, 182) = 0.54, p > .05$	$F(21, 68) = 1.14, p > .05$
	$R^2 = .172$	$R^2 = .409$
Subtitles	$F(1,182) = 8.05, p = .005$	$F(1,68) = 13.03, p = .001$
Grade	$F(2, 182) = 9.66, p = .001$	$F(1, 68) = 36.41, p < .001$
Type of education	$F(1,182) = 14.74, p = .001$	$F(1, 68) = 2.44, p > .05$
Grade * Type of education	$F(2, 182) = 0.72, p > .05$	$F(1, 68) = 0.79, p > .05$
	$R^2 = .167$	$R^2 = .403$
Active listening	$F(1,182) = 7.70, p = .007$	$F(1,68) = 12.02, p = .001$
Grade	$F(2, 182) = 11.35, p < .001$	$F(1, 68) = 37.64, p < .001$
Type of education	$F(1,182) = 15.21, p = .001$	$F(1,68) = 1.65, p > .05$
Grade * Type of education	$F(2, 182) = 0.77, p > .05$	$F(1, 68) = 0.64, p > .05$
	$R^2 = .179$	$R^2 = 400$

Table 5 (continued)

		Balance	
		Lower grades (1,2,3)	Upper grades (5, 8)
Songs		$F(1,182) = 0.52, p > .05$	$F(1,68) = 9.12, p = .004$
Grade		$F(2, 182) = 11.37, p < .001$	$F(1, 68) = 39.36, p < .001$
Type of education		$F(1,182) = 17.23, p < .001$	$F(1,68) = 2.34, p > .05$
Grade * Type of education		$F(2, 182) = 0.71, p > .05$	$F(1, 68) = 0.96, p > .05$
		$R^2 = .1620$	$R^2 = .399$
Post hoc analyses	Grade:	3, 2 > 1	8 > 5
	Type of education	Early-English > Mainstream	–

4 Discussion

The aim of this study was to investigate whether individual differences in Dutch primary school pupils' exposure to English outside the school environment was related to their English vocabulary knowledge. We investigated this question in pupils of different ages, ranging from four to twelve years old, and both in pupils who attended early-English or mainstream primary schools. It was found that for both groups of pupils, and for pupils of different ages, individual differences in out-of-school exposure were positively related to their English vocabulary knowledge. However, the kind of activities that they engaged in and that showed a relation with their vocabulary, differed depending on the age group.

Our first research question was to what extent primary school pupils of different ages are exposed to English outside of school, and what kind of activities they engage in. As might be expected on the basis of previous research (De Wilde et al. 2020; Lindgren and Muñoz 2013; Muñoz et al. 2018; Sylvén and Sundqvist 2012), the vast majority of the pupils was exposed to English in some form. Final-grade pupils were significantly more exposed to English outside the school than pupils in grades 1 to 5. Nevertheless, there were large individual differences, with both extremes being represented. One the one hand, some pupils did not have any exposure to English at all. This may be partly explained by the fact that 11 participants were from a protestant religious background. Previous research with secondary school students already showed pupils from a protestant denomination had significantly less exposure to English outside school than their peers with no such background, even when attending an English-Dutch bilingual school programme (Verspoor et al. 2011). On the other hand, other participants had up to as much as 54 hours of exposure per week. This does however not mean that children constantly actively engage in English activities. Listening to English songs, for example, may in fact mean that the radio is playing in the background while children are engaged in a totally different activity.

Second, we investigated whether out-of-school exposure to English differed between pupils of different grades, and whether older and younger pupils engaged in different English activities. We made a distinction between five types of activities: 'Subtitles', 'Educative activities', 'Games', 'Active listening', and 'listening to English songs'. We already showed that upper-grade pupils tend to spend more time on English activities than lower-grade pupils, but they indeed also engage in different activities. It appeared that pupils in the final grade spent more time than pupils in the lower grades on subtitled activities such as watching English movies, activities in which they had to listen actively like watching movies without subtitles, and listening to English songs. Just like grade-eight pupils, grade-five pupils spent more time on gaming activities in English than pupils in the lower grades, but grade-eight pupils even spent more time on this kind of activity than grade-five pupils. The only exception to the trend that older pupils engage more in English activities, was for activities that could be classified as 'educative'. Younger pupils, especially those in grade two, spent significantly more time on educative activities than older pupils. This is not very remarkable, however, since most of the activities in this category were specifically aimed at young children. We asked for example about whether children watched English tv for Dutch kindergartners. It may be that older children engage in educative activities as well, such as playing educative computer games. Future research may make a distinction between such computer games and other types of games.

That older pupils are more engaged in activities in English than younger pupils may not be surprising, given the fact that most of these activities involve exposure to screens and older children generally have more 'screen time' than younger children (Anderson et al. 2008). Older children engage, for example, more in video games and watching television than younger children. Our findings also match previous research results with Danish and Spanish children, that showed that 9-year-old children have more exposure to English outside school than 7-year-old children (Muñoz et al. 2018), and with a Flemish study that showed 11- and 12-year-old pupils engaged more in English activities than 10-year-olds (Puimège and Peters 2019). Previous research already showed that upper-grade primary school pupils are engaged in gaming in English, listening to English songs, watching English television shows, and even talking in English with their native Dutch-speaking friends (De Wilde et al. 2020; Leona et al. 2021). Our findings are largely in line with these findings, showing again that upper-grade primary school pupils engage in various English media.

For lower-grade primary school pupils, much less data from previous studies are available. Unsworth et al. showed that first-grade pupils were exposed to English activities outside school for 38 minutes per week on average, whereas second-year pupils were exposed to English for almost three hours per week (155 min), but large standard deviations showed there were large individual differences in this exposure (Unsworth et al. 2015). Kindergartner pupils in our study were exposed to English for many more hours. Mainstream grade one pupils were already exposed four-and-a-half hours per week to English, as opposed to six-and-a-half hours per week for early-English pupils. The difference between the study from Unsworth and colleagues and our study may be that Unsworth et al. only questioned parents about kindergartner-specific activities, such as watching English television shows aimed at kindergartners. We distributed one questionnaire to parents of pupils in all grades. Although this questionnaire included activities specifically aimed at kindergartners, it also included other activities that we thought would be more suitable for older children. It seems that younger pupils engage in such activities as well. Although significantly less than older pupils, young pupils also play English computer games, for example, or watch subtitled English television shows. This may seem surprising given the fact that most of these pupils are not able to read yet, but it may be that they engage in these types of activities because older siblings engage in such activities.

Our third and final research question was whether individual differences in out-of-school exposure were positively related to pupils' English vocabulary knowledge. We investigated this relation for lower-grade and upper-grade pupils separately, and in both groups we found evidence for a positive relation between informal exposure to English and English vocabulary performance. The type of English activities that were related to pupils' English vocabulary knowledge differed however for lower-grade and upper-grade pupils. For both groups of pupils, individual differences in the extent to which children were exposed to 'subtitled activities' or 'active listening activities' were positively related to English vocabulary knowledge. For lower-grade pupils, 'educative activities' in English were also related to their English vocabulary performance. For upper-grade pupils, gaming and listening to English songs were positively related to English vocabulary knowledge, whereas 'educative activities' were not.

There is ample evidence for a relation between English gaming activities and English vocabulary development (De Wilde et al. 2020; Lindgren and Muñoz 2013; Sylvén and Sundqvist 2012), and our findings corroborate with those previous findings, showing a relation between individual differences in gaming activities and English vocabulary development for pupils in the upper grades. For subtitled activities, results of previous studies are mixed. Some of those studies (Lindgren and Muñoz 2013) found a positive relation between watching English television that was subtitled, whereas other studies (De Wilde et al. 2020) did not. Just like the participants in the study of De Wilde et al., participants in our study are usually exposed to television series and movies that are subtitled rather than dubbed. What may explain the difference between the findings of their study and that of ours is that the Flemish children were questioned *directly* about their *daily* exposure, whereas we questioned *parents* about their child's *weekly* exposure. We distributed the same questionnaire amongst parents of younger and older pupils. As younger pupils are not able to read or write yet, the logical consequence was to ask all parents to fill in the questionnaire, including the parents of older pupils. Parents may however not always have a clear overview of what kind of activities their child engages in or for how long, especially when children have access to their own device. Moreover, it may have been difficult for parents to decide on how much time children spend on different game genres.

We also investigated whether any relations between type of education and out-of-school exposure to English existed. No relation was found between school type and total amount of informal exposure to English. Early-English pupils were equally exposed to English as mainstream pupils. When looking at the different types of activities (subtitles, gaming, educative activities, active listening, and English songs), it appeared that early-English pupils only engaged more in active listening activities than mainstream pupils. There were no differences between the groups for the other types of activities. It may be that early-English pupils are stimulated at school to engage in such activities in English in their spare time. It may also be that because they learn English at school, early-English pupils actively search for such activities. The active listening category consisted of 'English tv without subtitles', 'English films without subtitles', 'English stories', and 'English talks'. These activities require the pupil to have a certain level of English proficiency. Especially lower-grade early-English pupils had a significantly larger English vocabulary than their mainstream-school peers. It may thus be that this required level of English is more often reached by early-English than mainstream pupils.

The relation between out-of-school exposure to English and English vocabulary did not differ between early-English and mainstream pupils. These findings are contradicting those of Leona et al. (2021), who found that the relation between out-of-school exposure and English vocabulary in 10-year-old Dutch early-English pupils was moderated by pupils' linguistic self-confidence. When not taking into account linguistic self-confidence, however, there was a direct relation between out-of-school exposure and English vocabulary knowledge, just as for mainstream pupils (Leona et al. 2021). As we took no motivation measures into account, we cannot be sure whether motivation or any other relevant factors played a role in our data.

Our data are cross-sectional, meaning that we cannot draw too firm conclusions regarding pupils' English vocabulary development. Nevertheless, our data provide evidence that pupils in the higher grades are more often exposed to English outside the school environment than pupils in the lower grades, and show that for both younger and older pupils individual differences in out-of-school exposure are related to English vocabulary knowledge.

5 Conclusion

Our study shows that not only older, but also very young Dutch primary school pupils engage in a large variety of informal activities in English, and for a substantial number of hours. Although there are large individual differences, and some pupils seem to have no or very limited exposure to English outside the school environment, the majority engages in one or more types of activities in English. Individual differences in out-of-school exposure to English are related to English vocabulary knowledge. This shows that Dutch children between 4 and 12 years old do not only learn English at school through formal education, but also outside the school environment by playing English (computer) games, watching English television shows and movies, and reading English stories.

Appendix: Questionnaire

The following answers will only be used as background information for the study.
Which parents or caretakers are exist in your household?
Mother (or caretaker) and father (or caretaker)
- Only a mother (or caretaker)
- Ony a father (or caretaker)
- Two parents (or caretakers) of the same sex
- Other: ....

This questionnaire is filled out by:
- Mother (or caretaker) of the child
- Father (or caretaker) of the child

Name of my son/daughter: ....

Date of birth of my son/daughter (dd/mm/yyyy): ....

My son/daughter is in grade ....

The languages your child speaks

The following questions address the languages that your child is exposed to.

1. **Which languages does your child use most . . . (provide one answer per row)**

	Dutch	Frisian/dialect	Foreign language(s)	Not applicable
With u	O	O	O	O
With the other parent/caregiver	O	O	O	O
With siblings	O	O	O	O
With grandparents (1)	O	O	O	O
With grandparents (2)	O	O	O	O
With friends	O	O	O	O

2. **Does your child regularly speaks a foreign language, Frisian, or a dialect with someone? If yes, describe:**
   a. **Which language(s) your child speaks, and**
   b. **With whom your child speaks this language/those languages, and how often**

```
┌─────────────────────────────────────────────────┐
│                                                 │
│                                                 │
│                                                 │
└─────────────────────────────────────────────────┘
```

3. **How many hours OUTSIDE OF SCHOOL does your child weekly spend on . . . .**

If some of the activities below are not applicable to your child, please fill in 0 hours per week and circle n.a. (not applicable).

	Number of hours per week	How often this activity is done:
English stories	... hours a week	a. N.a. b. Mostly on one day c. Mostly on multiple days a week d. Almost all days a week
English conversations with family members/friends	.... hours a week	a. N.a. b. Mostly on one day c. Mostly on multiple days a week d. Almost all days a week
English sport games (e.g. Wii Sports)	... hours a week	a. N.a. b. Mostly on one day c. Mostly on multiple days a week d. Almost all days a week
English adventure or simulation computer games (e.g. SimCity)	... hours a week	a. N.a. b. Mostly on one day c. Mostly on multiple days a week d. Almost all days a week
Other (partly) English games: (indicate what game):	... hours a week	a. N.a. b. Mostly on one day c. Mostly on multiple days a week d. Almost all days a week
Dutch TV programs with English words (e.g. Dora)	... hours a week	a. N.a. b. Mostly on one day c. Mostly on multiple days a week d. Almost all days a week
English TV programs for Dutch toddlers/children (e.g. Muzzy)	... hours a week	a. N.a. b. Mostly on one day c. Mostly on multiple days a week d. Almost all days a week
English TV programs for English toddlers/children (e.g. Peppa Pig)	... hours a week	a. N.a. b. Mostly on one day c. Mostly on multiple days a week d. Almost all days a week
English TV programs for older children and adults (series or movies) *with subtitles*	... hours a week	a. N.a. b. Mostly on one day c. Mostly on multiple days a week d. Almost all days a week
English TV programs for older children and adults (series or movies) *without subtitles*	... hours a week	a. N.a. b. Mostly on one day c. Mostly on multiple days a week d. Almost all days a week

(continued)

	Number of hours per week	How often this activity is done:
English videos on for instance the computer or tablet (for instance via Youtube) *with subtitles*	. . . hours a week	a. N.a. b. Mostly on one day c. Mostly on multiple days a week d. Almost all days a week
English videos on for instance the computer or tablet (for instance via Youtube) *without subtitles*	. . . hours a week	a. N.a. b. Mostly on one day c. Mostly on multiple days a week d. Almost all days a week
English songs (e.g. pop music on the radio)	. . . hours a week	a. N.a. b. Mostly on one day c. Mostly on multiple days a week d. Almost all days a week
Repeating what your child learned at school (with respect to English)	. . . hours a week	a. N.a. b. Mostly on one day c. Mostly on multiple days a week d. Almost all days a week

References

Anderson, S. E., Economos, C. D., & Must, A. 2008. Active play and screen time in US children aged 4 to 11 years in relation to sociodemographic and weight status characteristics: a nationally representative cross-sectional analysis. *BMC Public Health* 8. 1–13. https://doi.org/0.1186/1471-2458-8-366

de Graaff, R. 2015. Vroeg of laat Engels in het basisonderwijs: Wat levert het op? [Early or late English in primary education: Does it matter?]. *Levende Talen Tijdschrift* 16(2). 3–15.

De Wilde, V., Brysbaert, M., & Eyckmans, J. 2020. Learning English through out-of-school exposure. Which levels of language proficiency are attained and which types of input are important? *Bilingualism: Language and Cognition* 23(1). 171–185. https://doi.org/10.1017/S1366728918001062

Dunn, L. M., & Dunn, D. M. 2007. *PPVT-4 Manual*. Minneapolis, Minnesota: NCS Pearson.

Dunn, L. M., Dunn, L. M., & Schlichting, L. 2005. *Peabody Picture Vocabulary Test-III-NL*, 2nd edn. Amsterdam: Pearson Assessment and Information.

Dutch Inspectorate of Education. 2019. Peil.Engels Einde basisonderwijs 2017–2018 [Level. English End of primary education 2017–2018]. *Dutch Inspectorate of Education*. https://www.onderwijsinspectie.nl/documenten/rapporten/2019/11/08/peil.engels-einde-basisonderwijs-2017-2018 (Accessed 1 July 2021)

Enever, J., Krikhaar, E., Lindgren, E., Lopriore, L., Lundberg, G., Mihaljevic Djigunovic, J., Muñoz, C., Szpotowicz, M., & Tragant Mestres, E. 2011. *ELLiE: Early Language Learning in Europe*. In J. Enever (ed.), United Kingdom: British Council.

Goriot, C., Broersma, M., McQueen, J. M., Unsworth, S., & van Hout, R. 2018. Language balance and switching ability in children acquiring English as a second language. *Journal of Experimental Child Psychology* 173. 168–186. https://doi.org/10.1016/j.jecp.2018.03.019

Goriot, C., McQueen, J. M., Unsworth, S., Hout, R. van, & Broersma, M. 2020. Perception of English phonetic contrasts by Dutch children: How bilingual are early-English learners? *PLOS ONE*, 15(3), e0229902. https://doi.org/10.1371/journal.pone.0229902

Goriot, C., Unsworth, S., van Hout, R., Broersma, M., & McQueen, J. 2021a. Differences in phonological awareness performance: Are there positive or negative effects of bilingual experience? *Linguistic Approaches to Bilingualism* 11(3). 418–451. https://doi.org/10.1075/lab.18082.gor

Goriot, C., Van Hout, R., Broersma, M., Lobo, V., Mcqueen, J. M., & Unsworth, S. 2021b. Using the peabody picture vocabulary test in L2 children and adolescents: Effects of L1. *International Journal of Bilingual Education and Bilingualism. Advance Online Publication* 24(4). 546–568. https://doi.org/10.1080/13670050.2018.1494131

Jenniskens, T., Leest, B., Wolbers, M., Bruggink, M., Dood, C., & Krikhaar, E. 2017. *Zicht op vroeg vreemdetalenonderwijs [Insight into early foreign language education]*. Nijmegen: KBA Nijmegen.

Leona, N. L., van Koert, M. J. H., van der Molen, M. W., Rispens, J. E., Tijms, J., & Snellings, P. 2021. Explaining individual differences in young English language learners' vocabulary knowledge: The role of Extramural English Exposure and motivation. *System* 96. 102402. https://doi.org/10.1016/j.system.2020.102402

Lindgren, E., & Muñoz, C. 2013. The influence of exposure, parents, and linguistic distance on young European learners' foreign language comprehension. *International Journal of Multilingualism* 10. 105–129. https://doi.org/10.1080/14790718.2012.679275

Lobo, V. R. 2013. *Teaching L2 English at a very early age: A study of Dutch schools* Utrecht: LOT dissertation.

Muñoz, C., Cadierno, T., & Casas, I. 2018. Different starting points for English language learning: A comparative study of Danish and Spanish young learners. *Language Learning* 68(4). 1076–1109. https://doi.org/10.1111/lang.12309

Puimège, E., & Peters, E. 2019. Learners' English vocabulary knowledge prior to formal instruction: The role of learner-related and word-related variables. *Language Learning* 69(4). 943–977. https://doi.org/10.1111/lang.12364

Sylvén, L. K., & Sundqvist, P. 2012. Gaming as extramural English L2 learning and L2 proficiency among young learners. *European Association for Computer Assisted Language Learning* 24. 302–321. https://doi.org/10.1017/S095834401200016X

Thijs, A., Tuin, D., & Trimbos, B. 2011. *Engels in het basisonderwijs: verkenning van de stand van zaken [English in primary education: an exploration of the current situation]*. https://www.slo.nl/downloads/2011/engels-in-het-basisonderwijs.pdf/

Unsworth, S., Persson, L., Prins, T., & de Bot, K. 2015. An investigation of factors affecting early foreign language learning in the Netherlands. *Applied Linguistics* 36. 527–548. https://doi.org/10.1093/applin/amt052

Verspoor, M., De Bot, K., & Van Rein, E. 2011. English as a foreign language: The role of out-of-school language input. In A. De Houwer & A. Wilton (Eds.), *English in Europe Today: Sociocultural and educational perspectives*, 147–166. Amsterdam: John Benjamins Publishing.

Rosa M. Jiménez Catalán
Lexical profiles of children and adolescent EFL learners in the semantic domain of animals

Abstract: This chapter looks at the English lexical output and word association of children and adolescent EFL learners in the semantic domain of animals. Research on the relation of age and the productive vocabulary of these groups is scarce and has focused on the comparison of scores obtained on tests or in the words used in compositions, showing a greater production in older learners than in young learners. However, the lexical output generated by EFL learners in response to cue-words in semantic categorization tasks has hardly been investigated, let alone the examination of qualitative aspects of their lexical output such as the strategies and associations that children and adolescent EFL learners use in word retrieval (clusters) and word search (switches). The present study contributes to fill this gap by considering the age-group as a factor of possible learning differences as observed in the words retrieved in a semantic fluency task by children and adolescents EFL learners. The quantitative results show differences concerning word production, clusters, and switches. Likewise, although similarities are observed concerning the most frequent words and association patterns, the qualitative analysis reveal inter and intragroup differences that need to be considered when researching individual language learning differences in English as a target. The findings also have implications for education as they provide teachers with actual words, and the associations produced by children and adolescent EFL learners when asked to generate words related to the semantic domain of animals.

Keywords: productive vocabulary, clusters and switches, semantic fluency task, age, EFL learners

Acknowledgments: This work was supported by the Spanish *Ministerio de Ciencia e Innovación, Fondos Feder, and Agencia Estatal de Investigación* (Grant PGC 2018-095260-B-100).

https://doi.org/10.1515/9783110743043-007

1 Introduction

The domain of animals is a universal semantic category commonly used in neuropsychological research to investigate speech alterations as well as to establish normative data for age and education levels across languages (Rosselli, Ardila, Salvatierra, Marquez, Matos and Weekes 2002). This domain is also included in lexical availability research to identify the available lexicons of learners of Spanish or English as second or foreign languages (see Jiménez Catalán 2014). Neuropsychological and lexical availability research differ concerning focus, but the tasks used in data collection share similar semantic categories as cue-words or stimuli to activate word responses from the mental lexicon. Both in neuropsychological and lexical availability research, the word responses are subsequently analysed to get insights into lexical retrieval, organization, and conceptualisation of speakers' lexicons. The present study combines both approaches to examine group and individual differences in the word production and associations uncovered by the clusters and switches in response to the cue-word ANIMALS generated by children and adolescents, learners of English as a foreign language (EFL). For the sake of clarity, we mark the semantic field in small letters (animals), the cue-word in capital letters (ANIMALS), and the word responses in italics (*cat*).

2 State of the art review

Clusters are groups of at least two words retrieved consecutively in response to the semantic category, as for example, *oranges*, and *pears*, in response to FRUITS. Clusters depend on the activation of words stored in memory and the subsequent retrieval of semantically related words until the category or subcategory is exhausted. When this occurs, there is a switch into a new subcategory (Troyer and Moscovitch 2006). Clusters and switches involve distinct parts of the brain and cognitive processes. The former require temporal-lobe processes related to memory such as word storage, while the latter depend on frontal-lobe processes responsible for adopting or inhibiting decisions related to strategic search (Troyer 2000; Kavé 2006; Troyer and Moscovitch 2006; Hurks, Schrans, Meijs, Wassenberg, Feron and Jolles 2011).

The neuropsychological research that has examined word production, clusters, and switches in typical children and adolescents is scarce in first languages and practically inexistent in foreign languages. In first languages, research has focused either on the effect of ageing or on the lexical performance of a wide range of age groups with speech pathologies compared to healthy (typical) samples. The present study takes as reference neuropsychological research on children (aged 11 to 12) and adolescents (aged 17 to 18) that have included the cue-word ANIMALS in a semantic fluency task (also called verbal fluency task). At first sight, the research on first languages (L1) summarised in Table 1 predicts variability in the results due to the wide range of target languages investigated, but the studies reveal similar findings in the gradual increase of word production, clusters, and switches as age increases, in favour of the older groups. However, there is also counter evidence as Chami, Munro, Kimberley, McGregor, Arciuli, Baker and Heard (2018) identified the existence of a plateau in the production of clusters and switches by Australian-English speaking children, and Sauzéon, Lestage, Raboutet, N' Kaoua, and Claverie (2004) reported an increase in the cluster size in French children, which stabilised at the age of 11 to 12. In a similar vein, Tallberg, Carlsson and Lieberman (2014) noted lack of significant differences in the cluster-size of, respectively, Swedish, and Malayalam children from different ages.

The above studies focused on first languages. We wonder whether the tendencies identified may also occur in a foreign language, and, if so, whether the lexical production and the semantic organization revealed by clusters and switches would differ in children and adolescents EFL learners. However, regarding foreign languages, the only published study on clusters and switches, we are aware of, was the one conducted by Palapanidi (2019) with Greek learners of Spanish at university. Focusing on the semantic domains of FOOD and DRINK, the author found that C1 learners produced more words, and more clusters, and switches than the B1 learners. Although this study focused on a different target language, semantic category, and age group, we might assume quantitative and qualitative differences in the words retrieved by children and adolescent EFL learners in response to ANIMALS. This assumption finds support in L1 semantic fluency research, as well as in the few studies that have looked at the relationship of age and the productive vocabulary of EFL learners. This research has mainly focused on the comparison of scores obtained on tests completed by early and later starters in English as a foreign language, showing a greater production of vocabulary in older learners than in young learners (e.g., Cenoz 2003; Lasagabaster and Doiz 2003; Miralpeix 2006). Similar results were found in studies comparing the words used in compositions by young and adult EFL learners (Agustín Llach and Jiménez Catalán 2014; Miralpeix 2007). More closely related to the current research are the results obtained by members of the GLAUR research group with EFL learners in the 6th grade of primary education (aged 11–12 years) and the 12th grade in post-obligatory education (aged 17–18 years) using lexical availability tasks in which the semantic category animals was included. For the sake of comparing the results of the present study, Table 1 shows the main characteristics and mean values of

Table 1: The age factor in neuropsychological L1 studies including ANIMALS in semantic/verbal fluency tasks.

Study	Language and Focus	Samples	Tasks	Mean values of responses to 'Animals'
Cohen et al. 1999	English Verbal fluency development Normative data	19 American English native speaking children Aged: 6 through 12 years	Verbal fluency test Receptive Vocabulary (PPVT-R) Expressive Vocabulary (WISC-III) Memory tests Reading, Spelling, Matching tests	Age (Years, Months) 12,0 to 12,11. Mean:30.42. SD: 5.81
Tombaugh, Kozak & Rees 1999	English Age Levels of education Normative data	1,300 Canadian English speaking (aged 16 to 95 years) Age groups: 16–59; 60–79; 80–95 Education: 0–8, 9–12, and 13–21 years	Phonological fluency task Semantic fluency task, category: Animals	Age range Mean: 67.0, SD: 19.8 Age 16–19 (years) Mean: 39.3. ST: 12.3 Years of education from 0 to 21. Mean: 11.4. SD: 4.4
Kavé 2006	Hebrew Naming and word fluency development	150 Hebrew speaking children distributed into age groups Aged: 8–9, 10–11, 12–13, 14–15, 16–17 30 native Hebrew adults Aged: 18 to 29	Naming test Phonemic fluency test Verbal Fluency task Category: Fruits and vegetables Vehicles; Animals	Age range 12–13. Mean:17.7. SD: 4.9 16.17. Mean: 20.9. SD: 4.7 18–29. Mean: 23.0. SD: 5.0

	Dutch Age/Grade Vocabulary production Normative data	295 native Dutch-speaking children Aged: 6.56 to 15.85	Verbal Fluency task Category: Animals Design Fluency (DF) Test	Grade 1: 12.86 (.57) Grade 3: 16.32 (.61) Grade 5: 18.74 (.62) Grade 7: 20.31 (.77) Grade 8: 22.01 (.76). Grade 9: 21.84 (.79)
Tallberg et al. 2011	Swedish Word production, clusters, switches, preservation errors Normative data	130 Swedish speaking children across kindergarten, 3rd grade, 6th grade, 9th grade	Letter fluency task Semantic fluency task Category: Animals	Kindergarten: 9.5 (3.2) Grade 3: 13.5 (4.0) Grade 6: 17.6 (4.4) Grade 9: 18.7 (3.9)
García et al. 2012	Spanish Verbal fluency development Normative data	1,032 Spanish speaking children Aged: 6 to 12; 11 to 12	Letter fluency task Semantic fluency task Category: Animals	Age range Group 1 (6.3–7.4) 10.82 (6.59) Group 2 (7.5–8.4) 13.11 (3.92) Group 3 (8.5–9.4) 14.15 (3.81) Group 4 (9.5–10.4) 16.20 (4.12) Group 5 (10.5–11.4) 16.20 (4.12) Group 6 (11.5–12.4) 17.79 (4.20)

(continued)

Table 1 (continued)

Study	Language and Focus	Samples	Tasks	Mean values of responses to 'Animals'
John & Rajasekhar 2014	Malayalam Word production Years of schooling Age	1,015 Malayalam-peaking children 5 to 15 years Grades: 1, 2,3,4,5	Letter fluency task Semantic fluency task Category: Animals	Grade Group 1 (Grade 1–2) Mean 7.38 (2.39) Group 2 (Grade 3–4) Mean 9.42 (2.85) Group 3 (Grade 5–6) Mean 11.75 (3.13) Group 4 (Grade 7–8) Mean 13.15 (3.38) Group 5 (Grade 9–10) Mean 14.24 (3.46)
Konstantopoulos et al. 2014	Cypriot Word production Years of schooling Age	749 Cypriot-speaking children and adolescents Aged 7–16 years old	Verbal semantic fluency task Categories: Animals, Fruits, and Objects	Age/years of education Mean age (11.22 years) Mean of years of education (5.57) Mean of VF: 19.76 words (SD: 8.17)

word responses to ANIMALS obtained in previous research with different samples. None of those studies addressed the age factor, but rather gender, or language profile. However, if we compare the means obtained in the sixth grade with those obtained in the ninth grade in the longitudinal research conducted by Agustín Llach and Fernández Fontecha (2014), we can see a significant word production increase in favour of the older group in all the semantic categories analysed. A similar increase is observed if we compare the means of 6th and 12th graders in lexical availability studies.

Table 2: EFL Lexical availability studies including the semantic category of ANIMALS.

Study	Focus	Samples	Tasks	Mean values of responses to 'Animals'
Jiménez Catalán & Ojeda 2009	Gender	210 Spanish sixth graders Hours of English tuition: 629 Age: 11 to 12	Background questionnaire Lexical availability task: 15 cue-words	Mean: 10.72, ST: 4.48 Girls: 11.45, ST: 4.40; Boys: 10.00, ST: 4.46
Agustín Llach & Fernández 2014	Gender Word increase	190 EFL learners at two collection times: 6th grade (Aged 11–12), Hours: 629 9th grade (Aged 14–15), Hours: 944	Background questionnaire Lexical availability task: 9 cue-words	6th grade Males: 10.82. Females: 11.88 9th grade Males: 14.16. Females: 16.4 No significant gender differences in 6th grade, but Significant increase in word production in 9th grade in the two sexes
Jiménez Catalán & Fernández 2019	Lexical availability output of L2 and L3 EFL learners	28 EFL learners: 14 monolinguals (English L2), 14 bilinguals (English L3)	Background questionnaire Lexical availability task: 10 cue-words	English L3. Mean: 16.07. SD: 4.269; Min 6, Max 21 English L2. Mean: 19.43. SD: 6.321 Min 9, Max 29

To our knowledge, except for the longitudinal study on the same learners at 6th and 9th grade, the comparison of the lexical output generated by EFL learners of different age ranges in response to ANIMALS is practically inexistent. Likewise, no research has been conducted on the strategies and associations that children and adolescent EFL learners may adopt in word search and production either in lexical availability or semantic fluency tasks. In the present comparison of children and adolescent EFL learners, our guess is that the latter will produce higher numbers of words, clusters, and switches than children as these may not yet have fully developed organisational skills (see Koren, Kofman and Berger 2005). Furthermore, as there is evidence of individual differences related to language and semantic memory in children and adolescents (see Weiner, Scheneider and Knopf 1988; Tomblin and Nippold 2014), we might expect patterns of individual lexical variation inter and intra groups. The present study contributes to Second Language vocabulary studies (lexical availability included) by considering the age/grade as a factor of possible individual learning differences, as observed in the words generated in a lexical availability/semantic fluency task by children at the end of primary school education (12-year-olds) and adolescents at the end of post-obligatory education (17-year-olds). Specifically, the study addressed three objectives. The first one was to determine if the two groups would differ in terms of three lexical parameters: (i) number of word types retrieved in response to ANIMALS, (ii) number of switches, and (iii) number of clusters observed in the words generated by each group. The second objective was to ascertain whether there were differences in the actual words produced in response to ANIMALS by children and adolescents. Finally, the third objective was to identify the word association patterns emerging in the clusters most frequently generated by each group (inter-group comparison), and those generated by learners of the same age group (intra-group comparison).

3 Method

3.1 Sample

We compared forty-five EFL learners at 6th grade of Spanish primary education (11–12 age) with forty-five EFL learners at 12th grade (17–18 age). The two groups attended state schools in a middle/low social class area in a middle-sized city located in the North of Spain.

3.2 Data collection and procedures

This study is part of a large-scale research project where we investigate the productive vocabulary of EFL learners by means of different tests, among them a production and association task referred to in our research indistinctly as semantic fluency task or lexical availability task. After obtaining permission from the school principals and teachers, the data collection was conducted in the students' classrooms, with the presence and collaboration of their English teachers. The instructions were provided in oral and written form in Spanish and were identical for the two groups. The learners were asked to write as many unique words as came to their mind in response to the cue-word ANIMALS in 2 minutes, as controlled by a stopwatch. The words generated by the two groups were processed in Excel spreadsheets. All the word responses were codified, edited, and lemmatised according to the criteria followed in our previous lexical availability studies (see Jiménez Catalán and Canga Alonso 2019), such as correcting spelling errors, counting repeated word responses to the same cue-word only once, removing Spanish words, lemmatising words in plural to their singular, changing verb forms to bare infinitives, keeping irregular verb forms, and counting compound words or lexical units as one word (e.g., Peacock, guinea pig, Panda bear).

Once lemmatised, we counted the number of words retrieved respectively by 6th and 12th grade EFL learners in equal time in response to ANIMALS. Then, the frequency of word types was obtained for each age group according to the number of learners who retrieved each word. Finally, we applied a qualitative analysis to the words generated by each learner as to identify clusters and patterns of associations. For the identification of clusters and switches we followed Troyer, Moscovitch, and Winocur (1997) and Troyer (2000). However, due to the nature of the samples in the current study, EFL learners rather than typical and non-typical samples of native speakers, it was deemed necessary to introduce some modifications. First, unlike neuropsychological research that allows 1 minute per semantic category, the present study allowed 2 minutes for the elicitation of the words generated by children and adolescent EFL learners. There were two reasons for this: One was that 2 minutes rather than 1 minute is the standard time in lexical availability tasks conducted in Spanish as L1, L2, and English as L2, L3, which provides a framework for comparing word production in similar ages and school grades. Second, all the English words generated by the learners were considered valid, regardless of whether the words were members of the semantic category animals or not. The reason for this is that their inclusion favours the identification of word association patterns. For example, in the clusters (*chicken egg*), and (*cat reliable*) it is possible to hypothesise the type of association made by the learner such as origin or consequence (e.g., chicken are born from eggs), or quality attribution (e.g., cats are reliable). Third, in contrast with Troyer and Mascovit (2006), who counted single words as clusters (size zero), and initiated counting the size of the cluster in the second word, in the present study, we initiated the counting in the first word of the cluster. For example, in the sequence – *tiger, monkey, cheetah, dog, cat, hamster* – the word dog is counted as a switch and as the first word of a new cluster consisting of three words. In addition, to counting the first word as a switch and as a part of the cluster, we counted as a switch unrelated single words between clusters as for example, *snake* in the following pattern: (*Cat, dog, hamster*) *snake* (*Chicken, pig*). In our opinion, the adoption of this decision facilitates the identification of patterns of association in clusters consisting of two words; otherwise, these associations would remain hidden in the data generated by EFL learners. This decision was in agreement with Mayr (2002), who observed that children tend to generate single words or two-word clusters rather than multi-word clusters.

Following, we calculated the totals and means of word types, clusters and switches retrieved, applying t-tests to determine the significance of the results. The word responses and the identification and classification of clusters into subcategories were done upon the definition provided for each animal in English dictionaries rather than by using a previous taxonomy of animals. The dictionaries used as reference were *The Cambridge Dictionary* and *Word Reference*. For example, *ant* was classified as an insect, *snake* as reptile, or *cat* and *dog* as pets following the definitions and examples provided in these dictionaries. Seven subcategories were identified in the two groups: Birds, Farm animals, Insects, Pets, Reptiles, Rodents, and Water animals. The final step was to conduct a qualitative analysis of the patterns of clusters produced by children and adolescent EFL learners with equal production of words in the two groups. The aim was to ascertain whether there were individual differences inter and intra groups.

4 Results

The total number of English words (tokens) produced by the children as a group (6th grade) was 579. In comparison, adolescents as a group (12th grade) produced a total of 723 words in response to ANIMALS. The means resulting from the number of unique words (types) generated by *each* learner (Table 3) suggest that the adolescents produced a higher number of words, clusters, and switches than children. However, as the t-test applied to the means indicates, the results were only significant for word production and clusters, but not for switches.

Table 3: Descriptive and inferential statistics for each group in words, switches, and clusters.

	Means and SD		Mean Difference	t-test		d
	6th graders	12th graders		t(88)	p-value **p < 0.01	
Words	12.87 (4.39)	16.07 (6.13)	−3.20	−2.85	0.005	−0.60
Switches	6.51 (1.96)	7.11 (2.53)	−0.60	−1.26	0.212	−0.26
Clusters	3.18 (1.51)	4.40 (1.86)	−1.22	−3.42	0.001	−0.72

Table 4 shows positive correlations among the three lexical indicators in the two groups. The values reveal that as the number of words increases, so do the number of switches and clusters.

Table 4: Correlation among words, switches, and clusters.

	n words	n Switches	n Clusters
Children (Grade 6)			
n Words	1		
n Switches	.404**	1	
n Clusters	.754**	.298*	1
Adolescents (Grade 12)			
n Words	1		
n Switches	.624**	1	
n Clusters	.821**	.616**	1

*p < 0.05, **p < 0.01.

The standard deviations revealed greater variability in the adolescent group in the three lexical parameters examined. Furthermore, dispersion in word production pointed to intra group differences, as nineteen adolescent EFL learners (46.6%) produced either the mean (two learners) or above the mean, while twenty-four (53.3%) produced below the mean. Likewise, individual differences emerged in the maximum and the minimum number of words generated in equal amount of time: whereas one learner generated 30 words (S59), another generated 5 words (S76). Focusing on children, the examination of the intra-group data showed individual differences in the maximum (26) and minimum (4) number of words, generated respectively by one (Sb10) and two learners (Sa25, and S6b11). However, great homogeneity was observed in the number of learners who produced the average number of words as well as those who produced above and below the mean. Specifically, we found fifteen learners who aligned with the mean (33.33%), fifteen who produced above the mean (33.33%), and fifteen who performed below the mean (33.33%).

We now move on to the second objective, namely, to examine the actual words generated by children and adolescents in response to ANIMALS. This analysis will be based on the unique or different words (types) retrieved by each group. The children as a group (Grade 6) generated a total of 90 word types, compared to the 165 word types produced by the adolescents as a group (Grade 12). In the two groups we found a predominance of names of living animals, but, also, names for extinct animals or fictious creatures, and word associations referring to the habitat and attributes to animals. Specifically, out of the 90 words generated by children, 80 were existing animals. As to the 165 words generated by the group of adolescents, 108 were names of existing animals. This issue will be commented further on in the Discussion section. Following, we compare the two groups in terms of the shared and non-shared words; then, we focus on the individual differences that emerge in the two groups. Combined, children and adolescents produced 57 shared word types, whereas 33 words were produced only by the children group, and 108 by the adolescent group. Table 5 displays the top 20 words ranked in decreasing order by the number of children and adolescents who retrieved each word. As can be inferred from the raw frequencies, there was a high degree of overlap in the words most frequently retrieved by the two groups, as 15 out of the top 20 were shared words. However, the comparison of the raw frequencies also uncovers differences concerning the number of learners who retrieved each of the shared words; more precisely, it showed a larger number of children compared to adolescents who retrieved *elephant* and *giraffe*, and vice versa, a larger number of adolescents who retrieved *horse* in comparison to children.

Table 5: Top 20 words in response to ANIMALS.

Children *n* 45					Adolescents *n* 45			
Dog	38	Whale	18	Dog	43	Cow	17
Cat	38	Crocodile	17	Cat	42	Bear	15
Elephant	34	Rabbit	15	Bird	33	Dolphin	15
Lion	31	Horse	14	Fish	31	Shark	15
Fish	29	Mouse	13	Snake	28	Turtle	15
Bird	26	Shark	12	Lion	27	Pig	13
Monkey	25	Hummingbird	12	Horse	27	Eabbit	12
Giraffe	24	Pig	12	Tiger	24	Giraffe	12
Tiger	23	Parrot	11	Crocodile	23	Hamster	11
Snake	20	Cheetah	10	Eephant	20	Mouse	11

Furthermore, if we consider the total production of each group, individual differences were revealed in the 39 words and 84 types generated only once (hapax legomena) respectively by children and adolescents. A close look at Table 6 reveals that in the first group, 30 words (77%) belonged to the semantic category of animals, compared to 46 words (55%) in the second group. Due to space limits, it is not possible to provide an inter and intra detailed analysis of these words, but just some exemplars to illustrate this differential tendency. For instance, regarding children, learner S6b10 retrieved 26 words, among them, five hapax legomena: *lizard, python, anaconda, whip snake, Komodo dragon*; while Sb13 retrieved 20 words including two hapax legomena: *alligator*, and *pangolin*. As for adolescents with similar word production to the two children compared above, that is, 26 words and 20 words, learner S49 generated two hapax legomena, *seal*, and *fox*, while S47 produced four: *goatee, rainforest, sea*, and *sea star*.

Table 6: List of Hapax Legomena word responses.

Children	*Alligator, Anaconda, Buffalo, Cast, Caterpillar, Chimpanzee, Cockroach, Crab, Croak, Komodo Dragon, Duck, Flamingo, Hippopotamus, Kangaroo, Killerfish, Ladybug, Lizard, Louse, Man, Nautilus, Octopus, Owl, Pangolin, Pony, Pulp, Python, Serpent, Blue Shark, Whip Snake, Spark, Squirrel, Steak, Toucan, Vampire, Wall, Wild, Worm, Zombie*
Adolescents	*Aisle, Albatross, Alligator, Amazon, Arachnid, Bacteria, Bad, Big, Bitch, Bite, Caiman, Calm, Cannibal, Carrion, Chimpanzee, Chinchilla, Circus, Clownfish, Cock, Cockroach, Crawly, Deer, Diversity, Dragonfly, Egg, Elk, Endanger, Environment, Falcon, Fox, Free, Freedom, Goatee, Goldfish, Grizzly, Hedgehog, Hen, Huge, Hunger, Jungle, Koala, Ladybird, Lamb, Lizard, Mammoth, Meat, Mice, Milk, Mockingbird, Nightingale, Octopus, Oviparous, Owl, Owner, Panther, Partner, Passion, Penguin, Pigeon, Rainforest, Reindeer, Reliable Reptile, Salamander, Scary, Scorpion, Sea, Sea star, Seal, Seed, Small, Sparrow, Species, Squirrel, Strange, Take Care of, Tiny, Tropical, Turkey, Unicorn, Vegetarian, Walk, Wheat, Wonderful.*

Finally, we present the findings related to the third objective, namely, to identify word association patterns from clusters generated by each group (inter-group comparison), as well as those generated by learners belonging to the same age group (intra-group comparison). The descriptive and inferential statistics of the cluster size per group will be presented first, followed by an exploratory analysis of clusters and association patterns in the word production of four learners, two for each group. For the youngest age group, the most frequent cluster size pattern was two consecutive semantically related words, identified in thirty-seven children, while the maximum cluster size was eight semantically related words, identified in the lexical production of one child. In the oldest age group, the most frequent cluster size was also two words, identified in forty adolescents, and the maximum size thirteen words, observed in one adolescent. As shown in Table 7, the comparison of the means of the most common clusters sizes in the two groups did not reveal any significant differences between groups.

Table 7: Description and comparison of cluster sizes for each age group.

	Means and SD		Mean Difference	t-Test		d
	Children	Adolescents		t	p-Value	
Csize2	2.05 (1.27)	2.38 (1.13)	−0.33	−1.18	0.243	−0.27
Csize3	1.38 (0.57)	1.76 (0.83)	−0.38	−1.95	0.056	−0.51
Csize4	1.07 (0.27)	1.29 (0.56)	−0.22	−1.33	0.193	−0.46
Csize5	1.17 (0.39)	1.00 (0.00)	0.17	1.03	0.317	0.52

At this point, we focus on the qualitative analysis of the clusters as to explore whether there were individual differences. For this purpose, we will rely on both children and adolescent EFL learners with nearly identical word production. Table 8 includes exemplars of the words generated by two children and two adolescents. For the sake of clarity, switches that develop into clusters are marked in bold and the whole cluster presented in brackets, whereas switches that do not turn into clusters appear without brackets. Thus, in the comparison of children we observed that both S6b2 and S6b16 generated clusters of two and three words associated to the same subcategories: pet animals, wild animals, and farm animals. However, individual differences were observed in the strategies adopted by each child. For example, S6b2 began by associating ANIMALS with pets by means of a prototypical association (e.g., *dog* and *cat*), then shifted to wild animals, returned to pets, shifted to farm animals, and closed with a switch to water animals that did not develop into a cluster. In comparison, S6b16 started with a switch associated with the subcategory of birds (*Hummingbird*), moved consecutively to the subcategories of wild animals, and domestic animals, returned to wild animals, and finally, switched to the subcategory of farm animals, without developing it in a cluster, closing the sequence with a cluster associated to water animals (*Shark Dolphin*). In the search and association strategies adopted by this learner, an idiosyncratic beginning (hapax legomena) stood out, as did the chaining of associations through two clusters (*Fish Bird*) and (*Tucan Wild*). Following the Spreading Activation theory (Collins and Loftus 1975), the words generated in these clusters could be considered as a priming effect of nodes that serve to activate in memory other nodes conceptually related. Thus, in the chaining we observe that the first word of the cluster, a superordinate (*fish*), activated the retrieval of another superordinate (*bird*), both conceptually related to animals. In turn, the second superordinate activated a member of the subcategory (*Tucan*), and one of the attributes of this member (*wild*). Likewise, individual differences emerged in the two adolescents under comparison. For example, the cognitive strategies adopted were radically different: S66 generated a long cluster related to the frame farm, and in addition to retrieving typical animals found in farms, the learner provided the word farm, as well as words associated to farm life. Furthermore, in the large frame generated by the learner it was possible to identify two sub-clusters metonymically related to farm labours and products such as (*wheat seed*), and (*chicken egg*). In comparison, the associations observed in adolescent S79 were closer to the ones observed in the children, not only on the shared subcategories of pets and wild animals, but also in the strategies adopted: the learner first searched into the subcategory of pets, then moved to wild animals, switched to farm animals without success, and shifted to wild animals again. Even though the size of the cluster was not as large as in the other adolescent, it was larger than those observed in children.

Table 8: Examples of clusters, and switches in children (6th grade) and adolescents (12th grade).

6th Grade: S6b2	(*Dog Cat*), (*Tiger Lion Deer*), (*Bird Fish Mouse*), (*Pig Horse Chicken*), Penguin
6th Grade: S6b16	Hummingbird, (*Lion Jaguar Monkey*), (*Fish Bird*), (*Tucan Wild*), Sheep, (*Shark Dolphin*)
12th Grade: S66	(**P**ig Cow Sheep Horse Bird Farm Wheat Seed Chicken Egg Milk Dog)
12th Grade: S79	(*Dog Cat Fish Bird*), (**S**nake Bear) Horse, (*Crocodile, Monkey, Tiger, Lion, Zebra*)

5 Discussion and conclusion

The first objective was to determine whether children and adolescent EFL learners differed in the number of words, clusters, and switches generated in response to the cue-word ANIMALS. The results showed significant age/grade differences as adolescents retrieved more words and clusters as well as a higher, although not significant, number of switches than children. The positive correlations between words, clusters, and switches indicate that as the number of words increases, the number of clusters and switches increases. These findings mirror previous neuropsychological research in L1, which showed an increase in the number of words parallel to an increase in age/grade in all the studies summarised earlier (Table 1). Similarly, the significant increase observed in the number of clusters generated by adolescents, as well as the absence of significant differences in the size of the clusters observed in the present study corroborate the findings reported by Tallberg, Carlsson and Lieberman (2014), Sauzéon, Lestage, Raboutet, N'Kaoua and Claveri (2004), John and Rajashekhar (2014), and Chami, Munro, Kimberley, McGregor, Arciuli, Baker and Heard (2017). As for the comparison with lexical availability research with EFL learners, the significant increase in the average number of words retrieved by adolescents in the present study confirms the significant increase observed by Agustín Llach and Fernandez Fontecha (2014) in word production in grade 9 as compared to grade 6. Also noteworthy is the close similarity of the means for animals found in this study and in previous lexical availability research with different samples. In our view, the similar incremental tendency observed in the current study and earlier research could be attributed to the fact that both neuropsychological and lexical availability research were conducted in school settings with informants of similar age and grade. In these learning contexts, age and grade go hand in hand, to the extent that it is difficult to disentangle the effect of age from that of grade. Bearing this in mind, we can cautiously attribute the word increase to the vocabulary input related to the semantic category of animals that EFL learners may have been exposed to through the teaching materials and classroom activities from sixth to twelfth grade. The word increase by grade was to be expected since there were five school years across these grades, which entailed more hours of instruction for the adolescent group, approximately 500 more as a minimum. Given the larger amount of English instruction that adolescents might have been exposed to, the increase seems rather small as it was only 3.20 words more on average. This may be due to the scarcity of vocabulary input related to the semantic field of animals that children and, particularly, adolescents might have been exposed to in their English textbooks. It may be the case that few new words were included throughout the grades. Evidence in favor of this interpretation is found in studies that have examined the vocabulary input of English textbooks (e.g. Nordlund 2016; Konstantakis and Alexiou 2012) where a considerable overlap of words was observed across grades. However, the increase might be also attributed to the nature of the semantic field of animals: A close category (Hernández Muñoz 2014) in comparison with other semantic categories in which new members might be added as, for example, health, or town. The examination of word production in relation to the input related to animals as well as other semantic fields that children and adolescents EFL learners were exposed to through textbooks and activities is pending. Meanwhile, we can only conclude that the production of adolescents is significantly higher than children at sixth grade.

The second objective was to determine whether there were any differences in the actual words generated in response to ANIMALS by children and adolescents. The results showed a high degree of overlap in the twenty most frequent words recalled by the two age groups. These words revealed similar organisation in the mental lexicon in terms of semantic subcategories. Furthermore, there was similarity in the type of words retrieved. Following the prototype theory postulated by Rosch (1975), who distinguished three levels of categorization, it is possible to classify the words generated by children and adolescents into basic words (e.g., *elephant, lion, monkey* . . .) superordinates (*bird, fish*), and prototypical words (*dog, cat*). Extending the analysis to the total words retrieved by each group, we also find exemplars for the subordinate level. For instance, *blue whale, anaconda, Komodo dragon, blue shark*, and *killer fish* retrieved by children, or *panda bear, anaconda, goldfish, sea star, clown fish* retrieved by adolescents. However, in comparison with the basic words that are frequently shared by other learners, most subordinates are hapax legomena. These words reveal individual differences in each group that might be due to exposure to English outside the school context. However, they might be also due to different episodic memories as well as to individual learners' preferences for specific animals or even feelings and emotions towards them, as can be noted in the words retrieved by adolescents. Hapax legomena are a recurrent phenomenon in corpus studies, where it has been observed that over half of the words only occur once in a corpus (Renouf 2016: 158). The higher number of hapaxes identified in the present study is in agreement with the tendencies observed in corpus studies. For Renouf, hapax legomena are related to creativity and can provide insights into the productivity of certain words. Similarly, we could interpret the retrieval of hapaxes as an indicator of higher lexical richness in the adolescent group, but also, in those children who retrieved hapaxes. These words need to be investigated in relation to vocabulary knowledge as to determine whether those learners who retrieve a higher number of hapaxes are those who have a large vocabulary size.

Finally, the third objective was to identify the word association patterns emerging in the clusters most frequently generated by children and adolescents as to determine whether there were inter-group and intra-group differences. The findings showed the existence of differential patterns in the clusters of children and adolescent EFL learners. Although, as we saw in the results section, in both groups the most frequent clusters were composed of two words, the tendency towards longer sequences and larger clusters was evident in the adolescents. These clusters provided key information for understanding the organisation of the mental lexicon and semantic memory in relation to animals of EFL learners at two different ages. The clusters and associations observed in adolescent EFL learners seem to be influenced by age as longer sequences and larger clusters involve higher cognitive maturation (Koren, Kofman and Berger 2005), higher episodic and semantic memory (Horn, Bayen and Michalkiewicz 2021), and, in our opinion, more encyclopaedic knowledge as revealed, for instance, by the hapaxes related to environmental issues retrieved by adolescents, but not by children. In comparison, some clusters generated by the children, although of similar size to the ones found in adolescents, tend to be influenced by form rather than meaning, for example, (*donkey monkey*), (*chick chicken*) and (*bee sheep*). Although these examples seem to point to the effect of age, in the interpretation of these data, again, it is necessary to be cautious since, as we saw in the comparison of examples of children and adolescents with identical word production, some children were able to produce long sequences and clusters. These findings suggest individual intra-group differences that may be due to a larger vocabulary size in some children, which in turn could be related to greater semantic memory and greater ability to search and associate words. For Meara (1996), the two fundamental dimensions of lexical competence in a second language are vocabulary size and lexical organisation. This means that children and adolescents with higher vocabulary knowledge might have been in a better position to draw connections between words and build strong associations and networks.

The findings of this exploratory study have implications for education, as the data was obtained from children and adolescents EFL learners, respectively in the final stages of primary and post-secondary education in Spain. At these educational stages, English is a compulsory subject in the Spanish curriculum and vocabulary knowledge may determine academic performance. There is evidence that vocabulary knowledge is a predictor of language level and academic success in education (Quian 2002; Bleses, Makransky, Dale, Højen and Ari 2016). Therefore, either in first or second/foreign languages, it seems of paramount importance to identify the words that learners can activate, associate, and produce in relation to specific semantic domains. With respect to animals, the identification of the words they can retrieve in this semantic field allows to diagnose the difficulties that individual learners may have in understanding and producing texts in content of curricular subjects related to ecology, environment or endangered species and their protection.

References

Bleses, Dorthe, Guido Makransky, Philip Dale, Anders Højen & Burcak Aktür Ari. 2016. Early productive vocabulary predicts academic achievement 10 years later. *Applied Psycholinguistics* 1(6). 1461–1476.
Cenoz, Jasone. 2003. The influence of age on the acquisition of English: general proficiency, attitudes, and code-mixing. In María Pilar García Mayo & María Luisa García Lecumberri (eds.), *Age and the acquisition of English as a foreign language*, 77–93. Multilingual Matters. Clevedon, Buffalo, Toronto, Sydney.
Chami, Sara, Natalie Munro, Kimberley Docking, Karla McGregor, Joanne Arciuli, Elise Baker & Rob Heard. 2018. Changes in semantic fluency across childhood: Normative data from Australian-English speakers. *International Journal of Speech-Language Pathology* 20(2). 262–273.
Cohen, Morris, Allison M. Morgan, Melanie Vaughn, Cynthia Riccio & Josh Hall. 1999. Verbal fluency in children: developmental issues and differential validity in distinguishing children with attention-deficit hyperactivity disorder and two subtypes of dyslexia. *Archives of Clinical Neuropsychology* 14(5). 433–443.
Collins, Allan M. & Elizabeth Loftus. 1975. A spreading-activation theory of semantic processing. *Psychological Review* 82(6). 407–428.
García, Eduardo, Cristina Rodríguez, Raquel Martín, Juan Jiménez, Sergio Hernández & Alicia Díaz. 2012. Test de Fluidez Verbal: datos normativos y desarrollo evolutivo en el alumnado de primaria. *European Journal of Education and Psychology* 5(1). 53–64.
Hernández Muñoz, Natividad. 2014. Categorías en el léxico bilingüe: Perspectivas desde el priming semántico interlenguas y la disponibilidad léxica. *Revista Electrónica de Lingüística Aplicada* 1. 19–38.
Horn, Sebastian S., Ute J. Bayen & Martha Michalkiewicz. 2021. The development of clustering in episodic memory: A cognitive-modelling approach. *Child Development* 92(1). 239–257.
Hurks, Petra P.M., D. Schrans, Celeste Meijs, Renske Wassenberg, Frans Feron & Jelle Jolles. 2011. Developmental changes in semantic verbal fluency: Analyses of word productivity as a function of time, clustering, and switching. *Child Neuropsychology* 16(4). 366–387.
Jiménez Catalán, Rosa María (ed.). 2014. *Lexical Availability in English and Spanish*. Springer.
Jiménez Catalán, Rosa María & Almudena Fernández Fontecha. 2019. Lexical availability output in L2 and L3 EFL learners: Is there a difference? *English Language Teaching* 12(2). 77–87.
Jiménez Catalán, Rosa María & Andrés Canga Alonso. 2019. The available English lexicon of male and female Spanish adolescents. *ELIA* 19. 157–176.
Jiménez Catalán, Rosa María & Julieta Ojeda Alba. 2009. Girls' and boys' lexical Availability in EFL. *ITL International Journal of Applied Linguistics* 158. 57–76.
John, Sunila & Bellur Rajashekharm. 2014. Word retrieval ability on semantic fluency task in typically developing Malayalam-speaking children. *Child Neuropsychology: A Journal on Normal and Abnormal Development in Childhood and Adolescence* 20(2). 182–195.
Kavé, Gitit. 2006. The development of naming and word fluency: Evidence from Hebrew-Speaking children between ages 8 and 17. *Developmental Neuropsychology* 29(3). 493–508.

Konstantopoulos, Kostas, Paris Vogazianos & E. Vayanos. 2014. The predictive nature of age and gender in the verbal fluency test in the Greek Cypriot children: Normative data. *Communication Disorders, Deaf Studies & Hearing Aids* 2 (3).1–5.

Koren, Rinat, Ora Kofman & Andrea Berger. 2005. Analysis of word clustering in verbal fluency of school-aged children. *Archives of Clinical Neuropsychology* 20. 1087–1104.

Meara, Paul. 1996. The dimensions of lexical competence. In Gillian Brown Gillian, Kirsten Malmkjaer & John Williams (eds.), *Performance and competence in second language acquisition*, 35–53. Cambridge: Cambridge University Press.

Lasagabaster, David & Aintzane Doiz. 2003. Maturational constraints on foreign-language written production. In María Pilar García Mayo & María Luisa García Lecumberri (eds.), *Age and the acquisition of English as a foreign language*, 136–160. Clevedon/Buffalo/Toronto/Sydney: Multilingual Matters.

LLach, Agustín, María Pilar & Almudena Fernández Fontecha. 2014. Lexical variation in learners' responses to cue words: The effect of gender. In Rosa María Jiménez Catalán (ed.), *Gender perspectives on vocabulary in foreign and second Languages*, 69–81. Dordrecht: Springer.

Llach, Agustín, María Pilar & Rosa María Jiménez Catalán. 2018. Teasing out the role of age and exposure in EFL learners' lexical profiles: A comparison of children and adults. *International Review of Applied Linguistics in Language Teaching* 56(1). 25–43.

Mayr, Ulrich. 2002. On the dissociation between clustering and switching in verbal fluency: comment on Troyer Moscovitch, Winocur Alexander & Stuss. *Neuropsychologica* 40. 562–566.

Miralpeix, Imma. 2006. Age and vocabulary acquisition in English as a foreign language (EFL). In Carmen Muñoz (ed.), *Age and the Rate of Foreign Language Learning*, 89–106. Clevedon/Buffalo/Toronto/Sydney: Multilingual Matters.

Miralpeix, Imma. 2007. Lexical knowledge in instructed language learning. The effects of age and exposure. *International Journal of English Studies* 7. 61–83.

Nordlund, Marie. 2016. EFL coursebooks for young learners: a comparative analysis of vocabulary. *Education Inquiry* 7(1). 47–68.

Palapanidi, Kiriaki. 2019. Manifestaciones de clusters y switches en el léxico disponible de aprendices griegos de ELE en diferentes niveles lingüísticos. *MarcoELE Revista de Didáctica Español Lengua Extranjera* 28. https://www.redalyc.org/journal/921/92157659004/html/

Qian, David. D. 2002. Investigating the relationship between vocabulary knowledge and academic reading performance: An assessment perspective. *Language Learning* 52(3). 513–536.

Renouf, Antoinette. 2016. Adverbial happax legomena in new text: Why do some coinages remain hapax? In María José López-Couso, Belén Méndez-Naya, Paloma Núñez-Pertejo & Ignacio Palacios-Martínez (eds.), *Corpus Linguistics on the Move. Exploring and Understanding English through Corpora*, 158–181. Amsterdam: Brill.

Rosch, Eleanor. 1975. Cognitive representations of semantic categories. *Journal of Experimental Psychology. General* 104. 192–233.

Rosselli Monica, Alfredo Ardila, Judy Salvatierra, Martha Marquez, Luis Matos & Viviana Weekes. 2002. A Cross-linguistic comparison of verbal fluency tests. *International Journal of Neuroscience* 112(6). 759–776.

Sauzéon, Hélène, Philippe Lestage, Catriona Raboutet, Bearnard N' Kaoua & B. Claverie. 2004. Verbal fluency output in children aged 7–16 as a function of the production criterion:

Qualitative analysis of clustering, switching processes, and semantic network exploitation. *Brain and Language* 89. 192–202.

Tallberg, Ing-Mari, S. Carlsson & M. Lieberman. 2011. Children's word fluency strategies. *Scandinavian Journal of Psychology* 52. 35–42.

Tombaugh, Tom N., Jean Kozak & Laura Rees. 1999. Normative data stratified by age and education for two measures of verbal fluency: FAS and animal naming. *Archives of Clinical Neuropsychology* 14(2). 167–177.

Tomblin, J. Bruce & Marilyn A. Nippold (eds.). 2014. *Understanding Individual Differences in Language Development Across the School Years*. London: Routledge.

Troyer, Angela. K. 2000. Normative data for clustering and switching on verbal fluency tests. *Journal of Clinical and Experimental Neuropsychology* 22. 370–378.

Troyer, Angela K. & Morris Moscovitch. 2006. Cognitive processes of verbal fluency tasks. In Amid M. Poreh (ed.), *Studies on Neuropsychology, Neurology and Cognition. The quantified process approach to neuropsychological assessment*, 143–160. London: Taylor & Francis.

Weiner Franz E., Wolfgang Schneider & Monica Knopf. 1988. Individual differences in memory development across life span. In Paul B. Bates, David L. Featherma & Richard M. Lerner (eds.), *Life-span Development and Behavior*, 39–85. London: Academic Press.

Ágnes Albert, Brigitta Dóczi, Katalin Piniel and Kata Csizér

The contribution of motivation and emotions to language learning autonomy in the Hungarian secondary school classroom: The results of a questionnaire study

Abstract: The aim of the research presented in this chapter was to investigate the extent to which emotions and motivation affect the autonomy of students learning English in secondary schools in Hungary. The rationale of our study is that although learner autonomy is increasingly seen as an important goal in education, Hungarian learners' autonomy seems to decrease rather than increase in higher grades (Albert et al. 2018a, 2018b). To shed light on the relationship of these constructs in the secondary school context, we designed a complex study, where students' autonomous learning behavior and their autonomous use of technology (Benson 2013), components of the L2 motivational Self System (Dörnyei 2005, 2009) and nine positive and negative emotions (Pekrun 2006) were measured with the help of a standardized questionnaire (N = 337). Based on regression analyses, our results show that emotions and motivation-related scales contribute to students' autonomous learning behavior and their autonomous use of technology in different ways, with the emotion of curiosity being the only scale with significant impact on both scales of autonomy. In addition, while positive emotions played a positive role in shaping autonomy, the contribution of negative emotions was mixed. Moreover, our findings suggest that in the Hungarian context negative language learning experiences are more likely to lead to autonomy than positive ones. As for pedagogical implications, we argue that classroom learning should provide the basis for enhancing learner autonomy by using activities and tasks that prompt learners' curiosity, that are motivating, and that allow for positive emotional experiences.

Keywords: emotions, learner autonomy, motivation

1 Introduction

Despite the fact that there is no shortage of studies investigating in what ways students' individual differences (IDs) contribute to language learning achievement (see for example, Dörnyei, Csizér and Németh 2006; Dörnyei and Ryan 2015;

Gardner 2010; Mills, Pajares and Herron 2007; Pawlak 2021), there are still relatively few studies mapping these variables in concert (Ryan 2019). Given that individual differences tend to influence the language learning process in different ways, examining their interrelationships might lead to a deeper understanding of the intricacies behind language learning success (Dörnyei and Ryan 2015). Therefore, the aim of the present study was to shed light on how two ID variables, motivation and emotions, influence autonomous learning behavior and autonomous use of technology in a secondary school context.

In Hungary, language instruction in school settings is often still characterized by frontal teaching and exam-oriented outcomes (Öveges and Csizér 2018), which are not really conducive to life-long learning and autonomous learning behavior. We think that a closer investigation of what leads to autonomy could play a key role in enhancing learners' language skills and improving their language knowledge in the long run, which creates the practical rationale for our study. In this sense both the broad concept of autonomy, which includes a set of "capacities which are necessary to carry out a self-directed learning programme" (Little 1991: 180) and the more specific capacity of self-regulation (Nakata 2014) appear to be relevant for us. Since self-regulation is one of the 21st century skills in education (Chalkiadaki 2018; Krskova et al. 2020; Shaw et al. 2014), it is necessary that language learners also take responsibility for their own language development in order to maximize language learning opportunities. If learners gain and seek autonomy, they themselves can take control of their language learning.

In this chapter, we will first provide a theoretical framework based on the individual difference variables of motivation, autonomy, as well as positive and negative emotions, and outline previous studies that investigated their interrelationship in pairs. This will be followed by our research questions, the methods of our study, and the results based on statistical analyses including two regression models. Finally, we elaborate on relevant pedagogical implications and possible future research directions.

2 Background to the study: Motivation, autonomy and emotions in language learning

In order to follow-up the call for investigating IDs as conglomerates, our study investigates three groups of ID variables: language learning motivation, autonomy and emotions. In this literature review, first we will define these concepts and then summarize some of the key studies focusing on their relationships.

Second language learning motivation has been defined in different ways in various research studies (Csizér 2020), but researchers agree that the core concept of motivation consists of choice, effort and persistence (Dörnyei and Ushioda 2011). As the amount of effort that students are willing to invest into learning seems to be central to the definition, many studies, including the present one, measure students' motivated learning behavior, that is, the intended effort invested into the day-to-day process of language learning. A somewhat related concept to motivation is language learning autonomy, which can be defined as the extent to which students are willing to take responsibility for their own learning processes (Benson 2007; Little 1999). While there is some disagreement regarding the extent to which control over various parts of the learning process, from selecting the content, planning and execution, are to be considered self-regulation or autonomy (Asztalos, Szénich and Csizér 2020), in the present study we conceptualized two dimensions for learner autonomy: autonomous learning behavior, i.e., taking responsibility for learning, as well as autonomous use of technology, i.e., the extent to which students are willing to use the internet- and computer-based opportunities on their own to improve their language skills and knowledge. Both of these attributes of autonomous learners were discussed by Benson (2001) and later studied on Hungarian samples (Csizér and Kormos 2012, 2014; Kormos and Csizér 2014). Finally, the last major construct in our study is emotions, more specifically emotions pertaining to classroom language learning, which have recently been defined as "affective experiences that are directly tied to language learning activities and resulting learning outcomes, a dynamic process which is determined by appraisals of socio-culturally shaped L2 learning tasks" (Shao et al. 2019: 2). In order to offer a complex view of learners' emotional experiences, we included a wide range of both positive and negative emotions in our study.

There are several research studies that investigated the interrelationships of the above defined concepts, although most of them have mapped only two of them. Out of the three constructs, the relationship between motivation and autonomy has been investigated the most extensively. Although initially it was proposed that autonomy is likely to lead to motivation (Deci and Ryan 1985; Dickinson 1995), in their mixed methods study Spratt and her colleagues (2002) found that the relationship of the two constructs is more complex than that, and it is also possible to argue that motivation might precede autonomy. The significant relationship between the two constructs is also supported by Liu's (2015) study on Taiwanese students' motivation and autonomy. In contrast, there is very limited research regarding the relationship between autonomy and emotions. One exception is Beseghi's (2018) qualitative study on university students, which established that the initial negative emotions of the learners turned into more positive ones as their autonomy increased over the course of a series of advising sessions.

On the other hand, the relationship between language learning motivation and different emotions has received more attention recently. In their questionnaire study, MacIntyre and Vincze (2017) examined correlations between a series of motivational variables, like Clément's (1986) socio-contextual variables, Gardner's (2010) integrative and instrumental orientations, and Dörnyei's (2005) L2 self-system, and a range of negative and positive emotions. Their findings indicated stronger relationships between motivation and positive emotions, and some of the highest correlations could be detected between motivation and the so-called positivity ratio (Fredrickson 2013), a figure describing the ratio of positive and negative emotions. In his more focused study on self-guides, Teimouri (2017) found that while in the regression analyses L2 joy was exclusively predicted by the ideal L2 self and L2 anxiety by the ought-to L2 self, L2 shame was linked to both to some extent, although its relationship with the ought-to L2 self was stronger. Finally, Saito and colleagues (2018) set out to investigate learners' language use and spoken language achievement relative to their motivation and feelings of anxiety and enjoyment. They found that students' motivation to learn English was dependent on their previous experiences while their positive emotions were mostly influenced by their recent experiences. Negative emotions were not linked to either previous or recent experiences in this study. However, learners' language achievement was more strongly influenced by anxiety than by their ideal L2 selves.

As for the Hungarian context, the relations between autonomy and motivation have been investigated, and it has been proved that there is a strong correlation between their dimensions (Csizér and Kormos 2012, 2014). Moreover, it was also shown that students' motivated learning behavior is linked to autonomous learning behavior as well as to autonomous use of technology (Kormos and Csizér 2014). Another relevant example is provided by Albert, Csizér and Piniel's (2018) analysis, which investigated relationships between positive emotions and autonomous learning behavior. They used partial correlations to illustrate how emotions might shape autonomy in direct and indirect ways. One intriguing result was that when the strong effect of enjoyment was partialled out, the negative impact of negative emotions changed into positive. This finding, on the one hand, highlights the complexity of emotional experiences and the intricate nature of their relationships; on the other hand, it draws attention to the necessity of more in-depth research in connection with them.

All three of the above mentioned concepts were investigated by Csizér et al. (2021). In this study, the authors used Dörnyei's (2005, 2009) L2 Motivational Self System to measure components of motivation. This model conceptualizes two self-related constructs: the *ideal L2 Self* and the *ought-to L2 self*. While the first one includes students' views about themselves as competent users of the L2, the second one subsumes the external pressures that students think they have to comply with. In addition, the model includes a third component *L2 learning experience*, which measures issues regarding the experience of learning the language. In terms of emotions, the study operationalized a number of positive and negative emotions in order to provide a more complex picture on emotion-related experiences in language learning than the usual representation of positive emotions with enjoyment and negative emotions with anxiety (Dewaele and MacIntyre 2014, 2016; Horwitz et al. 1991). The results indicated a number of important issues in connection with these ID variables. First, ideal and ought-to L2 selves correlated significantly with learner autonomy; therefore, the importance of future self-images in promoting learner autonomy cannot be denied. Second, in terms of emotions and autonomy, feelings of pride deriving from past experiences and feelings of hope connected to future achievements seemed to be defining for both autonomous learning behavior and autonomous use of technology. Third, emotions and motivation also showed high correlations. It seems that the positive emotions of hope, pride, and enjoyment are especially important.

Thus, the research gap we identified is as follows: motivation, autonomy, and emotions should be investigated in concert in future studies, since, based on previous research, it seems that these constructs are related (Csizér et al. 2021). Therefore, in our study we set out to measure Hungarian students' motivated learning behavior, their ideal and ought-to L2 selves, their learning experiences (Dörnyei 2005, 2009) and a variety of positive and negative emotions to gain insights as to how these constructs impact students' autonomous learning behavior and autonomous use of technology.

Based on our literature review and the research gap we identified, the following research questions guided the present study:
1. What characterizes Hungarian secondary school students' motivation, autonomous behavior and emotions concerning the English language?
2. What motivation- and emotions-related scales impact Hungarian students' autonomous behavior?

3 Methods

In order to answer our research questions, a quantitative study was devised. In the next part we will elaborate on the characteristics of the sample and the data collection instrument. This is followed by the data collection procedures and the steps we took to analyze our data.

3.1 Participants and context

Altogether 337 EFL learners from three different secondary schools in the capital city of Hungary participated in our study. The sample consisted of 118 male and 219 female learners, from grades 9 through 12, with a mean age of 16 years (ranging from 14 years to 19 years old). On average, the participants started learning English around the age of 10, which corresponds to the regulations of foreign language teaching in Hungary because the compulsory teaching of the first foreign language starts in grade 4, in elementary school (roughly at the age of 9–10) (Government decree 2003). At the time of data collection, 133 participants were learning English three lessons a week, 49 had four lessons a week, and 148 students had five English lessons each week in school. Out of the 337 learners, 77 were also taking extra-curricular English classes in some form.

3.2 Instrument

For our data collection purposes, we devised a self-report questionnaire in Hungarian, the first language of the participants. The instrument consisted of two parts: the first section assessed the individual differences variables referred to above, using five-point Likert scale items (where 1 signaled disagreement and 5 meant agreement with the items, indicating low or high levels of the associated constructs), whereas the second elicited biographical information related to the participants. The instrument ultimately comprised 15 scales. All of these scales were closely based on the findings of previous research (e.g., Piniel and Albert 2018; Piniel and Csizér 2013) and various other studies conducted in the Hungarian language learning context (Albert, Tankó and Piniel 2018a, 2018b; Csizér and Kormos 2009, 2012; Kormos and Csizér 2008; Öveges and Csizér 2018). Information on how the constructs were operationalized, the number of items used to measure the constructs, as well as the reliability of each scale in terms of Cronbach's alpha coefficients are reported below.

3.2.1 Motivation

Our instrument included four motivation-related scales, closely drawing on Dörnyei (2005, 2009), Kormos and Csizér (2008) and Csizér and Kormos (2012). These were the following:

Motivated learning behavior (5 items, α=0.80): the extent to which learners are ready to invest energy in their foreign language learning (example: *I can honestly say that I do everything I can to master the English language*).

Ideal L2 self (5 items, α=0.81): participants' vision about their future language use (example: *When I think of my future life, I imagine myself using English regularly*).

Ought-to L2 self (8 items, α=0.72): what participants perceive as expectations in terms of their own language learning (example: *For all the people around me, English proficiency is an important part of general knowledge*).

Language learning experiences (5 items, α=0.90): agreement with the items of this scale signals participants' positive experiences concerning learning English (examples: *I like the activities that we do in English lessons. I have a good time during English classes.*).

3.2.2 Autonomy

Two scales, based on Csizér and Kormos (2012), tapped into the autonomy of language learners:

Autonomous learning behavior (9 items, α=0.79): the extent to which participants are able to learn and practice English on their own (example: *I spend more time practicing elements in English that I find difficult to understand*).

Autonomous use of technology (5 items, α=0.85): learners' abilities to utilize the internet- and computer-based opportunities in order to improve their English knowledge (example: *I often use the Internet to improve my English*).

3.2.3 Emotions

The instrument employed in our study also measured a wide range of positive and negative emotions (Pekrun 2014; Pekrun et al. 2011) relevant in the English as a foreign language classroom context. We adopted these scales from Albert, Tankó and Piniel (2018a, 2018b) and Albert et al. (2019).

Enjoyment (5 items, α=0.71): refers to learners' feelings of enjoyment while taking part in the activities and topics during language lessons (example: *I enjoy the topics that we discuss in English lessons*).

Hope (6 items, α=0.75): measures how hopeful learners feel about achieving success in learning English at school (example: *I feel hopeful about overcoming challenges in the process of learning English*).

Pride (5 items, α=0.88): taps into the extent to which learners feel proud of their achievements in language learning (example: *I am proud of my achievements in language learning*).

Curiosity (6 items, α=0.78): the items measure how curious and interested learners feel about learning English, and the topics and activities they encounter during the English lessons (example: *In English lessons, we deal with topics that arouse my curiosity*).

Anxiety (5 items, α=0.67): measures learners' feelings of inhibition experienced in connection with English language activities in school lessons (example: *I get frustrated if I can't understand an English-language text*).

Boredom (5 items, α=0.76): the items measure to what extent learners feel bored during the activities and topics in the English language lessons (example: *I get bored by the activities in English lessons*).

Apathy (4 items, α=0.73): refers to learners' feeling of hopelessness related to success in English language learning in school (example: *I feel hopeless about ever mastering English in the school*).

Confusion (5 items, α=0.74): the items measure the extent to which learners feel confused about language learning in class (example: *Sometimes I feel confused because I don't understand what is happening in the English lessons*).

Shame (5 items, α==0.81): items tap into learners' feelings of shame about their achievement and actions during English lessons (example: *I feel ashamed if I can't answer a question during our English lessons*).

3.3 Data collection and data analysis

After having piloted and finalized the instrument (Albert, et al. 2019; Csizér and Öveges, 2019, 2020; Csizér et al. 2021), the required permissions and consent were obtained for data collection. With the presence of one of the researchers, the paper-based questionnaire was administered during the participants' respective English lessons. Participation in the study was voluntary, and the students were ensured of the anonymity of their responses. Subsequently, learners' responses were recorded and subjected to data analysis using IBM's SPSS software version 20.

In terms of our data analysis, we used descriptive statistics and paired sample t tests to answer the first research question. In the case of the second research question, since the use of multi-level analysis was not possible due to subsample size limitations, we ran regression analyses (stepwise method) separately for both autonomy-related scales in order to compare and contrast the results. Missing values were treated pairwise. Due to the sample size, the significance level was set at 5%.

4 Results and discussion

4.1 Hungarian secondary school students' motivation, autonomous behavior, and emotions related to the English language

Our first research question referred to the characteristics of Hungarian secondary school students' motivation, autonomy, and emotions. The means of the motivation scales (see Table 1) suggest an increased level of motivation, with the ideal L2 self showing the highest mean ($M = 4.54$, $SD = 0.58$), followed by the ought-to L2 self ($M = 4.03$, $SD = 0.63$). The relatively low standard deviation measures suggest that there is limited variation with regard to the importance of the future self-guides in the sample, which indicates that the majority of students tend to believe that English will have an important role in their future lives. The mean value of the language learning experience referring to the current classroom experiences of the learners is the lowest of the motivation scales ($M = 3.68$, $SD = 0.88$; see the results of the paired samples t tests in Table 1), and the mean of the motivated learning behavior scale displaying the effort students are willing to invest in language learning ($M = 3.82$, $SD = 0.73$) is only slightly above that. The higher dispersion figures found here suggest greater variation within the sample in these regards. By comparing the means of those motivation scales that were closest to one another with the help of paired-samples t tests, we were able to establish that the differences between all of the scales were statistically significant. These results are comparable to other Hungarian studies, as the ideal L2 self usually has a defining role in shaping students' motivation, and it often obtains the highest mean value in studies, followed by the ought-to L2 self and motivated learning behavior. In addition, it is not rare that negative learning experiences are reported when classroom learning experiences are tapped into (Csizér 2020).

Table 1: Descriptive statistics and paired samples t tests of the motivation scales (N = 337).

Scales	M	SD	Minimum	Maximum
Ideal L2 self	4.54	0.58	1.40	5.00
Ought to L2 self	4.03	0.63	1.63	4.88
Motivated learning behavior	3.82	0.73	1.80	5.00
Language learning experience	3.68	0.88	1.20	5.00
Paired samples t tests	*t*	*p*		
Ideal L2 self – Ought-to L2 self	14.02	<.001		
Ought to L2 self – Mot. l. beh.	4.57	<.001		
Mot. l. beh. – L. l. experience	2.48	.01		

The means of the autonomy scales (see Table 2) imply that while the students of the sample could be characterized by a moderate level of autonomous learning behavior ($M = 3.08$, $SD = 0.67$), they exhibited a higher level of autonomy with regard to the autonomous use of technology ($M = 3.96$, $SD = 0.97$). The difference between the means of the two scales was statistically significant based on the results of a paired samples t test ($t = 18.35$; $p < 0.05$; Table 2). These differences can be attributed to the fact that English teaching is still very often frontal and teacher-centered in Hungarian classrooms, where students' autonomy is not encouraged (Öveges and Csizér 2018). In addition, we can assume that the autonomous use of technology is often not related to classroom teaching but to issues pertaining to students' use of English outside the classroom. Interestingly, comparing our results to a similar Hungarian study conducted about a decade ago (Csizér and Kormos 2012), we can see similar results when students' autonomous learning behavior is considered, but it seems that students' autonomous use of technology has increased over the years.

Table 2: Descriptive statistics and paired samples t tests of the autonomy scales (N = 337).

Scales	M	SD	Minimum	Maximum
Autonomous use of technology	3.96	0.97	1.00	5.00
Autonomous learning behavior	3.08	0.67	1.33	4.89
Paired samples t tests	*t*	*p*		
	18.35	<.001		

When looking at the means of the emotions' scales in Table 3, it can be seen that all positive emotions had higher mean values than negative emotions in our sample. The differences between the means were checked using paired samples t tests on those scales closest to one another, and the results of the tests suggest statistically significant differences between the means of all scales except for shame and anxiety (see the results of the paired samples t tests in Table 3).

What appears to be an encouraging sign is that the means of all positive emotions are above three while the means of all negative ones are below, so on average, secondary school students tend to experience more positive emotions in the classroom than negative ones. Since according to an updated interpretation of the positivity ratio "when considering positive emotions, more is better, up to a point" (Fredrickson 2013: 820), it is reassuring to see that positive emotional experiences tend to characterize the EFL classroom. This way students might be able to reap the benefits of these positive emotions, which "reshape who people are by setting them on trajectories of growth and building their enduring resources for survival" (p. 815).

The emotion with the highest mean and the lowest standard deviation in Table 3 is hope (M = 4.29, SD = 0.57), which suggests that secondary students of this sample mostly felt hopeful towards their future English achievements. The next two emotions were enjoyment (M = 3.86, SD = 0.61) and pride (M = 3.66, SD = 0.98), while curiosity (M = 3.23, SD = 0.71) had the lowest mean of the positive scales. While hope already appeared as a potentially important emotion in the EFL classroom in other studies (Albert et al. 2019; Csizér et al. 2021), recent research on emotions tend to emphasize the feeling of enjoyment almost exclusively (Dewaele and MacIntyre 2014, 2016; Saito et al. 2018; Teimouri 2017). Our results indicate that although the feeling of enjoyment is a characteristic emotion in the EFL classroom, pride and especially hope appear to be just as important. As regards curiosity, its relatively low mean value should be discouraging in any educational context, but it might be hypothesized that in this case it is related to the unfavorable language learning experiences that often characterize the Hungarian context (Öveges and Csizér 2018; Csizér 2020).

With regard to negative emotions, we found the same level of shame (M = 2.69, SD = 0.99), and anxiety (M = 2.69, SD = 0.80) and somewhat less confusion (M = 2.56, SD = 0.80) among the Hungarian students comprising our sample. The least characteristic negative emotions among the learners were boredom (M = 2.35, SD = 0.77) and apathy (M = 2.21, SD = 0.87). The relatively high mean value of anxiety lends support to its already well-documented importance in the language learning context (Horwitz et al. 1991), but it also highlights the presence of other potentially important emotions, such as shame and confusion. Boredom and apathy appear to be less characteristic of the EFL classroom, although the slightly higher dispersion measures in the case of negative emotions seem to suggest greater variation among the learners.

Table 3: Descriptive statistics and paired samples t tests of the emotion scales (N = 337).

Scales	M	SD	Minimum	Maximum
Hope	4.29	0.57	2.00	5.00
Enjoyment	3.86	0.61	1.50	5.00
Pride	3.66	0.98	1.00	5.00
Curiosity	3.23	0.71	1.50	5.00
Shame	2.69	0.99	1.00	5.00
Anxiety	2.69	0.80	1.00	5.00
Confusion	2.56	0.80	1.00	5.00
Boredom	2.35	0.77	1.00	4.80
Apathy	2.21	0.87	1.00	4.75
Paired samples t tests	*t*	*p*		
Hope – Enjoyment	12.59	<.001		
Enjoyment – Pride	4.16	<.001		
Pride – Curiosity	7.50	<.001		
Curiosity – Shame	8.27	<.001		
Shame – Anxiety	.16	.86		
Anxiety – Confusion	3.24	<.001		
Confusion – Boredom	3.43	<.001		
Boredom – Apathy	3.38	<.001		

4.2 Emotions and motivation-related scales affecting students' autonomous learning behavior

In order to answer our second research question about the contribution of motivation and emotion scales to the two aspects of learner autonomy examined by us, we ran separate regression analyses with autonomous learning behavior and autonomous use of technology as dependent variables and the emotions and motivation-related scales as independent ones. Based on our results presented in Tables 4 and 5, a number of interesting points can be highlighted. It becomes apparent at first glance that the two autonomy-related scales are shaped by different motivational and emotion constructs. While autonomous learning behavior is positively affected by motivated learning behavior, learning experience and curiosity, the autonomous use of technology is shaped by the ideal L2 self, pride, curiosity, and somewhat surprisingly, boredom in a positive way. As for negative influences, autonomous learning behavior is negatively influenced by positive learning experiences, suggesting that learner autonomy can be expected to increase as a result of negative learning experiences, while the autonomous use of technology is shaped negatively by confusion. These differences can be explained by the fact that autonomy, similarly to many other ID variables, is a complex construct and its complexity is illustrated by the fact that various aspects of autonomy are influenced by different ID variables.

When autonomy is conceptualized as general student-initiated behavior, other behavioral type variables, such as motivated learning behavior, have an influencing role, as well as positive emotions associated with the said behavior: enjoyment and curiosity. These relationships lend support to findings of previous studies, where links between motivation and autonomy (Csizér and Kormos 2012, 2014; Kormos and Csizér 2014; Liu 2015; Spratt et al. 2002), and autonomy and positive emotions (Beseghi 2018) were already revealed. Enjoyment in particular has been frequently identified as an affective correlate of language learning (Dewaele and MacIntyre 2014, 2016; Piniel and Albert 2018). In this regression analysis, it is the negative influence of the learning experience on autonomous learning behavior which is a truly novel finding. We hypothesize that it might be explained by the general negative language learning experiences in the Hungarian context (cf. Csizér 2020; Nikolov 2001) as well as the presence of exam-focused frontal teaching in Hungary (Öveges and Csizér 2018), which might not give much room to developing learner autonomy. It is possible that it is precisely the autonomy reducing effect of classroom experiences that might be held accountable for the decline in autonomy among school children in compulsory education reported in the Hungarian context (Albert, Tankó and Piniel 2018a, 2018b; D. Molnár 2014).

As regards our second autonomy construct, the autonomous use of technology, it might be fraught with more challenges resulting in a complex interplay of various factors. First of all, relationships with a future related self, that is the learners' ideal L2 self, as well as positive emotions linked to past achievement, like pride, can be witnessed here. This is in line with previous studies reporting links between the ideal L2 self and autonomy (Kormos and Csizér 2014), and the presence of positive emotions should also be expected in connection with autonomy (Beseghi 2018). Moreover, pride was already identified as an emotion positively correlating with autonomy in a previous study in the Hungarian context (Csizér et al. 2021). It also seems quite evident that confusion as a negative emotion has a negative effect on the autonomous use of technology since this activity can be quite perplexing sometimes. Therefore, feelings of confusion might discourage students from engaging in such activities. The intriguing point here is the positive effect of boredom on the autonomous use of technology. A plausible explanation here might be that since the emotions tapped by our questionnaire referred to the classroom context, students' boredom probably has arisen in connection with classroom tasks and activities. It can be hypothesized that students bored by these might turn to other activities that they find more engaging, such as the autonomous use of technology.

A further noteworthy finding is that the only scale that influenced both types of autonomy was curiosity, highlighting the importance of the basic emotion of interest in the learning process, which is considered as one of the six primary emotions by Izard (2007). The association of this emotion with autonomy should probably not come as a surprise since curiosity appears to be the driving force behind the exploration of the environment (Voss and Keller 2013), which can be hypothesized as an indispensable precondition of any autonomous action. Significant positive correlations between the emotion of curiosity and the two facets of autonomy examined were already reported in previous work by Csizér et al. (2021), as well.

Table 4: Results of the regression analysis (stepwise method) of the motivational and emotions scales with autonomous learning behavior as the dependent scale (N = 337).

	Final model		
Scales	B	SE B	β
motivated learning behavior	.554	.037	.602*
enjoyment	.260	.068	.235*
learning experience	−.143	.043	−.188*
curiosity	.159	.055	.168*
R^2		.57	
F for change in R^2		111.577*	

*p <.05.

Table 5: Results of the regression analysis (stepwise method) of the motivational and emotions scales with autonomous use of technology as the dependent scale (N = 337).

	Final model		
Scales	B	SE B	β
confusion	−.396	.058	−.326
ideal L2 self	.494	.073	.298
pride	.224	.050	.226
boredom	.250	.078	.198
curiosity	.209	.088	.153
R^2		.42	
F for change in R^2		48.304*	

*p <.05.

5 Conclusions and pedagogical implications

The findings of our study indicate that students are generally highly motivated especially with regard to their ideal L2 self and ought-to self; however, they have lower dispositions towards their language learning experiences in the classroom. In terms of emotions, a positive finding is that the students in this sample experienced positive feelings to a greater extent than negative ones: we found hope, enjoyment, pride and curiosity to be the prevalent emotions in the Hungarian EFL classroom. On the other hand, negative emotions, such as shame, anxiety and confusion were present but were shown to be less characteristic. Our participants displayed moderate levels of autonomous behavior but somewhat higher levels of autonomous use of technology, which might be attributed to language use outside of the classroom rather than actual classroom teaching.

Regarding the influence of motivation and emotions on autonomy in our research, motivated learning behavior, learning experience, and curiosity had positive effects on autonomous learning behavior, whereas the autonomous use of technology appeared to be shaped by the ideal L2 self, pride, as well as curiosity. In terms of the negative effects, autonomy was found to be negatively influenced by learning experiences, while the autonomous use of technology was negatively impacted by confusion. The above-mentioned differences all point to the complex nature of autonomy and call for further investigation in relation to the links between various ID variables.

As for the pedagogical implications of our study for the Hungarian context, we have to highlight that learner autonomy should ideally not be the result of negative classroom experiences; it should not appear as the alternative solution to those who are motivated and are seeking other ways to improve their language knowledge. On the contrary, classroom learning should provide the basis for enhancing learner autonomy by using activities and tasks that prompt learners' curiosity, that are motivating, and that allow for positive emotional experiences. Furthermore, students should not be expected to know how to use technology for language learning purposes. Helping students to become more autonomous language learners, even in their use of technology, necessitates scaffolding in order to avoid such negative emotions as confusion. Therefore, it is important to stress that learners should be explicitly assisted in becoming autonomous rather than just be expected to take responsibility for their learning, or be pushed into becoming autonomous as a response to negative classroom experiences. It would also be interesting to see what findings similarly complex studies conducted in other countries might reveal about the relationships of autonomy, motivations and emotions.

Obviously, these findings raise several questions as to their wider pedagogical implications. The role of several positive emotions, such as enjoyment, hope, pride, and curiosity should be examined jointly in the future because they might play a vital role in creating an atmosphere in the classroom that could lead to enhanced language development, which would be an important aim in the Hungarian context. It would also be important to investigate how teachers could trigger these emotions and how teachers' and students' emotions might interact. In addition to this, since autonomy and self-regulation are 21st century skills which should be developed in all fields of education including language learning, it is all the more important to pay attention to ensuring that students take more control of their language learning.

There are some limitations to the present study that also point to further research directions. First of all, due to the number of participants and the number of schools, we cannot claim that the findings would be generalizable for the Hungarian secondary school context. In addition, we need to highlight the fact that this study focused on instructed settings; thus, in contexts outside the classroom different results might have emerged. Finally, our quantitative results presented a cross-sectional approach to the issue, so related processes and the sources of the relationships could not be investigated here.

In terms of future research directions, we believe that with the help of teacher and student interviews, we could gain a deeper insight into how autonomy and autonomous use of technology can be fostered and what keeps them actively going in the long run. Furthermore, it is still relatively unclear how students utilize technology inside and outside the classroom precisely, so this would also be a topic worthy of investigation. Since students typically spend four years in secondary school, it would also be interesting to examine whether students belonging to certain age groups differ in terms of their autonomy, motivations, or emotions. Moreover, studying the same constructs and their relationships in connection with other languages and contrasting these with our findings about English might also be highly informative, as such comparative studies have already been carried out in connection with English and Italian (Dewaele and Proietti Ergün 2020) and English and Dutch in CLIL and non-CLIL contexts (De Smet et al. 2018).

Appendix

Correlation among the scales (N = 337).

Scales	1	2	3	4	5	6	7	8	9	10	11	12	13	14	15
1. Autonomous use of technology	1	.478	.440	.439			.419	.222	.472		-.245	-.404	-.489		-.153
2. Autonomous learning behavior		1	.718	.377	.127	.145	.397	.459	.429	.366		-.213	-.259	-.183	
3. Motivated learning behavior			1	.555	.248		.503	.381	.478	.260		-.282	-.300	-.123	-.591
4. Ideal L2 self				1	.401		.381	.209	.276	.110		-.219	-.196		-.367
5. Ought to L2 self					1	-.121					.283	.208	.182		.156
6. Language learning experience						1	.306	.688	.242	.702	-.148	-.194	-.114	-.752	-.459
7. Hope							1	.453	.692	.244	-.342	-.514	-.528	-.115	-.321
8. Enjoyment								1	.457	.741		-.239	-.189	-.630	-.455
9. Pride									1	.261		-.430	-.467	-.143	
10. Curiosity										1	-.319			-.735	
11. Shame											1	.657	.428		.261
12. Anxiety												1	.621		.294
13. Confusion													1		.285
14. Boredom														1	.532
15. Apathy															1

Note. Only results significant.

Note

This study was supported by the NKFIH – 129149 research grant.

References

Albert, Á., Csizér, K., & Piniel, K. 2018. The relationship between foreign language learning autonomy and emotions: The results of a nationwide study in Hungary. Presentation at the *Autonomy in language learning and teaching: The case of target language skills and subsystems* conference. Konin, 7–9 May, 2018.

Albert, Á., Piniel, K., & Lajtai Á. 2019. Középiskolás diákok angolórákkal kapcsolatos érzelmei egy kérdőíves felmérés tükrében [Investigating high school students' emotions in connection with their English classes with the help of a questionnaire study]. *Modern Nyelvoktatás* 25(2). 27–41.

Albert, Á., Tankó, Gy., & Piniel, K. 2018a. A tanulók válaszai a 7. évfolyamon [Answers of Grade 7 students]. In E. Öveges & K. Csizér (Eds.), *Vizsgálat a köznevelésben folyó idegennyelv-oktatás hatékonyságáról [An investigation of the foreign language teaching in the compulsory education in Hungary]*, 93–163. Budapest: Oktatási Hivatal.

Albert, Á., Tankó, Gy., & Piniel, K. 2018b. A tanulók válaszai a 11. évfolyamon [Answers of Grade 11 students]. In E. Öveges & K. Csizér (Eds.), *Vizsgálat a köznevelésben folyó idegennyelv-oktatás hatékonyságáról [An investigation of the foreign language teaching in the compulsory education in Hungary]*, 93–163. Budapest: Oktatási Hivatal.

Asztalos, R., Szénich, A., & Csizér, K. 2020. Foreign language teaching and autonomous language learning – an overview and innovative practices in Hungary. In C. Ludwig, M. G. Tassinari & J. Mynard (Eds.), *Navigating foreign language learner autonomy*, 299–316. Hong Kong: Candlin & Mynard e-publishing.

Benson, P. 2001. *Teaching and researching learner autonomy in language learning.* London: Longman.

Benson, P. 2007. Autonomy in language teaching and learning. *Language Teaching* 40. 21–40. https://doi.org/10.1017/S0261444806003958

Benson, P. 2013. *Teaching and researching: Autonomy in language learning.* New York: Routledge.

Beseghi, M. 2018. Emotions and autonomy in foreign language learning at university. *Educazione Linguistica. Language Education* 7(2). 231–250. https://doi.org/10.30687/ELLE/2280-6792/2018/02/003

Chalkiadaki, A. 2018. A systematic literature review of 21st century skills and competencies in primary education. *International Journal of Instruction* 11(3). 1–16.

Clément, R. 1986. Second language proficiency and acculturation: An investigation of the effects of language status and individual characteristics. *Journal of Language and Social Psychology* 5(4). 271–290. https://doi.org/10.1177/0261927X8600500403

Csizér, K. 2020. *Second language learning motivation in a European context: The case of Hungary.* New York: Springer.

Csizér, K., Albert, Á, & Piniel, K. 2021. The interrelationship of language learning autonomy, self-efficacy, motivation and emotions: The investigation of Hungarian secondary school students. In M. Pawlak (Ed.), *Investigating individual learner differences in second language learning*, 1–21. New York: Springer.

Csizér, K., & Kormos, J. 2009.Modelling the role of inter-cultural contact in the motivation of learning English as a foreign language. *Applied Linguistics* 30. 166–185.

Csizér, K., & Kormos, J. 2012. A nyelvtanulási autonómia, az önszabályozó stratégiák és a motiváció kapcsolatának vizsgálata [The investigation of language learning autonomy, self-regulatory strategies and motivation in Hungarian]. *Magyar Pedagógia* 112. 3–17.

Csizér, K., & Kormos, J. 2014. The ideal L2 self, self-regulatory strategies and autonomous learning: A comparison of different groups of English learners. In K. Csizér & M. Magid (Eds.), *The impact of self-concept on language learning*, 73–86. Clevedon: Multilingual Matters.

Csizér, K., & Öveges, E. 2019. Idegennyelv-tanulási motivációs tényezők és a nyelvi vizsgák Magyarországon: összefüggések vizsgálata egy kérdőíves kutatás segítségével [Motivation to learn a foreign language and language exams in Hungary: Studying their relationships with the help of a questionnaire study]. *Modern Nyelvoktatás* 25. 86–101.

Csizér, K., & Öveges, E. 2020. Nyelvtanulási autonómia és nyelvi tervezés: egy vegyes módszerű kutatás eredményei [Language learning autonomy and language planning: Results of a mixed methds study]. *Modern Nyelvoktatás* 36. 44–58.

D. Molnár, É. 2014. Az önszabályozott tanulás pedagógiai jelentősége [The importance of self-regulatory learning]. In A. Buda & E. Golnhofer (Eds.), *Tanulmányok a neveléstudomány köréből 2013: Tanulás és környezet* [Studies in pedagogy, 2013: Learning and context], 29–54. Budapest: MTA Pedagógiai Tudományos Bizottság.

De Smet, A., Mettewie, L., Galand, B., Hiligsmann, P., & Van Mensel, L. 2018. Classroom anxiety and enjoyment in CLIL and non-CLIL: Does the target language matter? *Studies in Second Language Learning and Teaching* 8. 47–71. https://doi.org/10.14746/ssllt.2018.8.1.3

Deci, E. L., & Ryan, R. M. 1985. *Intrinsic motivation and self-determination in human behavior*. New York: Plenum.

Dewaele, J.-M., & MacIntyre, P. D. 2014. The two faces of Janus? Anxiety and enjoyment in the foreign language classroom. *Studies in Second Language Learning and Teaching* 4. 237–274. https://doi.org/10.14746/ssllt.2014.4.2.5

Dewaele, J.-M., & MacIntyre, P. D. 2016. Foreign language enjoyment and foreign language classroom anxiety: The right and left feet of FL learning? In P. D. MacIntyre, T. Gregersen & S. Mercer (Eds.), *Positive psychology in SLA*, 215–236. Clevedon: Multilingual Matters.

Dewaele, J.-M., & Proietti Ergün, A. L. 2020. How different are the relations between enjoyment, anxiety, attitudes/motivation and course marks in pupils' Italian and English as foreign languages? *Journal of the European Second Language Association* 4(1). 45–57. https://doi.org/10.22599/jesla.65

Dickinson, L. 1995. Autonomy and motivation a literature review. *System* 23. 165–174. https://doi.org/10.1016/0346-251X(95)00005-5

Dörnyei, Z. 2005. *The psychology of the language learner: Individual differences in second language acquisition*. Mahwah: Lawrence Erlbaum.

Dörnyei, Z. 2009. *The psychology of second language acquisition*. Oxford: Oxford University Press.

Dörnyei, Z., Csizér, K., & Németh, N. 2006. *Motivation, language attitudes and globalisation: A Hungarian perspective*. Clevedon: Multilingual Matters.

Dörnyei. Z., & Ryan, S. 2015. *The psychology of the language learner revisited*. New York: Routledge.

Dörnyei, Z., & Ushioda, E. 2011. Teaching and researching motivation, 2nd edn. Harlow: Longman.

Fredrickson, B. L. 2013. Updated thinking on positivity ratios. *American Psychologist* 68. 814–822. https://doi.org/10.1037/a0033584

Gardner, R. C. 2010. *Motivation and second language acquisition: The socio-educational model*. New York: Peter Lang.

Government decree No. 243/2003 (XII.17). On the issuance, implementation and application of the National Core Curriculum. Retrieved on 8 February 2021 from http://www.nefmi.gov.hu/letolt/kozokt/nat_070926.pdf

Horwitz, E. K., Horwitz, M. B., & Cope, J. A. 1991. Foreign language classroom anxiety. In E. K. Horwitz & D. J. Young (Eds.), *Language anxiety: From theory and research to classroom implications*, 27–36. Englewood Cliffs: Prentice Hall.

Izard, C. E. 2007. Basic emotions, natural kinds, emotion schemas, and a new paradigm. *Perspectives on Psychological Science* 2(3). 260–280. https://doi.org/10.1111/j.1745-6916.2007.00044.x

Kormos, J., & Csizér, K. 2008. Age-related differences in the motivation of learning English as a foreign language: attitudes, selves and motivated learning behaviour. *Language Learning* 58. 327–355. https://doi.org/10.1111/j.1467-9922.2008.00443.x.

Kormos, J., & Csizér, K. 2014. The interaction of motivation, self-regulation and autonomous learner behavior in different learner groups. *TESOL Quarterly* 48. 275–299. https://doi.org/10.1002/tesq.129

Krskova, H., Wood, L. N., Breyer, Y. A., & Baumann, C. 2020. FIRST: Principles of discipline for 21st century skills. In L. N. Wood, L. P. Tan, Y. A. Breyer & S. Hawse (Eds.), *Industry and higher education: Case studies for sustainable futures*, 265–289. New York: Springer.

Little, D. 1991. *Learner autonomy 1: Definitions, issues and problems*. Dublin: Authentik e-publisher.

Little, D. 1999. Learner autonomy is more than a Western cultural construct. In S. Cotterall & D. Crabbe (Eds.), *Learner Autonomy in Language Learning: Defining the Field and Effecting Change*, 11–18. New York: Peter Lang.

Liu, H. J. 2015. Learner autonomy: The role of motivation in foreign language learning. *Journal of Language Teaching and Research* 6. 1165–1174. http://dx.doi.org/10.17507/jltr.0606.02

MacIntyre, P. D., & Vincze, L. 2017. Positive and negative emotions underlie motivation for L2 learning. *Studies in Second Language Learning and Teaching* 7(1). 61–88. http://dx.doi.org/10.14746/ssllt.2017.7.1.4

Mills, N., Pajares, F., & Herron, C. 2007. Self-efficacy of college intermediate French students: Relation to achievement and motivation. *Language Learning* 57(3). 417–442. https://doi.org/10.1111/j.1467-9922.2007.00421.x

Nakata, Y. 2014. Self-regulation: Why is it important for promoting learner autonomy in the school context? *Studies in Self-Access Learning Journal* 5(4). 342–356.

Nikolov, M. 2001. A study of unsuccessful language learners. In Z. Dörnyei & R. Schmidt (Eds.), *Motivation and second language acquisition*, 149–170. The University of Hawaii, Second Language Teaching and Curriculum Center.

Öveges, E., & Csizér, K. 2018. Vizsgálat a köznevelésben folyó idegennyelv-oktatás kereteiről és hatékonyságáról [An investigation of the foreign language teaching in the compulsory education in Hungary]. Budapest: Oktatási Hivatal.

Pawlak, M. (Ed.) 2021. *Investigating individual learner differences in second language learning*. New York: Springer.

Pekrun, R. 2006. The control-value theory of achievement emotions: Assumptions, corollaries, and implications for educational research and practice. *Educational Psychology Review* 18(4). 315–341. https://doi.org/10.1007/s10648-006-9029-9

Pekrun, R. 2014. *Emotions and learning (Educational Practices Series, Vol. 24)*. Geneva: International Academy of Education (IAE) and International Bureau of Education (IBE) of the United Nations Educational, Scientific and Cultural Organization (UNESCO).

Pekrun, R., Goetz, T., Frenzel, A. C., Barchfeld, P., & Perry, R. P. 2011. Measuring emotions in students' learning and performance: The Achievement Emotions Questionnaire (AEQ). *Contemporary Educational Psychology* 36(1). 36–48. https://doi.org/10.1016/j.cedpsych.2010.10.002

Piniel, K., & Albert, Á. 2018. Advanced learners' foreign language related emotions across the four skills. *Studies in Second Language Learning and Teaching* 8(1). 127–147. https://doi.org/10.14746/ssllt.2018.8.1.6

Piniel, K., & Csizér, K. 2013. L2 motivation, anxiety and self-efficacy: The interrelationship of individual variables in the secondary school context. *Studies in Second Language Learning and Teaching* 3(4). 523–550. https://doi.org/10.14746/ssllt.2013.3.4.5

Ryan, S. 2019. Motivation as an individual difference. In M. Lamb, K. Csizér, A. Henry & S. Ryan (Eds.), *Palgrave Macmillan handbook of motivation for language learning*, 163–182. London: Palgrave.

Saito, K., Dewaele, J. M., Abe, M., & In'nami, Y. 2018. Motivation, emotion, learning experience, and second language comprehensibility development in classroom settings: A cross-sectional and longitudinal study. *Language Learning* 68(3). 709–743. https://doi.org/10.1111/lang.12297

Shao, K., Pekrun, R., & Nicholson, L. J. 2019. Emotions in classroom language learning: What can we learn from achievement emotion research? *System* 86. 102–121. https://doi.org/10.1016/j.system.2019.102121

Shaw, K., Holmes, K., Preston, G., Smith, M. & Bourke, S. 2014. Innovative teaching and learning: From research to practice. *Scan* 33(2).

Spratt, M., Humphreys, G., & Chan, V. 2002. Autonomy and motivation: Which comes first? *Language Teaching Research* 6(3). 245–266. https://doi.org/10.1191/1362168802lr106oa

Teimouri, Y. 2017. L2 selves, emotions, and motivated behaviors. *Studies in Second Language Acquisition* 39(4). 681–709. https://doi.org/10.1017/S0272263116000243

Voss, H. G., & Keller, H. 2013. *Curiosity and exploration: Theories and results*. Amsterdam: Elsevier.

Mark Christianson and Kota Ohata

Effects of authentic communication experiences on linguistic self-confidence: Individual differences in perceptions among Japanese primary school students

Abstract: This paper is a preliminary exploration into Japanese primary school age learners' beliefs regarding their self-confidence in language learning. One hundred and seven (107) Japanese primary school students studying English as a foreign language (EFL) in a private school near Tokyo participated in a questionnaire-based study following a week-long exchange visit to their school by students from the United Kingdom. During the visit, the Japanese students (ages 11 to 12) had several opportunities to engage in conversations with the UK students in lessons as part of the school's EFL curriculum as well as in various situations outside of lessons in more informal contexts. Following the exchange, the students were given a short questionnaire focusing on their perceptions of motivation and self-confidence in terms of their own language learning and intercultural communication. The results indicate that most students felt that their motivation and self-confidence for learning and using English was higher as a result of their contact and communication with the UK students, but not in all cases. Salient factors the learners referred to in terms of their motivation and confidence are explained using the participants' self-reflective quotations. Also, implications for how instructors in primary school EFL situations may help their students develop a robust self-confidence regarding their own second language development are discussed.

Keywords: SLA, EFL young learners, linguistic self-confidence, motivation, anxiety

1 Introduction

Opportunities for contact and communication with native speakers may be welcome and stimulating to some foreign language learners but anxiety-provoking to others, regardless of age or education level. In such opportunities, there exists the potential for a rewarding experience, but also a risk that the learner's current competence in the second or foreign language may be inadequate for successfully engaging in the expected communication at hand. There is also the potential for overwhelming anxiety that one may be negatively evaluated by others in the same environment in comparison to more capable speakers, or even in comparison to one's own ideal of oneself as a successful language learner (Ehrman 1996). As Horwitz et al (1986) note, "[A]ny performance in the L2 is likely to challenge an individual's self-concept as a competent communicator and lead to reticence, self-consciousness, fear, or even panic" (p. 128).

As one Japanese learner reflected,

> Every time I stumbled in my second language, I suspected that I might be misrepresented in English, in the ways that I would neither imagine nor expect I could be. It's like I've lost control of myself, always at the mercy of others' whimsical ways of perception as to what I have said and done in my unstable and shaky English. How many times did I wish that I could convince myself or make myself believe that the person who was speaking in that pitiful English was not really a true "myself" but just a separate entity!

The personal account of this university age learner, drawn from Ohata's (2004) study on language learning anxiety, depicts the deeply seated affective nature of second or foreign language learning experiences (Brown 1994), which may involve a threat to the learners' self-concept or self-expression to the extent that they may feel a loss of their self-esteem along with acute anxious feelings (Cohen and Norst 1989; Horwitz et al. 1986).

Given the fact that language anxiety occurs in various contexts of foreign language learning and may involve a great deal of emotional vulnerability on the part of language learners (Arnold and Brown 1999: 9), how can learners manage such emotional turmoil? How can they stay motivated to make their learning sustainable? One issue particularly relevant to the questions above is the issue of L2 self-confidence, or the personal belief of efficacy in one's own language learning. Please note that "L2" will be used below to refer to both second language and foreign language contexts except when a distinction is required.

Although the issue of learner self-confidence in L2 learning has been discussed, the phenomenon has not been fully described yet, especially in the ways that are particularly relevant to specific L2 learning contexts (e.g. Japanese primary school EFL). Certainly, L2 self-confidence and its related constructs (e.g., self-efficacy, self-concept, self-esteem, or locus of control) have been investigated in studies on language learning motivation (Clement, Dornyei, and Noels 1994; Crookes and Schmidt 1991; Dornyei 1994; Mills 2014; Oxford and Shearin 1994). As with other psychological constructs, one's self-confidence depends on individual differences and the differences in the setting (Ehrman 1996; Skehan 1989). That is, each individual's frame of reference, whether it be culturally or personally rooted, plays a role in shaping one's sense of efficacy in reaction to particular situations or contexts (Pekrun 1992; Bandura 1986). In this connection, this study seeks to understand individual differences among Japanese primary school age EFL learners in their beliefs and perceptions regarding their L2 self-confidence.

Thus far, research into the self-confidence beliefs of Japanese primary school EFL learners has been largely limited. This study, therefore, is an attempt to explore learner confidence among Japanese primary students as a potential source of their motivation as language learners in an EFL context. It is assumed that an understanding of how the learners believe they can develop as language learners can contribute to a clearer understanding of how such learners may be able to sustain their motivational drive in tackling further challenges in their EFL studies both during and beyond primary school.

1.1 Research questions

The main research questions in this exploratory, action-research based study are:
1) How will Japanese primary school students react to an opportunity to interact with similarly-aged native speakers who visit their school? What individual differences will emerge?
2) Will their sense of motivation to study English become stronger and, if so, what individual reasons or factors will they give for their response?
3) Will their self-confidence in their own ability to use English for communication become stronger, and if so, what reasons or factors will they each give?
4) At the primary school level in EFL contexts, how might authentic experiences of personal face-to-face contact and communication in a foreign language (such as the visit by UK students presented here) be utilized effectively so that students gain in motivation and self-confidence?

2 Review of literature

2.1 Self-efficacy beliefs in language learning

Learner self-confidence in L2 learning has previously been discussed in terms of self-perceptions of L2 competence or efficacy (Clément, Dörnyei and Noels 1994; Leaver, Ehrman, and Shekhtman 2005; Mills 2014). Bandura's (1997) social cognitive theory defines perceived self-efficacy as "beliefs in one's capabilities to organize and execute the course of action required to produce given attainments" (p. 3). That is, perceptions of self-efficacy are based on one's personal judgment of what one believes may be accomplished with the abilities that one possesses. Bandura (1993) also notes the existence of domain-specific perceptions of self-efficacy, which are different in nature from a more general form of self-efficacy or self-confidence. For example, one may not necessarily have a strong sense of self-efficacy for a specific situation or task (e.g., the upcoming spelling test), but in general possess a self-confident identity as a capable EFL learner.

Although there is a good possibility that a sense of efficacy in specific areas will overflow into one's general feelings of self-worth or self-esteem (Ehrman 1996: 137), self-efficacy beliefs imply that there exists some degree of control, or "locus of control," within oneself. Locus of control, as Williams and Burden (1999: 194) note, "relates to whether individuals see the events that happen in their lives as lying within their control or outside of it" (Wang 1983 as cited in Williams and Burden 1999). Beliefs of personal efficacy, thus, relate to a sense of control (Bandura 1993, 1997), based on the individual's appraisal of a certain situation as being threatening or not. That is, if the situation is perceived as potentially threatening, and beyond one's ability to deal with, anxiety results as a natural consequence. In sum, the ways in which individuals experience anxiety will depend on their perceptions of self-efficacy and whether they consider themselves sufficiently in control of that particular situation (Pappamihiel 2002).

In particular, the question of how self-efficacy relates to specific L2 learning contexts is an issue that demands further research. As Graham (2004) notes, the construct of self-efficacy has been "applied widely in general educational contexts" (p. 173), especially in relation to academic achievements or outcomes (Multon, Brown, and Lent 1991; Schunk 1991) but only "to a lesser extent in the study of language learning motivation" (Graham 2004: 173).

The relevance of learner self-efficacy beliefs to L2 learning is quite apparent, as noted above, and this has naturally led to the self-efficacy construct being incorporated into various studies of second language learning motivation (Clément, Dörnyei, and Noels 1994; Clément, Gardner, and Smythe 1980; Gardner, Tremblay, and Masgoret 1997; Wong 2005). Tremblay and Gardner (1995), for instance, noted that the learner's self-efficacy is "an important antecedent to motivational behavior in language learning (e.g., persistence)" (as cited in Graham 2004: 173), defining it as "an individual's beliefs that he or she has the capacity to reach a certain level of performance or achievement" (p. 507). A series of studies by Eccles and Wigfield (e.g., Eccles 1984; Wigfield 1994; Wigfield and Eccles 1992) also implied that "motivation is based on how much students expect to succeed at a task and how much they value that success" (Ehrman, Leaver, and Oxford 2003: 321). That is, if students are given intrinsically motivating tasks which are interesting yet challenging, they can gain a sense of enjoyment, accompanied by a feeling of competence (self-efficacy) in doing the tasks as a sort of reward (Deci and Ryan 1985).

2.2 Defining L2 self-confidence

As somewhat different from the task-specific type of self-efficacy described above, L2 self-confidence or "linguistic self-confidence" proposed by Clément et al. (1980, 1985, 1994) describes the learner's overall belief in one's competence in the L2 use. According to MacIntyre, Clément, Dörnyei, and Noels (1998: 551), L2 self-confidence is comprised of two componential factors:
1) self-evaluation of one's L2 skills, as the cognitive component, and
2) anxiety, as the affective component.

The cognitive component corresponds to the learner's "perceived competence" (Baker and MacIntyre 2000; MacIntyre and Charos 1996) or "a judgment made by the speaker about the degree of mastery achieved in the L2" (MacIntyre et al. 1998: 551). The affective component corresponds to "language anxiety, especially the discomfort experienced when using a L2" (MacIntyre et al. 1998: 551). In Clément's model of L2 acquisition (Clément 1978, 1980, 1984, 1986; Clément and Kruidenier 1985; Sampasivam and Clément 2014), L2 self-confidence is defined as "self-perceptions of communicative competence and concomitant low levels of anxiety in using the second language" (Noels et al. 1996: 255). Furthermore, in that model, L2 self-confidence is described as serving as "the most important determinant of attitude and effort expended toward L2 learning" (Clément et al. 1994: 422).

2.3 Anxiety in language learning

The concept of anxiety in relation to second language use is a key component of L2 self-confidence. Horwitz, Horwitz, and Cope (1986) define language anxiety as "a distinct complex of self-perceptions, beliefs, feelings, and behaviors . . . arising from the uniqueness of the language learning process" (p. 28). Language anxiety, as often instantiated in the form of performance anxiety, such as communication apprehension, fear of negative evaluation, or test anxiety (Horwitz 1986; MacIntyre and Gardner 1991), is also known to be highly related to student motivation. Ehrman (2003: 323) notes that overly anxious learners "are less motivated to perform in ways that bring active attention to themselves in the classroom or in natural language-use settings". Thus, the concepts of motivation, anxiety and L2 self-confidence are closely linked.

2.4 L2 self-confidence and willingness to communicate (WTC)

Self-confidence in L2 learning is associated not just with L2 learning motivation in general (Gardner et al. 1997; Hashimoto 2002), but more specifically with other variables such as Willingness to Communicate (WTC) (MacIntyre et al. 2002), which are positively correlated with L2 motivation. Thus, as Clement and others (1994) note, language anxiety is a central factor in determining learner self-confidence and a lack of anxiety is thereby an important attribute of motivated learners (Papi 2010). In light of the fact that the essential components of language anxiety include various forms of performance anxiety (i.e., communication apprehension), L2 self-confidence is also considered a key determinant of learners' willingness and readiness to participate in communicative activities in language classrooms (MacIntyre et al. 1998; Yashima, Zenuk-Nishide, and Shimizu 2004).

According to MacIntyre et al.'s (1998) model of variables that influence the construct of WTC in the L2, there are two aspects of self-confidence; that is, one is characterized as rather transient and situational and described as state communicative self-confidence, while the other more stable and enduring form is L2 self-confidence. This differentiation of aspects of self-confidence roughly corresponds to Bandura's (1993) conceptualization of domain specific perceptions of self-efficacy on the one hand and a more general form of self-efficacy beliefs on the other. Under the overarching construct of WTC, MacIntyre et al. (1998) propose that overall L2 self-confidence can be built up over time in various communicative situations (e.g., intergroup and social communicative settings). In such situations, affective elements such as social and individual motivation interact with one another to influence state or situational-level self-confidence, facilitating the process of learners' willingness to communicate. In this connection, Yashima (2002) and Yashima et al. (2004) reported that L2 motivation and learner self-confidence in L2 communication were both strongly related to the levels of L2 WTC among Japanese EFL learners at the college and high-school level. In particular, learners who have a high level of 'international posture,' were found to be more motivated and willing to communicate in the L2. According to Yashima et al. (2004), the construct of international posture refers to the kind of motivational attitudes that learners of predominantly mono-cultural backgrounds (e.g., Japanese EFL learners), tend to possess as an alternative to Gardner's (1985) integrative motivation.

As Edwards and Roger (2015) point out, L2 self-confidence, WTC, and L2 communicative competence can potentially be developed as a cyclical process, and given the studies by Yashima and others (2002, 2004), which incorporate the social and cultural aspects of learner motivation, it is apparent that there exists a complex network of factors influencing the ways L2 self-confidence can develop within individual learners.

2.5 L2 self-confidence among primary school students

Despite a global trend toward starting English study at a younger age (Crystal 2009), studies into L2 self-confidence among young English language learners (YELLs) in various learning contexts still seem to be limited, but have yielded a number of preliminary insights. For example, Leona et al (2021) researched the relationship between extramural English exposure and motivation and found that linguistic self-confidence was a factor in predicting L2 performance among the 262 10-year-old YELLs studied in the Netherlands. Within the Japanese context, research such as that by Carreira et al (2013) has explored various factors weighing on Japanese primary school children's motivation, but specific research exploring perceptions of self-confidence among Japanese primary age students engaged in L2 learning still seems needed.

3 Methodology

3.1 The context and participants

The 107 participants in this questionnaire-based study were students of 11 or 12 years old (Mean=12.04, SD=0.24), and all in the sixth grade of the same private primary school located near Tokyo, Japan. Students in this group had studied English within the school's EFL curriculum for one class period of 45 minutes per week in grades 1, 2, 3 (ages 6 to 9) and two periods of 45 minutes per week in grades 4, 5, 6 (ages 9 to 12). Thus, as of October of their sixth year when this study was conducted, the total number of EFL lessons the students had completed was approximately 280 periods. The class size for EFL lessons at the school is set at 18 students, and each lesson is taught by a teacher who is an advanced user of English and specializes in teaching EFL. It should be noted that one of the authors of this paper is such an instructor.

The English proficiency of almost all students was at a beginner level (CEFR A1 or A2, basic users), as assessed by the researchers based on student performance on spoken and written assessments used in the school. The number of students who had clearly attained intermediate or advanced English proficiency (B1 or higher) were a minority (just 6 out of 107). Each of these six had either lived abroad for more than a year or attended an English immersion pre-school prior to entering the primary school. It should be noted that other students in the school (approximately 30%) had also engaged in some type of substantial English learning outside of the school lessons (e.g. English language schools, summer English camps, or tutors at home) to varying degrees, but their proficiency would be best rated as A1 or A2 (basic users).

3.2 The visit by the UK students

The focus is of this study is the perceptions of the Japanese students following the visit by the UK students to their school in Japan. The questionnaire for this study was conducted several days after the conclusion of a week-long visit by students from the United Kingdom (UK) to the Japanese primary school. This visit by UK students was part of an intercultural exchange program with two schools in the United Kingdom. The first ever exchange between the Japanese school and the UK schools occurred in the previous year (2018), and the exchange related to the students participating in this research project took place in 2019 and was the second such exchange. Each year, a group of students travel to the other country and do homestays and attend classes for an equal period of 9 nights, 10 days.

From Japan, a selected number of students (16 in the year this study was conducted) had visited the schools in the UK and stayed in homes of their homestay partners, commuted to school to experience school life in the UK, and gone on excursions to see famous sights in London and surrounding areas. On the other hand, the same number of UK students (16, or eight from each of two schools) traveled to Japan, stayed in the home of their homestay partner for 9 nights, experienced Japanese school life and visited famous places in the greater Tokyo area in excursions.

The Japanese sixth grade students had several chances to engage in personal conversations with the 16 UK students during the time they were visiting the Japanese school (five school days). Since none of the UK students could use Japanese for anything more than basic greetings, the medium of communication was English in all cases. In some instances, communication was assisted by English proficient persons in the environment such as classmates, teachers, and parents, or via the use of paper and electronic dictionaries and translation applications. It should be noted that, for all 9 nights, the 16 UK students stayed in homes of the 16 Japanese students who had gone to the UK, and thus those 16 Japanese students had more opportunity for contact than their classmates.

Interaction between the UK students and the Japanese students occurred both inside the EFL classroom in organized activities, and outside of the EFL classroom informally.

3.3 Interaction within lessons

Within the classroom, all of the Japanese students had two periods of 45 minutes to interact with UK students in structured activities. Based on the lesson schedule, two groups of 18 Japanese students had class simultaneously, and therefore the 16 UK students split into two groups of eight, making a ratio of 18 to 8, eighteen Japanese students to eight UK students in each session.

In both periods, after short ice breakers and a mini-lesson time for the Japanese students to teach the UK students Japanese, the main activity was timed small-group conversations. In the timed small-group conversations, usually with a time limit of six minutes per conversation, two or three Japanese students would interact with one of the UK students, with Japanese students initiating topics they had previously studied, including *"What is your favorite sport?" "What do you like to do in your free time?" "Do you have pets?" "What time do you usually go to school?"* and *"When you grow up, what do you want to be?"* For many of the Japanese students, this was their first time to ever have a personal conversation with a non-Japanese person other than their English teachers at the school.

Based on observations by one of the researchers, it can be said that most conversations proceeded smoothly, but with communication breakdown occurring from time to time when pronunciation difficulties or a lack of vocabulary interfered with understanding. When breakdown occurred, Japanese students used several types of repair and clarification strategies they had studied to try to repair the conversation. Strategies including asking for a slower repetition, a definition, spelling or drawing, and asking for a moment while they checked a dictionary to figure out the meaning.

3.4 Interaction outside of lessons

Communication between the UK students and some Japanese students also occurred in various situations outside of the English lessons, in most cases unobserved by instructors. These situations including lunch time, break time, and after school in free play or club activities. One of the days during the exchange was Sports Day, and the UK students participated in foot races and other events along with Japanese students. Informal interaction also took place in non-English lessons such as music, art or science classes which were conducted in Japanese, with the UK students doing their best to participate, assisted by teachers and students. As has been noted above, the 16 Japanese students who had been selected for the UK Exchange (by lottery) had opportunities for further communication with their homestay partner during commute times, at home, and on school or family outings.

3.5 The questionnaire and data analysis

Following the exchange, the Japanese students were given a questionnaire focusing on their perceptions of the exchange as well as their own motivation and self-confidence in their own language learning and English abilities (See Appendix A). The questionnaire was administered by a Google Form, and 107 students (all students in the year group) filled in their ideas into the Google Form using iPads in the classroom in a lesson several days after the UK students had returned to the UK. The questionnaire required students to give their names. Students were aware that their responses would be seen by their teachers and the authors of this paper, and consented to having their responses used for research, with the explicit guarantee of confidentiality in that any release of the data would be in an anonymous way that ensured no identifying information is included.

Comments by the students on the open-ended questions were translated from Japanese into English and analyzed qualitatively according to the constant comparative method (Strauss and Corbin 1998) for key themes. All names preceding the quotations have been altered for confidentiality.

4 Findings

Based on the results of the questionnaire, the students' perceptions of their interactions with the UK students and how those interactions may or may not have had an influence on their motivation and self-confidence as a language learner are presented below.

4.1 Amount of interaction

Regarding interaction within the English classes, 58 students responded that they were able to interact and converse "a lot" and 46 students "a little." Two students said they spoke "Just Greetings" and one relatively reserved student responded that he was unable to interact at all (see Figure 1). In a group of two or three, it is possible for a reserved student to mainly watch and listen and let the other members do the conversations. However, in almost all groups, all students were actively engaging in communication and the questionnaire result reflects this.

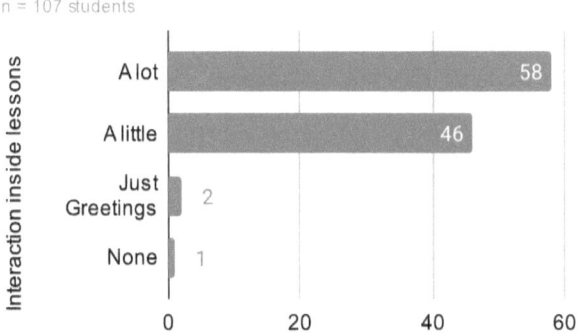

Figure 1: Results for questionnaire Q1: "*In English class lessons, how much did you converse with the UK students?*".

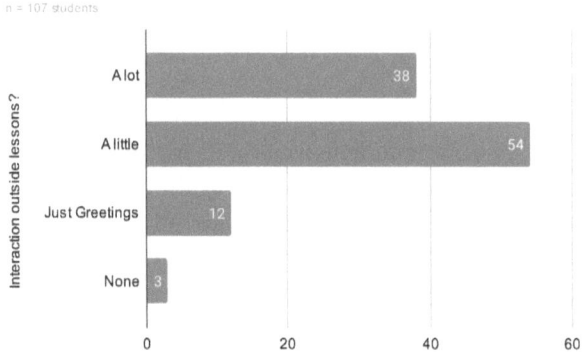

Figure 2: Results for questionnaire Q2: "*Outside of English class lessons, how much did you converse with the UK students (during breaks etc.)?*".

In general, compared to in-class interaction where an opportunity to converse was facilitated by the instructors, out-of-class interaction was less frequent for some students. As Figure 2 shows, only 38 students answered that they interacted "a lot" while 54 answered that they interacted "a little." The number whose interaction was limited to "just greetings" increased to 12 students, and 3 students answered they had no interaction outside of lessons at all. Although potential opportunities for communication during breaks or lunch or club activities existed, the Japanese students needed to initiate their own communication in those situations, and that seems to have made it difficult for some students.

4.2 Levels of nervousness

On the multiple-choice question regarding their nervousness or anxiety when communicating with the UK students, the students' responses were as follows:

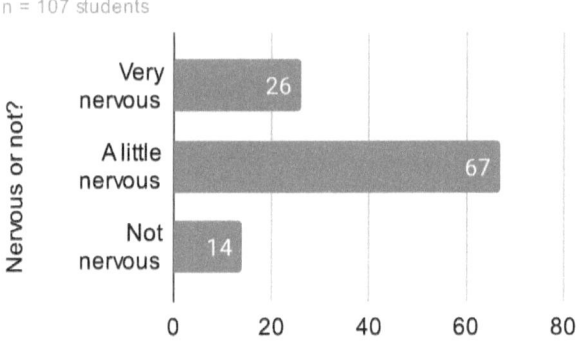

Figure 3: Results for questionnaire item: *"How was your experience of conversing with the UK exchange students?"*.

The majority expressed that they were "a little nervous" (67) or "very nervous" (26), with just 14 students choosing the item "not nervous at all" (see Figure 3). This is understandable when considering the fact that almost all students only had very basic conversational English proficiency, and many were meeting non-Japanese peers from another country face-to-face for the first time in their lives.

Of the 14 students who chose "not nervous at all," 8 were part of the group of 16 students who had travelled to the UK in May that year as part of the exchange program. In this case, the choice of "not nervous at all" seems natural since they had lived in the UK for ten days, attended the exchange program schools for a week, and were already familiar with the UK students who came to Japan. The other 6 students who chose "not nervous at all" tended to have higher English proficiency than their classmates either due to experiences of living abroad or extensive English study outside of school such as attending an English immersion pre-school.

On the other hand, the students who indicated they were "very nervous" when interacting with the UK students tended to either have relatively lower English proficiencies within the English class, struggling with both conversation tasks and literacy over the years, or generally more reserved, quiet personalities (as observed by the researcher who is also one of their instructors). Thus, it is understandable that their first attempt to converse with a group of native speakers made them highly nervous.

4.3 Increase in motivation

The questionnaire also asked the Japanese sixth graders about their perceived sense of motivation toward improving their English to communicate more as a result of the exchange experience.

As Figure 4 shows, the result for the multiple-choice item of the question was that 66 chose "Very much," and 39 chose "Somewhat." The two students who chose "Not at all" both had near native-speaker English proficiency due to having lived abroad, and explained that they felt their English proficiency was already at a level where they did not need a chance to converse with native speakers to feel further motivation of study.

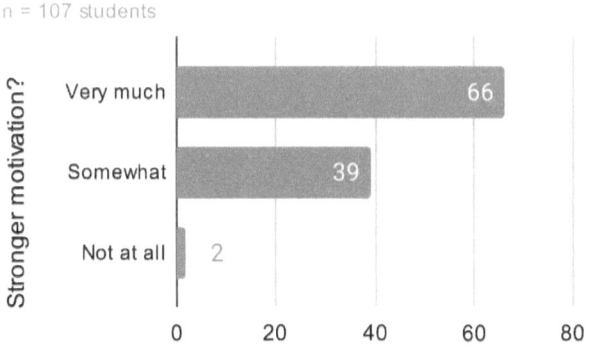

Figure 4: Results for questionnaire's Q4. *"As a result of interacting with the UK exchange students, do you feel that your "motivation" (interest) for English study and intercultural communication is stronger? In other words, do you feel that you want to improve your English and communicate more?"*.

In the open-ended response item on why they felt so, the students who expressed that they felt motivated "Very much" or "Somewhat" by the experience gave the following main types of reasons for their answer:
1) Interacting and becoming friends with the UK students was enjoyable (38 responses)
2) It was difficult or frustrating, and thus an impetus to study further (31 responses)
3) It made them want to learn more about other cultures (23 responses)

Firstly, one main theme in the reasons mentioned by those who chose "Very much" was that they enjoyed the interactions they had with the UK students during the visit. In other words, they felt they wanted to learn English more and engage in more communication because it was exciting and fun to get to know the UK students. References to the enjoyment included not only the conversations they had in and outside of classes, but also through other aspects such as playing sports or games together.

For example, as Rurika, a very shy student wrote:

> My English is not good, so I was a little bit afraid of the idea of trying to communicate with real native speaker kids. However, when I met the students from the UK, they were smiling, and so I wasn't as nervous as I thought I would be. I was able to find my courage and communicate, and I had fun playing with them. I want to be able to communicate more with them.

Another common reason given for feeling a stronger motivation was "frustration" they felt in the communication.

Sayaka expressed this as follows:

> I am very interested in developing my ability further because I felt a lot of frustration when I tried to communicate with the exchange students. For example, when we were teaching the UK students how to fold origami, there were many things that I wanted to say, but I couldn't find the words. I want to study really well and become able to say many things.

Yuno wrote her reason with a similar idea.

> I want to study and improve a lot because I couldn't answer many of the questions my partner from the UK asked. I was trying to say my answer many different ways, many different times, but she just frowned and looked confused each time I said something. That was frustrating. But I also had many times when we were able to understand each other, so I really want to be able to communicate well in the future.

Thirdly, many students attributed their stronger sense of motivation to a stronger desire to know more about other countries and cultures that emerged as a result of the intercultural experience with the UK students.

As Waka related:

> Speaking with the exchange students helped me learn that other countries and cultures are very interesting. I also enjoyed teaching the UK students about Japan and Japanese culture. In the future, I hope I can have more opportunities for intercultural communication.

Thus, almost all students seemed to feel that the opportunity they had for interacting with the UK students led to a stronger desire to communicate well. Different students cited different reasons for this perception, but the most common themes in the comments on this item were that they found that they can enjoy intercultural communication, they felt a desire to know more about the UK and other cultures, and they felt frustration with their lack of ability to communicate in the way that they wanted to.

4.4 Perceptions of increased confidence?

Figure 5 shows that almost all students (103 out of 107) indicated the experience of communicating with the UK students led to a strengthening of their self-confidence as users of the language to some extent. Students that chose "Very much" were 36 and the number of those who chose "Somewhat" was 67.

On the other hand, four students indicated that the opportunity to interact did not strengthen that their own linguistic self-confidence. Two of these were the same students who felt their English level was too high to feel further motivation, and their reasons were similar for saying that they did not gain in confidence as a result of communicating with the UK students. As for the other two, their reasons will be discussed below.

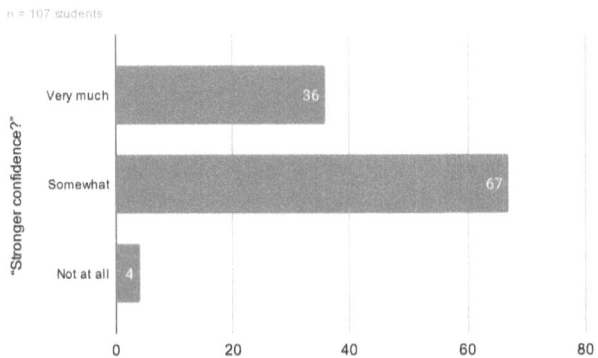

Figure 5: Results for the questionnaire item: "*As a result of interacting with the UK students, do you feel that your "confidence" to communicate in English became stronger?*".

In terms of reasons, an analysis of the responses to the open-ended section of the question shows that students tended to cite the following types of reasons to explain their choice of "Very much" or "Somewhat":
1) Their English communication was successful, often more than they thought (94 responses)
2) They overcame their fear or anxiety of communication (5 responses)

Each factor is illustrated with quotations from the data below.

Firstly, the vast majority of the students attributed their perception of stronger self-confidence to the fact that they experienced success in their communication efforts, often in a way that exceeded their initial expectations.

For example, Ichiro, a diligent but relatively shy student, who had only experienced English learning through the program at his school and who had never had a chance to talk with a similar-aged peer from an English-speaking country prior to the exchange, wrote:

> I was able to talk a lot with the UK students in class, and a little bit outside of class too. I was very nervous each time, but I found that I could enjoy communicating with people from a different country, and I could learn many, many things. My confidence is a little stronger. I have studied English hard in my lessons, but I get very nervous when I need to speak in English, so I don't think I have much confidence yet. After the UK students left, I decided to study English harder. I want to be fluent. Honestly speaking, when I watched some of my classmates speak fluently with the UK student, it made me feel overwhelmed, like maybe I should just give up . . . but I am going to work hard and do my best in my own way.

The phrase translated above as "give up" in Japanese was *zasetsu* (挫折), which has a meaning of a spirit being broken or defeated. Despite a sense of anxiety felt in comparison to his more capable classmates, Ichiro writes that he discovered a small but sure sense of self-confidence that he had not felt before.

Maya wrote about a particular episode of communication that sparked her confidence:

> One of the UK students had a really cute bag, and I was able to ask her about it such as where she bought it and how much it cost, and I was so happy because my English got through! It was the moment I felt a little confidence in my English communication ability. When you can communicate, it is fun, and you want to learn more so that you can communicate even more.

Another reason for a stronger confidence seemed to that the arrival of the UK students provided an opportunity to overcome a fear of communication that several students had.

For example, Nana, a student who expressed that she was "Very nervous" about meeting the UK students, wrote:

> I did not have any courage at all to talk with the UK students, but I was able to at least exchange greetings and get a smile. That is why I feel I have more confidence than before.

On the other hand, two students who had relatively weak English proficiency indicated that the opportunity to interact did not strengthen their own linguistic self-confidence, and they could not enjoy the exchange interaction very much.

As Keita, a somewhat shy student wrote:

> I really wanted to communicate with the UK students when they came, but I don't think my confidence got stronger at all. I just felt overwhelmed . . . and that there was so much I don't know in terms of vocabulary or grammar or expressions, and I couldn't really communicate with them very much. I couldn't smile at all.

Satoshi also chose "Not at all" and explained:

> During the time with the UK students, there were times when my attempts at English communication completely failed. I tried to say something, but I got blank looks. I think if my communication skill in English increases, I will be able to talk about many things with them and have fun, but I can't say I am confident in any way yet.

4.5 Making self-confidence stronger

Finally, the last question in the questionnaire was: *What do you think would make your confidence in your English ability stronger?* Interestingly, those who responded mainly used the item to reflect on the difficulties they had experienced in their communication during the exchange visit, and to set corresponding goals for future improvement.

For example, Fumi wrote:

> Prior to this exchange week, I had never known for sure whether I could actually use English to truly communicate with someone. Now I have some idea of what I can and cannot really do, and I feel I really need to learn a greater variety of reactions (not just "I see"), and want to know more phrases to be able to ask more interesting questions to the UK students, and not just the ones we learn in class.

Other students mentioned various needs for improvement that they had discovered. Some of the frequently mentioned items included a need for better pronunciation, more conversation practice, and a stronger vocabulary. Thus, the students see self-confidence as potentially increasing by improving in areas in which they felt they were lacking, as identified in a high-stakes situation where they felt a desire to perform.

Rento, a thoughtful, reserved student who chose "Very nervous" as his feeling toward communicating with the UK students, expressed his discovery as follows:

> Through this exchange, I have found some confidence because I was able to confirm that I can use English to communicate. However, my weakness is that I get very nervous, and I can't say what I want to say. To be more confident, I need to learn to relax, and not hesitate to start a conversation. I think that will improve my communication.

In sum, the results of the questionnaire indicate a variety of individual responses and perceptions among the Japanese primary students in connection to their experience of communicating with the UK students. In general, many students expressed that they felt a strong sense of motivation to improve their English communication skill either because they enjoyed the interaction or because they felt frustrated with not being able to communicate well. In terms of self-confidence, many, but not all, students felt that their self-confidence as a user of English became stronger due to their experience of being able to successfully communicate with the UK students more than they had expected.

5 Discussion

This exploratory, small-scale study has sought to shed light on how Japanese primary school age learners in an EFL context would respond to one week of face-to-face contact and communication with native speakers of English from the UK, and what individual differences would emerge in terms of how they perceive their own motivation and self-confidence in relation to that experience.

5.1 Issues in student anxiety

As the findings indicate, though almost all students expressed that the contact with the UK students led to a stronger sense of motivation in terms of wanting to study English and improve their ability to communicate more, some students felt a strong degree of nervousness or anxiety during the exchange. For some of the students who answered the questionnaire, there was a feeling of being overwhelmed by the encounter with the UK students and by seeing their classmates more capably interacting with the native speakers.

In such an environment, being evaluated might serve as a reminder of the learner's current limited level of L2 competence in comparison to others' or idealized images of him/herself as a successful language learner (Ehrman 1996;

Dörnyei 2009). Thus, the issue of anxiety seems to be closely related to the learner's self-identity or self-concept in the very sense that anxiety serves as both a source and effect of the learner's self-efficacy beliefs and L2 self-confidence (Mills, Pajare, and Heron 2006; Papi 2010). Moreover, considering the fact that the essential components of language anxiety include various forms of performance anxiety (i.e., communication apprehension), L2 self-confidence is also considered a key determinant of learners' willingness/readiness to participate in L2 communicative activities in the classrooms (MacIntyre et al. 1998; Yashima, et al 2004).

From a pedagogical point of view, sensitivity to such perceptions of anxiety seems thus needed. For example, as steps that can be taken by the instructor, anxiety held by the students hopefully can be reduced by means such as stressing that there is no need to compare oneself with others, and to emphasize the importance of not feeling afraid to make mistakes. Emotional support for students who may be more reserved, or feeling less proficient than other students should be provided as well.

More specifically, it may be helpful for such students if the instructor mentions to the whole class and to the arriving exchange-program students that such feelings of anxiety are natural, and that all members should be supportive of each other to provide a positive experience of intercultural communication for all students involved. Furthermore, as computer-mediated communication becomes more easily available, various forms of synchronous and asynchronous communication with users of English from other cultures via computer devices may be one avenue of opportunity. Compared to face-to-face contact, computer mediated contact may be a way to help students with relatively high anxiety feel comfortable with their first steps in using their foreign language in non-classroom situations (Arnold 2007).

5.2 Issues in developing L2 self-confidence

The students' responses showed how engaging in communication with students from another country can lead to frustration and difficulty, but that the desire to overcome such difficulties can also lead to motivation to try to use the language, and that the experience of actually succeeding in intercultural communication led to self-confidence. Thus, providing opportunities for students to have contact with other users who are not in their usual group, and encounter communication challenges they have not faced before, especially in a supportive environment, seems one key to developing L2 self-confidence in an EFL context (Sampasivam, Sinthujaa, and Clément 2014). The students in the study showed that they had a strong "willingness to communicate" (WTC) (Yashima 2002) and a strong "international posture" (Yashima et al. 2004), as can be seen by the number of responses indicating that one reason they felt motivated was that the exchange led to a desire to know more about other countries and cultures. One way to see language learning and language pedagogy is as a series of L2 confidence-building episodes. In other words, the learner can develop L2 competence via a cycle of 1) development of more self-confidence leading to more motivation, 2) more motivation leading to more effort and persistence in learning and gaining new abilities in the foreign language, and then 3) use of the abilities leading to further self-confidence (Dörnyei 2001; Ehrman, Leaver, and Oxford 2003). Thus, pedagogically speaking, the facilitation of contact with students from other countries and cultures, either face-to-face or via computer, seems to be a promising area of future development and research for seeing how student motivation, L2 self-confidence, and L2 competence build on each other, with due consideration to the anxieties and other obstacles each individual learner faces in their development as an intercultural communicator.

5.3 Limitations of the study and future directions

Similar studies in the future could consider several changes and improvements to build upon the findings presented here. The number of primary-age learners participating in this study was few, and all students were from only one school. Furthermore, only a week-long exchange visit by a group of native speaker children was specifically considered in terms of the effects it may have on the self-perceptions of the participants, and only a very simple, exploratory questionnaire was conducted. Ideally, questionnaires with a greater variety of items would be given several times over a certain period including pre-event and post-event for significant events, and follow up interviews to try to understand the feelings underlying the written responses would be scheduled as well. As Dörnyei (2001: 49) aptly points out, more qualitative and interpretive approaches (e.g., in-depth-interviews or case studies) need to be employed to further understand and explore "the internal dynamics of the intricate and multilevel construct of student motivation", and they can also provide a more holistic picture of closely related constructs of learner self (e.g., learner self-confidence, self-concept, self-esteem, or self-identity). The questionnaires and interviews would benefit from adding items to consider other variables such as personality, self-esteem, motivation level in general including perceptions about the importance of English learning and how the learners' hope to use the foreign language in the future. Furthermore, another limitation was that, in this study, no control group was employed.

Future studies would benefit from a design that includes comparable data from a group of students who do not participate in the exchange event.

6 Conclusion

Though this study is but a preliminary exploration, the findings from the student responses in the questionnaire provide some insights into Japanese primary school age learners' beliefs regarding their own L2 self-confidence. As a result of having several chances to engage in authentic communication in personal conversations with the UK students inside and outside of lessons, almost all indicated on the questionnaire that their motivation and self-confidence for using English was higher. To some extent, this shows that such "authentic" opportunities for interpersonal communication using the foreign language can be highly valuable for promoting motivation and self-confidence among primary EFL learners. Individual factors which may explain this phenomenon, based on the student's comments, included a sense of personal enjoyment related to getting to know similar-aged students from another culture, the increase of a desire to know more about other cultures, and a sense of frustration experienced in not being able to communicate as well as desired.

At the same time, the results show that not all students felt their motivation and confidence were strengthened. Students with a relatively high level of proficiency compared to other students did not feel the experience led to any further motivation or confidence, and some students with relatively weak skills or less outgoing personalities felt that they could not use the experience as well as other students and felt high levels of anxiety during the visit by the UK students. Instructors hoping to design similar intercultural exchanges to boost confidence and motivation would benefit from taking into account both of those affective difficulties in order to accommodate such individual differences.

Appendix

Questionnaire *(English Translation Added)*

Class _____   Name _____

Q1. 授業内の交流がありましたが、どのぐらい会話や交流をしましたか?
In class, how much did you converse or interact with the UK students?
できなかった / あいさつだけ / すこし会話ができた / たくさん会話ができた
None / Just greetings / A little / A lot

Q2. 授業外(休み時間、給食、通学、放課後、クラブ)の交流はどうでしたか?
Outside of class, how much did you converse or interact with the UK students? (during breaks, lunch, after school, in clubs)
できなかった / あいさつだけ / すこし会話ができた / たくさん会話ができた
None / Just greetings / A little / A lot

Q3. 留学生と英語で会話する経験はどうでしたか?緊張しましたか?
How was your experience of conversing with the exchange students? Were you nervous?
とても緊張した / 少し緊張した / 緊張しなかった
Very nervous / A little nervous / Not nervous at all

Q4. 英国の留学生と交流した結果、英語でもっとコミュニケーションしたい、できるようになりたい、という意味で英語学習や異文化交流への「意欲」は強まったと思いますか?
As a result of interacting with the UK exchange students, do you feel that your "motivation" for English study and intercultural communication is stronger? In other words, do you feel that you want to improve your English and communicate more?
全く思わない / 少し強まった / とても強まった
Not at all / A little / Very much

どうしてそう思いますか? *Why do you think so?*

Q5. 英国の留学生と交流した結果、自分は英語でコミュニケーションできるという「自信」は強まったと思いますか?
As a result of interacting with the UK exchange students, do you feel that your "confidence" to communicate in English became stronger?
全く思わない / 少し強まった / とても強まった
Not at all / A little / Very much

どうしてそう思いますか? *Why do you think so?*

Q6. どうしたら自分の英語力にもっと自信をもてると思いますか?
What do you think would make your confidence in your English ability stronger?

References

Arnold, J., & Brown, H. D. 1999. A map of the terrain. In J. Arnold (ed.), *Affect in language learning*, 1–27. NY: Cambridge University Press.
Arnold, N., 2007. Reducing foreign language communication apprehension with computer-mediated communication: A preliminary study. *System* 34(4). 469–486.
Baker, S. C., & MacIntyre, P. D. 2000. The role of gender and immersion in communication and second language orientations. *Language Learning* 50(2). 311–341.
Bandura, A. 1986. *Social foundations of thought and action: A social cognitive theory.* Englewood Cliffs, NJ: Prentice Hall.
Bandura, A. 1993. Perceived self-efficacy in cognitive development and functioning. *Educational Psychologist* 28(2). 117–148.
Bandura, A. 1997. *Self-efficacy: The exercise of control.* New York: W. H. Freeman.
Brown, H. D. 1994. *Principles of language learning and teaching*, 3rd edn. Englewood Cliffs, NJ: Prentice Hall.
Carreira, J. M., Ozaki K., & Maeda, T. 2013. Motivational model of English learning among elementary school students in Japan. *System* 41(3). 706–719.
Clément, R. 1978. *Motivational characteristics of Francophones learning English.* Quebec: Université Laval, International Centre for Research on Bilingualism.
Clément, R. 1980. Ethnicity, contact and communicative competence in a second language. In H. Giles, W. P. Robinson, & P. M. Smith (eds.), *Language: Social psychological perspectives*, 147–154. Oxford, England: Pergamon.
Clément, R. 1984. Aspects socio-psychologiques de la communication interethnique et de l'identite sociale [Social psychological aspects of interethnic communication and social identity]. *Recherches Sociologiques* 15. 293–312.
Clément, R. 1986. Second language proficiency and acculturation: An investigation of the effects of language status and individual characteristics. *Journal of Language and Social Psychology* 5. 271–290.
Clément, R., Dörnyei, Z., & Noels, K. A. 1994. Motivation, self-confidence, and group cohesion in the foreign language classroom. *Language Learning* 44(3). 417–448.
Clément, R., Gardner, R. C., & Smythe, P. C. 1980. Social and individual factors in second language acquisition. *Canadian Journal of Behavioral Science* 12. 293–302.
Clément, R., & Kruidenier, B. G. 1985. Aptitude, attitude and motivation in second language proficiency: A test of Clément's model. *Journal of Language and Social Psychology* 4. 21–37.
Cohen, Y., & Norst, M. J. 1989. Fear, dependence and loss of self-esteem: Affective barriers in second language learning among adults. *RELC Journal* 20. 61–77.
Crookes, G., & Schmidt, R. W. 1991. Motivation: Reporting the research agenda. *Language Learning* 41. 469–512.
Crystal, D. 2009. *English as a Global Language.* Cambridge: Cambridge University Press.
Deci, L., & Ryan, M. 1985. *Intrinsic motivation and self-determination in human behavior.* New York: Plenum.
Dörnyei, Z. 1994. Motivation and motivating in the foreign language classroom. *Modern Language Journal* 78. 373–384.
Dörnyei, Z. 2001. New themes and approaches in second language motivation research. *Annual Review of Applied Linguistics* 21. 43–59.

Dörnyei, Z. 2009. The L2 motivational self system. In Dörnyei, Z. and Ushioda, E. (eds.), *Motivation, language identity and the L2 self*, 9–42. Bristol: Multilingual Matters.

Eccles, J., Adler, T., & Meece, J. 1984. Sex differences in achievement: A test of alternate theories. *Journal of Personality and Social Psychology* 46. 26–43.

Edwards, E. & Roger, P. 2015. Seeking out challenges to develop L2 self-confidence: A language learner's journey to proficiency. *TESL-EJ* 18(4). 1–24.

Ehrman, M. E. 1996. *Understanding second language learning difficulties*. Thousand Oaks, CA: Sage.

Ehrman, M.E., Leaver B. L., & Oxford, R. L. 2003. A brief overview of individual differences in second language learning. *System* 31. 313–330.

Gardner, R., Tremblay P., & Masgoret, A.M. 1997. Towards a full model of second language learning: an empirical investigation. *The Modern Language Journal* 81(3). 344–362.

Gardner, R.C. 1985. *Social psychology and second language learning: The role of attitudes and motivation*. London: Edward Arnold.

Graham, S. J. 2004. Giving up on modern foreign languages? Students' perceptions of learning French. *Modern Language Journal* 88(2). 171–191.

Hashimoto, Y. 2002. Motivation and willingness to communicate as predictors of reported L2 use: the Japanese context. *Second Language Studies* 20(2). 29–70.

Horwitz, E. K. 1986. Preliminary evidence for reliability and validity of a foreign language anxiety scale. *TESOL Quarterly* 20. 559–562.

Horwitz, E. K., Horwitz, M. B., & Cope, J. 1986. Foreign language classroom anxiety. *Modern Language Journal* 70. 125–132.

Leaver, B. L., Ehrman, M. E., & Shekhtman, B. 2005. *Achieving success in second language acquisition*. Cambridge: Cambridge University Press.

Leona, N., Koert, M., Van der Molen, M., Rispens, J., Tijms, J. & Snellings, P. 2021. Explaining individual differences in young English language learners' vocabulary knowledge: The role of Extramural English Exposure and motivation. *System* 96. https://www.sciencedirect.com/science/article/pii/S0346251X20307624

MacIntyre, P.D., Baker, S.C., Clément, R., Donovan, L.A. 2002. Sex and age effects on willingness to communicate, anxiety, perceived competence, and L2 motivation among junior high school French immersion students. *Language Learning* 52. 537–564.

MacIntyre, P.D., Clément, R., Dörnyei, Z., & Noels, K.A. 1998. Conceptualizing willingness to communicate in a L2: A situational model of L2 confidence and affiliation. *The Modern Language Journal* 82(4). 545–562.

MacIntyre, P. D., & Charos, C. 1996. Personality, attitudes, and affect as predictors of second language communication. *Journal of Language and Social Psychology* 15(1). 3–26.

MacIntyre, P. D. & Gardner, R. C. 1991. Language anxiety: Its relation to other anxieties and to processing in native and second language. *Language Learning* 41. 513–534.

Mills, N., Pajares, F., Heron, C. 2006. A reevaluation of the role of anxiety: Self-efficacy, anxiety, and their relation to reading and listening proficiency. *Foreign Language Annals* 39(2). 276–295

Mills, N. 2014. Self-efficacy in second language acquisition. In S. Mercer & M. Williams (eds.), *Multiple perspectives on the self in SLA*, 6–19. Bristol: Multilingual Matters.

Multon, K. D., Brown, S. D., & Lent, R. W. 1991. Relation of self-efficacy beliefs to academic outcomes: A meta-analytic investigation. *Journal of Counseling Psychology* 18. 30–38.

Noels, K. A., Pon, G., & Clément R. 1996. Language, identity, and adjustment: The role of linguistic self-confidence in the acculturation process. *Journal of Language and Social Psychology* 15(3). 246–264.

Ohata, K. 2004. *Cultural as well as personal aspects of language learning anxiety: A case study of seven Japanese individuals' reflective accounts of language anxiety experiences in the U.S.* Unpublished doctoral dissertation, Indiana University of Pennsylvania.

Oxford, R. L., & Shearin, J. 1994. Language learning motivation: Expanding the theoretical framework. *Modern Language Journal* 78. 12–28.

Papi, M. 2010. The L2 motivational self system, L2 anxiety, and motivated behavior: A structural equation modeling approach. *System* 38. 467–479.

Pappamihiel, N. E. 2002. English as a second language students and English language anxiety: Issues in the mainstream classroom. *Research in the Teaching of English* 36. 327–355.

Pekrun, R. 1992. Expectancy-value theory of anxiety: Overview and implications. In D. Forgays & T. Sosnowski (eds.), *Anxiety: Recent developments in cognitive, psychophysiological, and health research*, 23–39. Washington, DC: Hemisphere.

Sampasivam, S. and Clément, R. 2014. The dynamics of second language confidence: Contact and interaction. In Mercer, S. and Williams, M. (eds.), *Multiple perspectives on the self in SLA*, 23–40. Bristol: Multilingual Matters.

Schunk, D. H. 1991. Self-efficacy and academic motivation. *Educational Psychologist* 26. 207–231.

Skehan, P. 1989. *Individual differences in second-language learning*. London: Edward Arnold.

Strauss, A., & Corbin, J. 1998. *Basics of qualitative research: Techniques and procedures for developing grounded theory*, 2nd edn. Thousand Oaks, CA: Sage.

Tremblay, P. F., & Gardner, R. C. 1995. Expanding the motivation construct in language learning. *Modern Language Journal* 79. 505–520.

Wang, M. 1983. Development and consequences of students' sense of personal control. In J. M. Levine & M. C. Wang (eds.), *Teacher and student perceptions: Implications for learning*, 213–247. Hillsdale, NJ: LEA.

Wigfield, A. 1994. Expectancy-value theory of achievement motivation: a developmental perspective. *Educational Psychology Review* 6. 49–78.

Wigfield, A., & Eccles, J. 1992. The development of achievement task values: a theoretical analysis. *Developmental Review* 12. 265–310.

Williams, M., & Burden, R. 1999. Students' developing conceptions of themselves as language learners. *Modern Language Journal* 83. 193–201.

Wong, S-L. M. 2005. Language learning strategies and language self-efficacy: Investigating the relationship in Malaysia. *RELC Journal* 36(3). 245–269.

Yashima, T. 2002. Willingness to communicate in L2: The Japanese EFL context, *Modern Language Journal* 86. 54–66.

Yashima, T., Zenuk-Nishide, L., & Shimizu, K. 2004. The influence of attitudes and affect on willingness to communicate and second language communication. *Language Learning* 54. 119–152.

Susan Sayehli, Rakel Österberg and Jonas Granfeldt

Emotion and motivation in younger learners' second foreign language acquisition

Abstract: Reports and studies repeatedly indicate that foreign languages other than English are facing major challenges in European educational systems (European Commission 2012). While young learners' motivation to learn a second foreign language (SFL) is often reported to be low (Tholin and Lindqvist 2009), studies have only recently started to take emotional factors into account in order to better understand how young learners experience foreign language learning and use. Learners' emotions might particularly influence younger learners' behaviour such as mitigating their willingness to communicate despite being engaged and motivated learners (MacIntyre 2002; Teimouri 2017). In this study we therefore examined 9th grade Swedish SFL (French, German and Spanish) learners' (N=120) foreign language classroom anxiety (FLCA; Horwitz et al 1986), their SFL motivation (Dörnyei 2009; Gardner and Lambert 1972), and their willingness to communicate (WTC; McCroskey and Baer 1985). As only few studies have examined motivations and emotions of students who study different SFLs, we also asked to what extent emotions and motivation are language-specific or learner-general in SFL learners within the same educational system. Results indicate that differences between learners of different SFLs are few and that FLCA together with learners' motivation is the strongest predictor for their willingness to communicate. Results indicate further that there are persistent gender differences between girls' and boys' emotions and motivations in SFL learning. Taken together the findings of our study point to the importance of including emotions into studying motivation and use of SFLs also in younger learners.

Keywords: motivation, emotion, willingness to communicate, foreign language classroom anxiety, second foreign languages

1 Introduction

Foreign language (FL) learning is a highly emotional experience. Most people who have tried learning a new language will recognize just how emotional it can be to experience communicative success or failure when trying to use the

FL in any given situation. Consequently, narratives based on learners' own accounts of their language learning trajectories stemming from a variety of settings and moments in life are often highly emotional (Norton 2000; Swain et al. 2010). Adolescence is a stage in life particularly marked by biological, social and psychological transitions and therefore it could be considered unsurprising that research in social psychology shows that adolescents' behaviours and perceptions are particularly influenced by emotional states (Moksnes et al. 2010).

Against this backdrop, some SLA scholars have pointed out for some time that the role of emotions in FL learning should be given more attention in L2 research (Dewaele 2005) and that emotions are under-researched compared to, for example, cognitive aspects of SLA (Swain 2013). To date, research on emotions and FL learning has to a large extent focused on the language learner, including such factors as gender (e.g., Dewaele et al. 2016), personality (e.g., Dewaele & Al-Saraj 2015) and more recently multilingualism (e.g., Dewaele and Greiff 2020). In the bulk of this research, the sole target language has been English, which is commonly the first foreign language in the European context (Boo et al. 2015), but some research has also compared English to a further second foreign language (SFL) (Dewaele 2002). However, only few studies have examined motivations and emotions of students who study different SFLs within the same school system. SFLs face common challenges in educational systems, but they often enjoy different popularity and status among students. We know for example from research on language attitudes and perception that the reasons for choosing a particular language vary from one language to another (Williams et al. 2002).

In this paper we aim to investigate to what extent emotions and motivation are language-specific or learner-general in SFL learners within the same educational system and to what degree emotions influence younger learners' behaviour such as their willingness to communicate and its relation to motivation.

2 Background

2.1 Affective variables in language learning

Language learning has often been considered to be primarily a cognitive endeavour of producing and perceiving target language meaning (Prior 2019). Emotions have played, if any, a secondary role. Since the 1980s, however, Krashen's concept of the "affective filter" inspired researchers to more closely examine the impact of negative emotions on language learning (Dewaele and Li 2020; Krashen 1982). The development of a validated instrument to measure levels of anxiety in language learners, *the Foreign Language Classroom Anxiety scales* (Horwitz et al. 1986) spurred this attempt further and allowed systematic research into the topic. Also, researchers of motivation in language learning have called for the inclusion of emotion in motivation research (Dörnyei and Ushioda 2009; MacIntyre and Gregersen 2012). Today, the study of emotions in language learning is an established line of research, and affective variables and motivation are considered to be crucial in order to understand how learners choose, learn and keep learning foreign languages (MacIntyre and Vincze 2017; MacIntyre et al. 2019). However, young learners' emotions and motivation have not yet been studied in SLA to the same extent as in adult learners (Lamb 2017; Mihaljević Djigunović 2012).

Negative feelings, most importantly *Foreign Language (Classroom) Anxiety*, were the first ones to be explored starting from the 1980's on and are today the most researched emotions in the field (MacIntyre and Gregersen 2012) even though also positive emotions such as joy and excitement are nowadays frequently studied (Dewaele and Dewaele 2017; MacIntyre et al. 2019). Horwitz et al. (1986: 127) define foreign language classroom anxiety (FLCA) as the total of three fears: 1) communication apprehension 2) test anxiety 3) fear of negative evaluation, which all three might be triggered particularly but not only in the foreign language classroom. In the foreign language classroom, communication situations can be perceived as test situations, and as such be particularly prone to causing anxiety among learners. Also, the social climate in the classroom has been shown to be an important factor for the development of FLCA particularly in oral production (Mihaljevi Djigunovic 2015; Nilsson 2020) as well as the concern of giving a bad impression or the urge to deliver a perfect performance (Gregersen and Horwitz 2002).

Procrastination and avoidance that are often reactions to anxiety have negative impacts on foreign language training and learning. Negative associations between anxiety and learner strategies have, for example, been observed by Liu and Chen (2014) and Lu and Liu (2011). Similarly, much research has examined the relation between anxiety and language learning outcomes, finding overall support for the negative association between anxiety and language achievement (e.g., Dewaele and Ip 2013; Horwitz 2001; Nilsson 2020; for a meta-analysis see Teimouri et al. 2019; but see Chastain 1975; Edwards et al. 2015; Hardy and Hutchinson 2007; Owens et al. 2014 for a discussion on potential positive learning effects of mild anxiety). FLCA has been found to correlate with gender (Dewaele et al 2016; Tuncel 2020) and gender together with age (Hye-Kyoung et al. 2017). Dewaele et al. (2016) found, for example, that females seemed to enjoy FL studies more than males even though they experienced a mild form of FLCA.

2.2 Motivation and emotion

Motivation in instructed language learning has been conceptualized in different theoretical strands. For many decades, Gardner's socio-educational model was one of the leading models in which integrativeness, that is, the identification with a specific, target language speaker group and the wish to become part of their culture, together with instrumentality, that is, the pragmatic external reasons to learn a language, were the main concepts. Motivation was partly defined by positive attitudes towards the speakers, language and the learning contexts (Gardner and Lambert 1972; Gardner 1985, 2019). Recently, and as an elaboration of Gardner's socio-educational model, the *Second Language Motivational Self System* (L2MSS; Dörnyei 2005, 2009) expanded particularly the concept of integrativeness. One of the reasons was that a clearly defined, external group to identify with, as for example in the case of learning Global English, was lacking (Busse 2017). Instead, motivation has been conceptualized in relation to future internal self-guides, that is, in relation to how people wish to be in the future. It combined the psychological theory of Possible selves (Markus and Nurius 1986) and Self-discrepancy theory (Higgins 1987) in that motivation is assumed to be generated by the perceived discrepancy (if reasonably sized) between the real self and future ideal selves (Higgins 1987). Dörnyei's model is built upon different components, but particularly the *ideal L2 self*, the interpersonal and emotional side of motivation which occurs when learners desire to resemble to and imagine themselves as competent speakers of the target language, has been shown to be positively associated with language learning outcomes (Dörnyei and Al-Hoorie 2017; see Li and Zhang 2021 for a review).

As already noted above, research on language learning motivation has so far focused more on cognitive aspects of motivation with emotions playing only a minor role (MacIntyre 2002). However, this does not mean that emotions have been completely absent in the study of language learning motivation. Gardner's *Attitude/ Motivation Battery Test* (AMBT, Gardner, 1985), for example, used positive or negative emotions related to FL learning in a few items in order to elicit attitudes and motivations. In the more recent theory of the Second Language Motivational Self System (L2MSS, Dörnyei 2005, 2009) emotions are sometimes argued to contribute to a more elaborate and robust possible self (Henry 2012). Emotions are however usually not measured separately. Therefore, researchers have already some time ago called for a more comprehensive inclusion of emotions in language motivation research (Dewaele 2005; Dörnyei and Ushioda 2009; MacIntyre and Gregersen 2012).

2.3 Willingness to communicate

Much research has used students' intended effort to measure behavioural effects of learners' motivation and emotion in language learning (e.g., Al-Hoorie 2018; Papi 2010). In recent studies *Willingness to Communicate* (WTC) has been used for these purposes (e.g., Teimouri 2017).

WTC was first examined by McCroskey and Baer (1985) within first language (L1) communication research and defined as a personality trait. As the WTC in L2 was found to be more variable than in L1, MacIntyre et al. (1998) suggested it to not only be a disposition but also to be dependent on situational factors (Wang et al. 2021). They defined WTC as "a readiness to enter into discourse at a particular time, with a specific person, using a L2" (MacIntyre et al. 1998: 547). WTC is a dynamic, and volitional process (MacIntyre 2007) and complex in so far as it is directly or indirectly promoted or impeded by an array of factors. In the WTC literature different cognitive, emotional and situational factors have been identified to be related to WTC (e.g., Collins 2013; MacIntyre et al. 1999; Munezane 2013). Among emotional factors, language speaking anxiety and confidence have been the most researched ones showing negative and positive effects on WTC respectively (e.g., Asmali 2016; Hashimoto 2002; see Shirvan et al. 2019 for a meta-analysis). There are several studies showing that a well-developed ideal L2 self increases learners' WTC (e.g., Teimouri 2017; Öz and Bursali 2018; but see Shirvan et al. 2019 claiming that the association is under-researched). Usually participants in these studies have been university students.

Studies with younger learners suggest a more complex picture of relations between FLCA, motivation and WTC. While for example a study on younger British learners of German, French and Spanish as FL (N=189) by Dewaele and Dewaele (2018) showed that a low level of FLCA together with high proficiency in the FL and the learners' age were the strongest predictors of WTC, a study by MacIntyre et al. (2002), on the other hand, found a different pattern of associations. They examined WTC in a cross-sectional study of younger learners in a French immersion class at ages 12–14 (N=268) and observed that the WTC increased even when anxiety levels were stable and motivation dropped over time. Teimouri (2017) used WTC as a criterion measure to examine the effects of motivation conceptualized in the L2MSS model and studied young learners (12 to 18 years old) of English as an FL in Iran (N=524). He found that even though learners were highly motivated, WTC was mitigated by negative emotions. In sum, the available research on factors affecting WTC in different populations is not conclusive and more research is needed.

2.4 Gender differences in motivation, FLCA and WTC

Gender differences have often been reported in motivation and emotion research. Particularly in motivation research, girls usually score higher on motivational scales than boys. In fact, only few studies show no gender differences (but see e.g., MacIntyre et al. 2002). Interestingly gender differences seem to be context-independent in motivation research. Differences were found in a wide range of disparate cultures (e.g., Canada: Kissau 2006; China: You et al. 2016; Hungary: Dörnyei et al. 2006; Japan: Oga-Baldwin and Fryer 2020; Sweden: Henry 2009; Henry and Cliffordson 2013; Taiwan: Lay 2008; Turkey: Öztürk and Gürbüz 2013; the United Arabic Emirates: Calafato and Tang 2019). Furthermore, gender effects have been found irrespective of the motivational aspect or theoretical construct under scrutiny. Particularly females score higher on ideal L2/L3 selves, integrative oriented and intrinsic motivation (e.g., Calafato and Tang 2019; Iwaniec 2019; Kissau 2006; Williams et al. 2002).

Even though gender differences seem to be persistent, only few studies have tried to explain them. Henry and Cliffordson (2013) associated them with different ways of constructing one's self-concept. Self-concepts were categorized into interdependent (socially oriented) or independent ones (uniqueness oriented). As females were argued to construct their identity interdependently, i.e. socially, language as a tool of communication was suggested to be more important to this group. Furthermore, they claimed that females have a greater capacity and interest to project into future social life, and therefore have a more elaborated ideal L3 self. Chaffee et al. (2020) on the other hand, have argued that stereotype forming is at the core of gender differences and that the subject foreign language learning is traditionally stereotyped as being feminine. In an experiment, they found that men who held traditional gender ideologies in their masculinity expressed more negative attitudes towards foreign languages and less interest in learning them when threatened in their masculinity than men whose masculinity had been affirmed or who held less traditional gender ideologies from the beginning. Accordingly, stereotypes and gender ideologies affect the motivation to study languages.

Gender differences have also been studied concerning emotions in foreign language learning. Dewaele et al. (2016) found gender differences in a large international survey using the FLCA scale. Females seemed to enjoy FL studies more than boys even though they experienced mild FLCA. The higher emotional sensibility was argued to benefit language learning. Gender differences were also found studying FLCA in association with WTC. A longitudinal study by MacIntyre et al. (2002) found that whereas boys' measures of WTC and FLCA remained similar over time, girls' WTC increased once anxiety decreased.

In the Swedish context Henry and Cliffordson (2013) found gender-related variance in the L3 ideal self when they studied Swedish SFL learners in grade 9 to the effect that girls scored higher on L3 ideal self than boys. Gender differences are also observed more generally in the Swedish school context. Females are more prone to choose SFLs than boys and Spanish is the language which nowadays attracts most boys (National Agency for Education 2021; SOU 2010: 91).

3 Current study and its context

Taking stock of previous research on emotions and motivation in learners of a foreign language, the current study was designed to focus on young learners of three different second foreign languages – French, German and Spanish – within lower secondary school in Sweden. Before outlining the research questions, we will briefly present the situation for second foreign languages within the Swedish school system in general and for each of the three languages in particular.

In Sweden the study of an SFL is not mandatory and previous reports have suggested that the motivation for learning an SFL is low (European Commission 2012). The study of an SFL has been an entitlement for all in secondary school since 1962, but remains an individual choice. About 80% of all students choose to start studying an SFL at age 12 (6th grade), but the attrition rate is relatively high (about 20–25% according to Tholin & Lindqvist, 2009). As a response to the declining interest in the study of SFLs, the Swedish government decided in 2007 to introduce a system of incentives labelled *Grade Point Average Enhancement Credits* (GPAEC) (*meritpoäng* in Swedish (Government bill 2004/05:162). The goal of this incentive measure was to raise the general interest in studying SFLs, to reduce the number of dropouts and to encourage pupils to continue study at higher levels of SFLs in upper secondary school. In brief, the system means that completed higher levels of SFLs (with a pass grade) can increase the pupils' GPA scores when applying to university. The system has been revised on several occasions during 2010–2015. Initially the measure only targeted the transition between upper secondary school and university, but in 2014 it was expanded with a similar measure targeting the transition between lower and upper secondary school. While there has been no official evaluation of the GPAEC measure, Granfeldt et al. (2021) have shown that it is likely that the measure has had a positive effect on enrolments to SFL classes, but mostly so in areas and social groups where transition rate to university among young people is high. Currently, about 72% of all students study an SFL at the end of lower-secondary school which is an increase of about 10% since 2000 (Granfeldt et al. 2021).

English is studied mandatorily from Year 3 at the latest, but often introduced earlier.

Even though studying an SFL is not mandatory in the Swedish educational system, it is compulsory to make what is called a 'language choice' (*språkval*) at the latest in the year preceding year 6 (age 12 years). Students can choose one of the SFLs offered by the respective school or an alternative.[1] The most common SFLs studied in Sweden are French, German and Spanish. Schools are required by law (School ordinance) to offer at least two of these three SFLs with the majority offering all three even though French is offered less in Northern Sweden and smaller municipalities (Granfeldt et al. 2019, 2021). Historically, German and French have been the two SFLs that have been offered as choices in lower-secondary school with German being the most popular. Only in 1994 Spanish was added to the standard choices in upper-secondary school. In the early 2000's Spanish saw a considerable increase in popularity, mainly at the expense of German, and today more pupils study Spanish (about 42%) than German (about 18%) and French (about 13%) together (Granfeldt et al. 2021). Against the background that studying an SFL is not compulsory in Sweden and that not all languages are offered, students' motivations become particularly relevant (Sayehli et al. 2021; Parrish 2020).

As evidenced by the literature review above, there are several studies examining motivation and emotions in foreign language learning. However, there are only few studies that compare what motivates students within the same school system to study different SFLs and to our knowledge none in the Swedish context. Differences in spread and status of SFLs suggest that there might be motivational differences between them. To know whether there are learner-general or language-specific motivational and emotional profiles across learners is important in order to understand students' language choice, to be able to effectively motivate them and eventually to keep them from dropping out from SFL studies and to help them become successful language learners. Similarly, it is important to examine how emotions are related particularly to younger learners' intended behaviour such as mitigating their willingness to communicate despite being engaged and motivated learners.

The current study therefore sets out to compare students' motivations and emotions and their willingness to communicate studying different SFLs (French, German or Spanish), in Swedish lower-secondary schools while taking gender differences into account.

---

[1] Alternatives are usually subjects such as mother tongue instruction (if other than Swedish), remedial Swedish or English (or a combination of both) or Swedish sign language.

More specifically the research questions of the current study are:
(1) Are there motivational and/or emotional differences between young learners of different SFLs?
(2) How are young language learners' emotion and motivation related to their motivated behaviour as measured by WTC?
(3) Are there gender differences in SFLs' motivations and emotions?

4 Material and methods

4.1 Participants

Participants were L3/SFL learners of French, German or Spanish in grade 9 coming from 15 different schools in Sweden. The schools were randomly selected from a representative and randomly stratified sample of 416 schools considering five parameters (geographical spread, school type, educational level of the students' parents, students' foreign language background and school year).[2] All learners were Swedish L1 speakers and had learnt English since at least school year 4. Participant characteristics are summarized in Table 1.

Table 1: Participant characteristics.

language	n	age	Gender		
			girls	boys	others
French	52	15	36	16	0
Spanish	31	15	17	14	0
German	37	15	18	18	1
Total	120		71	48	1

Note. The last three columns give number of participants' self-reported gender.

4.2 Questionnaire

Using an electronic questionnaire, we examined emotional and motivational constructs. The motivational constructs were based on Dörnyei's L2 Motivational Self

---

[2] The stratified sample was made by Statistics Sweden. Statistics Sweden is a government agency that produces official statistics.

System (Dörnyei 2009) and Lambert and Gardner's socio-educational model (Gardner and Lambert 1972). More specifically we used items referring to the students' *ideal L3 self* (Dörnyei 2009; Henry 2012; Rocher Hahlin 2020) and their *instrumental motivation* (Gardner and Lambert 1972). The instrumental motivation focused on students' immediate future (their final grades). The emotional construct was *foreign language classroom anxiety* with items from the Foreign Language Classroom Anxiety Scale (Horwitz et al. 1986). We also tested participants' *willingness to communicate* with items from McCroskey and Baer (1985). All items were piloted twice with different learner groups in two parts of the country. Number and wording of the items were recalibrated after each pilot. Positively and negatively worded items were rated on a five-point Likert scale with five indicating strong and one no agreement. Negatively worded items were reverse coded prior to analysis. Cronbach's alphas for all but the *instrumental motivation* scale were over .80 (see Table 2 for Cronbach's alphas).

Table 2: Questionnaire constructs.

construct	# items	Cronbach α
ideal L3 self	9	.91
instrumentality	4	.69
foreign language classroom anxiety (FLCA)	8	.87
willingness to communicate (WTC)	9	.88

4.3 Procedure

The study was approved by the Ethics Review Board of Southern Sweden (approval number 2017/745). Students gave their informed consent. If students were under age 15 additional parental consent was obtained. The electronic questionnaire was part of a bigger test battery and carried out as the first of four other tests (a written c-test and two oral tasks). It was administered online on students' own computer or school devices during school hours and took 20–30 minutes to complete. Its first section was on students' linguistic background, its second on motivation, emotions and attitudes. Students could skip items and still finish the questionnaire.

4.4 Analyses

The data were anonymized. For each participant and construct data were aggregated and a mean (M) was calculated. Participants who missed data on one item, missed data for the entire variable. To examine research question 1, that is, to what extent emotions and motivation were language-specific or similar in SFL learners within the same educational system and in order to examine research question 3 whether there were gender effects, four two-way ANOVAs with *ideal L3 self, instrumental motivation, foreign language classroom anxiety* and *willingness to communicate* as the respective dependent variable (DV) and with *languages* (French, German and Spanish) and *gender* (male, female) as independent variables (IV) were conducted. Assumptions of ANOVA were met as the data was normally distributed as assessed by Shapiro-Wilk'stest ($p > .05$) apart from German females' FLCA ($p = .024$) and French females' Ideal L3 selves ($p = .013$) (Maxwell and Delaney 2004). There was homogeneity of variances as assessed by Levene's test for equality of variances for all four ANOVAs ($p > .05$). To examine research question 2, that is, how young language learners' emotion and motivation were related to their motivated behaviour (WTC), correlations between the four motivational and emotional variables were calculated on the whole group and split by *language* and *gender*. Multiple regressions were performed to test which variables best predict learners' WTC.

5 Results

Table 3 summarizes the descriptive results for the four DVs across languages and gender. The averages for the different constructs are overall slightly above a middle value (2.5 of a 5 point-Likert scale) circling round 3.0. On the whole students score slightly positive in all categories. Differences are overall small.

Table 3: Descriptive results.

		Ideal L3 self	Instrumentality	FLCA	WTC
French	girls	3.50 (.77)	2.88 (.82)	3.22 (.82)	2.56 (.88)
	boys	2.72 (.93)	2.82 (.54)	2.78 (.88)	2.88 (.94)
	total	3.26 (1.09)	2,86 (.74)	3.09 (.86)	2.66 (.90)
Spanish	girls	3.46 (.77)	3.41 (1.02)	3.23 (1.05)	2.37 (.85)
	boys	3.28 (.92)	3.50 (.93)	2.75 (.81)	2.82 (1.10)
	total	3.38 (.83)	3.45 (.97)	3.02 (.97)	2.56 (.97)
German	girls	3.13 (.86)	2.96 (1.09)	3.16 (.95)	2.32 (.80)
	boys	2.97 (1.05)	2.82 (1.14)	2.39 (.68)	2.98 (1.05)
	total	3.04 (.96)	2,89 (.95)	2.78 (.91)	2.65 (.98)
Girls		3.40 (.97)	3.03 (.95)	3.21 (.90)	2.45 (.85)
Boys		2.97 (.98)	3.02 (.95)	2.62 (.79)	2.90 (1.01)
Total		3.22 (.99)	3.02 (.95)	2.98 (.90)	2.63 (.94)

Note. Averages given in columns, standard deviations in parentheses.

Four separate two-way ANOVAs were performed to examine the effect of *language* and *gender* on the *ideal L3 self, instrumentality, foreign language classroom anxiety* (FLCA) and *willingness to communicate* (WTC). There were no statistically significant interactions between the effects of *language* and *gender* on any of the emotional or motivational variables. There was a main effect of language on instrumentality $F(2, 110) = 4.308$, $p = .016$; partial $\eta^2 = .073$ to the effect that Spanish learners tended to be more instrumentally motivated than learners of German ($p = .044$) and French ($p = .018$) who did not differ from each other. There were also statistically significant differences for *gender* and FLCA, $F(1, 110) = 10.994$, $p = .001$; partial $\eta^2 = .091$, and *gender* and WTC $F(1, 111) = 6.978$, $p = .009$; partial $\eta^2 = .059$ showing that girls had higher levels of FLCA and lower WTC than boys. There was also a trend towards a significant difference for *ideal L3 self* and *gender*: $F(1, 104) = 3.732$, $p = .056$; partial $\eta^2 = .035$ to the effect that girls had a stronger ideal L3 self than boys (see Table 4).

Table 4: Two-way ANOVA results with instrumentality, ideal L3 self, FLCA and WTC as criterion.

DV	IV	Sum of squares	df	Mean Square	F	p	Partial η^2
ideal L3 self	gender	3.523	1	.876	3.732	.056	.035
	language	1.753	2	1.140	.928	.398	.018
	gender X language	2.280	2	.944	1.208	.303	0.23
instrumentality	gender	.033	1	.033	.038	.846	.000
	language	7.489	2	3.745	4.308	.016	.073
	gender X language	.206	2	.103	.118	.889	.002
FLCA	gender	8.287	1	8.287	10.994	.001	.091
	language	1.152	2	.576	.764	.468	.014
	gender X language	.612	2	.306	.406	.667	.007
WTC	gender	5.960	1	5.960	6.978	.009	.059
	language	.265	2	.133	.155	.856	.003
	gender X language	.588	2	.294	.344	.710	.006

Note. DV = dependent variable, IV = independent variable, df = degrees of freedom.

Correlations among the emotional and motivational variables across all learners suggested that *ideal L3 self* was positively associated with *WTC*, and negatively with *FLCA*. The correlation between FLCA and ideal L3 self was only weak (below $r = .4$) and could therefore be entered as separate predictors into a multiple regression testing their effects on WTC. *WTC* and *FLCA* were negatively associated (see Table 5).

Table 5: Correlations across learners.

	Ideal L3 self	Instrumentality	FLCA	WTC
ideal L3 self				
instrumentality	.09			
FLCA	−.36**	−.07		
WTC	.50**	.02	−.69**	

Note. Pearson's *r* correlations. **p < .01.

Correlations performed split by language suggested that there was a different pattern of significant correlations depending on the language learnt. While for all language learners FLCA and WTC were negatively associated, only French learners showed significant positive associations between *ideal L3 self* and *instrumentality*. Spanish learners were the only ones who did not show positive associations between *ideal L3 self* and WTC, and German learners were the only group who did not show negative associations between *ideal L3 self* and FLCA (see Table 6).

Correlations performed split by gender suggested that both girls and boys showed significant negative associations between ideal L3 self and FLCA and between WTC and FLCA. For both groups ideal L3 self and WTC were positively associated (see Table 6).

Table 6: Correlations per language (French / Spanish / German) and per gender (girls / boys).

	Ideal L3 self	Instrumentality	FLCA	WTC
ideal L3 self		.23/−.13	−.38**/−.63**	.51**/.65**
instrumentality	.35**/−.30/.02		−.14/.08	−.12/−.13
FLCA	−.43**/−.48/−.26	−.09/−.02/−.21		−.67**/−.69*
WTC	.51**/.34/.62**	.18/.19/−.21	−.74**/−.72**/−.61**	

Note. Above the diagonal Pearson's *r* correlations split by gender (girls / boys), under the diagonal Pearson's *r* correlations split by language (French / Spanish / German). *p < .05, **p < .01.

A multiple regression analysis was carried out to investigate whether FLCA, ideal L3 self, and instrumental motivation could significantly predict learners' level of WTC. The results of the regression indicated that the model explained 54% of the variance in WTC ($R^2 = .54$) and that the model was a significant predictor of levels of WTC, $F(2,104) = 60.94$, $p < .000$). While FLCA and ideal L3 self contributed significantly to the model, instrumental motivation did not (see Table 7).

Table 7: Regression coefficients of predictors of WTC.

Variables	B	SE	t	p	95%CI
constant	3.672	.401	9.147	.000	[2.876, 4.469]
FLCA	−.600	.072	−8.302	.000	[−.743, −.457]
ideal L3 self	.261	.065	4.047	.000	[.133, .390]
instrumental	−.044	.064	−.693	.490	[−.170, .082]

6 Discussion

This study aimed to find out whether there are motivational and/or emotional differences between young learners of different SFLs within the same school system considering that different SFLs enjoy different popularity among students. A basic question we are asking is the following: Do learners studying a very popular SFL like Spanish in Sweden have different emotions and motivations compared to learners studying less popular languages like French and German? A related question is if learners of different SFLs display different motivational and emotional profiles. Potential differences were examined studying their SFL motivation (conceptualized as the ideal L3 self; Dörnyei 2009 and as instrumental motivation; Gardner and Lambert 1972), foreign language classroom anxiety (FLCA; Horwitz et al. 1986) and their willingness to communicate (WTC; McCroskey and Baer 1985). We were also interested in how emotions might influence younger learners' behaviour such as their willingness to communicate in relation to their motivation and whether there are gender differences in the learners' motivational and emotional set-up.

The results can be summarized as follows. First, considering the constructs individually, results show that there is only little systematic variability between students' language-learning motivation and emotions that can be associated with the different SFLs. We found that Spanish learning students had higher instrumental motivation than those learning French or German, but learners of the three different SFLs did not differ in the strengths of their L3 self, their classroom anxiety or their willingness to communicate in the SFL. Second, when we considered associations between motivation and emotions, we found more differences between learners of different languages. Even though all students showed that the more anxious they were, the less willing they were to communicate in the SFL, only French and Spanish learners' ideal L3 self was associated with anxiety levels such that the more developed their L3 self was, the less anxious they were. German learners did not display that association. The ideal L3 self of the German learners was however positively associated with their willingness to communicate, similarly to French learners, but unlike Spanish learners. And finally, only French learners displayed a positive association between ideal L3 self and instrumentality. Third, we found across all learners that FLCA was the strongest predictor for younger learners' behaviour and thus mitigating their willingness to communicate despite being overall motivated learners. Finally, we found persistent gender differences between girls' and boys' emotions and motivations in SFL learning. Despite the fact that girls showed more developed L3 selves than boys, the girls displayed higher anxiety levels and were less willing to communicate in their SFL than the boys. As association patterns between the constructs found in correlations split by gender were similar across gender, results suggest that girls' motivation and emotions in SFL were not different in kind but generally stronger than those of boys.

Answering our first research questions, our results suggest that motivational and emotional patterns among the students who opted to study them are generally similar, even though there are some differences to which we come back below. Different observations might explain this situation. First of all, the task of learning a second foreign language, with its tensions and joy and its cognitive challenges such as learning a new grammar and new words might be basically the same for all SFLs, and therefore the differences between SFLs are small. Furthermore, the SFLs examined in this study have in common that they are the students' preferred choice irrespectively of the exact SFL they chose. Preference might contribute to generating similar emotional and motivational shapes. A further commonality between the studied SFLs is that they all are only little visible in social, cultural and media life in Sweden (in contrast to for example, English, see e.g. Sundqvist 2009). As learners' main contact with the SFLs is within the classroom, SFLs might be less perceived as different languages in the sense of being a means of communication and rather as one single school subject with different branches. This tendency might also be supported by the fact that all the three SFLs have equal status in the educational context. In the Swedish school system, they all have one single curriculum under the name 'moderna språk' (Modern languages) and learning targets, progression and incentives (grade point average enhancement credits, GPAEC, *meritpoäng*) work in the same way for all three languages. Taken together the similarity of the learning task and the similarity of the SFLs' societal and educational status might underlie the similar emotional and motivational patterns we found.

Still we found some interesting differences. Spanish students displayed higher scores on instrumentality than students in French or German. More specifically, the prospect to eventually gain higher final grades (through grade point average enhancement credits, GPAEC) motivated more students in Spanish than in French and in German. Similar results have been found in Norway (Carrai 2014) where students also were found to be more instrumentally motivated to study Spanish. The results corroborate with observations that Spanish is sometimes perceived as the easiest among the three languages (Riis and Francia 2013) and might therefore particularly attract students who are instrumentally motivated with the aim to obtain higher grades. The introduction of the GPAEC system in 2007 that went more or less hand in hand with the Spanish boom in Sweden, might have spurred this tendency. With the GPAEC system, a clear instrumental incentive measure (see above), more students chose to study an SFL (Granfeldt et al. 2021) and many of them probably chose Spanish. Often practitioners and also researchers, such as Riis and Francia (2013), expect students of Spanish to show higher integrative motivation due to the existing Spanish heritage language community in Sweden, Spain being a frequent Swedish holiday destination and Latin music being fairly popular. These circumstances did however not translate into higher L3 selves among the Spanish learners in our study.

Further differences between the SFLs were however found in the strengths of associations between emotions and motivations. High ideal L3 selves were associated with lower FLCA only for Spanish and French learners possibly because different factors underlie FLCA in Spanish and French as opposed to German. Due to typological similarity, Swedish learners of German often report less pronunciation difficulties which might reduce FLCA in production. Supposedly then, learners of German do not need to be equally highly motivated in order to avoid anxiety, but this needs to be further investigated in future research. French learners on the other hand were the only ones showing a significant association between ideal L3 self and instrumental motivation, supporting anecdotal evidence that French studies attract ambitious and motivated students. The association that prevailed across languages (and gender see beneath) was that the more anxious learners are, the less willing they are to communicate.

This finding leads us to our second research question: how young language learners' emotion and motivation relate to their motivated behaviour when measured by WTC. We found that the strongest predictor of WTC was FLCA together with the learners' ideal L3 self. The less anxious they were and the more developed the learner's ideal L3 self was, the more they were willing to communicate. These results are in line with previous findings and underscore that motivation is not alone sufficient to promote intended motivated behaviour, even when both motivation and intended behaviour imply communication. In other words, the fondness of picturing one's ideal self in communicative activities does not necessarily translate into the willingness to actually communicate in real situations. It thus explains why some learners despite having motivational goals do not intend taking the action that they envisage and that would get them closer to their goals (cf., Teimouri 2017). Reducing anxiety together with developing learners' ideal L3 self is thus important also from a teacher perspective, especially since some research has found that higher WTC is associated with higher learning outcomes (e.g., Al-Murtadha 2021; Menezes and Juan-Garau 2015; but see Joe et al. 2017 for results to the contrary). This might be particularly important for girls as we found them – examining our third research question – to be significantly more anxious and less willing to communicate than boys, even though their L3 selves were more developed. Possibly young learners might be extra affected as "keeping face" is crucial and emotions are particularly intense in that phase of life.

7 Conclusion

This study has shown that there are few motivational and emotional differences between young learners studying different SFLs within the same educational system, despite the fact that French, German and Spanish enjoy different popularity among students generally. Factors such as the similarity of the language learning task, the similar (non)-saliency of the three SFLs in socio-cultural life, and their equal status in the educational contexts are argued to contribute to our results. Nevertheless, we also found some language-specific differences that suggest that incentives, such as the GPAEC, and perceived or experienced difficulty to learn a language might have different effects on motivation and emotions of learners of different SFLs. Importantly, this study provided evidence that learners' emotions predict learners' intentional behaviour such as their willingness to communicate to the effect that it mitigates the intended behaviour of otherwise well motivated learners. This is suggested to pertain particularly to girls. In sum then, this paper adds to the evidence that emotions are central in understanding both the learning and the use of second foreign languages.

References

Al-Hoorie, A. 2018. The L2 motivational self-system: a meta-analysis. *Studies in Second Language Learning and Teaching* 8. 721–754.
Al-Murtadha, M.A. 2021. The relationships among self-reported and observed first language and second language willingness to communicate and academic achievement. *Language, Culture and Curriculum* 34(1). 80–94.

Asmali, M. 2016. Willingness to communicate of foreign language learners in Turkish context. *Procedia – Social and Behavioral Sciences* 232. 188–195.

Boo, Z., Dörnyei, Z., & Ryan, S. 2015. L2 motivation research 2005–2014: understanding a publication surge and a changing landscape. *System* 55. 147–157.

Busse, V. 2017. Plurilingualism in Europe: exploring attitudes toward English and other European languages among adolescents in Bulgaria, Germany, the Netherlands, and Spain. *The Modern Language Journal* 101(3). 566–582.

Calafato, R., & Tang, F. 2019. Multilingualism and gender in the UAE: a look at the motivational selves of Emirati teenagers. *System* 84. 133–144.

Carrai, D. 2014. *Fremmedspråk på ungdomstrinnet. En analyse av motivasjon og andre faktorer involvert i elevenes fagvalg og tilfredshet med faget*. Doctoral dissertation, Institutt for lærerutdanning og skoleforskning, Oslo universitet, Norway.

Chaffee, K.E., Lou, N.M., Noels, K.A., & Katz, J.W. 2020. Why don't "real men" learn languages? Masculinity threat and gender ideology suppress men's language learning motivation. *Group Processes & Intergroup Relations* 23(2). 301–318.

Chastain, K. 1975. Affective and ability factors in second language acquisition. *Language Learning* 25. 153–161.

Collins, J. B. 2013. Willingness to communicate and international posture in the L2 classroom: an exploratory study into the predictive value of willingness to communicate (WTC) and international posture questionnaires, and the situational factors that influence WTC. *Polyglossia* 25(1). 61–81.

Dewaele, J. 2002. Psychological and sociodemographic correlates of communicative anxiety in L2 and L3 production. *International Journal of Bilingualism* 6(1). 23–38.

Dewaele, J. M. 2005. Investigating the psychological and emotional dimensions in instructed language learning: obstacles and possibilities. *The Modern Language Journal* 89(3). 367–380.

Dewaele, J. M., & Al-Saraj, T. M. 2015. Foreign language classroom anxiety of Arab learners of English: the effect of personality, linguistic and sociobiographical variables. *Studies in Second Language Learning and Teaching* 5(2). 205–228.

Dewaele, J.-M., & Li, C. 2020. Emotions in second language acquisition: a critical review and research agenda. *Foreign Language World* 196(1). 34–49.

Dewaele, J.-M., & Dewaele, L. 2017. The dynamic interactions in foreign language classroom anxiety and foreign language enjoyment of pupils aged 12 to 18. A pseudo-longitudinal investigation. *Journal of the European Second Language Association* 1. 12–22.

Dewaele, J.-M., & Dewaele, L. 2018. Learner-internal and learner-external predictors of willingness to communicate in the FL classroom. *Journal of the European Second Language Association* 2(1). 24–37.

Dewaele, J. M., & Greiff, S. 2020. The power to improve: effects of multilingualism and perceived proficiency on enjoyment and anxiety in foreign language learning. *European Journal of Applied Linguistics* 8(2). 279–306.

Dewaele, J.-M., & Ip, T. S. 2013. The link between foreign language classroom anxiety, second language tolerance of ambiguity and self-rated English proficiency among Chinese learners. *Studies in Second Language Learning and Teaching* 3(1). 47–66.

Dewaele, J. M., MacIntyre, P. D., Boudreau, C., & Dewaele, L. 2016. Do girls have all the fun? Anxiety and enjoyment in the foreign language classroom. *Theory and practice of second language acquisition* 2(1). 41–63.

Dörnyei, Z. 2005. *The psychology of the language learner: individual differences in second language acquisition*. Mahwah: Lawrence Erlbaum.

Dörnyei, Z. 2009. The L2 Motivational Self System. In Z. Dörnyei & E. Ushioda (Eds.), *Motivation, language identity and the L2 self*, 9–42. Bristol: Multilingual Matters.

Dörnyei, Z., & Al-Hoorie, A.H. 2017. The motivational foundation of learning languages other than Global English: theoretical issues and research directions. *Modern Language Journal* 101(3). 455–468.

Dörnyei, Z., & Ushioda, E. (Eds.). 2009. *Motivation, language identity and the L2 self*. Bristol: Multilingual Matters.

Dörnyei, Z., Csizér, K., & Németh, N. 2006. *Motivation, language attitudes and globalisation: a Hungarian perspective*. Bristol: Multilingual Matters.

Edwards M.S., Moore P., Champion J.C., & Edwards E.J. 2015. Effects of trait anxiety and situational stress on attentional shifting are buffered by working memory capacity. *Anxiety Stress Coping* 28(1). 1–16.

European Commission. 2012. *Europeans and their languages* (Special Eurobarometer 386. Report).

Gardner, R. 1985. *Social psychology and second language learning. The role of attitudes and motivation*. London: Edward Arnold.

Gardner, R. 2019. The Socio-educational Model of second language acquisition. M. Lamb, K. Csizeìr, A. Henry, & S. Ryan (Eds.), *The Palgrave Macmillan handbook of motivation for language learning*, 21–37. Berlin: Springer.

Gardner, R. C., & Lambert, W. E. 1972. *Attitudes and motivation in second language learning*. Rowley, MA: Newbury House Publishers.

Government bill. 2004. Ny värld – ny högskola [New world – new university]. Proposition 2004/05:162. https://data.riksdagen.se/fil/A7324622-9134-487C-8C8F-735A8C1EFB03 (accessed 22 November 2021).

Granfeldt, J., Sayehli, S., & Ågren, M. 2019. The context of second foreign languages in Swedish secondary schools: results of a questionnaire to school leaders. *Apples – Journal of Applied Language Studies* 13(1). 27–48.

Granfeldt, J., Sayehli, S., & Ågren, M. 2021. Trends in the study of Modern languages in Swedish lower secondary school (2000 – 2018) and the impact of grade point average enhancement credits. *Education Inquiry* 12(2). 127–146.

Gregersen, T., & Horwitz, E. K. 2002. Language learning and perfectionism: anxious and non-anxious language learners' reactions to their own oral performance. *The Modern Language Journal* 86(4). 562–570.

Hardy L., & Hutchinson A. 2007. Effects of performance anxiety on effort and performance in rock climbing: a test of processing efficiency theory. *Anxiety Stress Coping* 20(2). 147–161.

Henry, A. 2009. Gender differences in compulsory school pupils' L2 self-concepts: a longitudinal study. *System* 37(2). 177–193.

Henry, A. 2012. *L3 motivation*. (Doctoral dissertation). Gothenburg Studies in Educational sciences, Gothenburg university. https://gupea.ub.gu.se/handle/2077/28132

Henry, A., & Cliffordson, C. 2013. Motivation, gender, and possible selves. *Language Learning* 63(2). 271–295.

Higgins, E. T. 1987. Self-discrepancy: a theory relating self and affect. *Psychological Review* 94, 319–340.

Horwitz, E. K. 2001. Language anxiety and achievement. *Annual Review of Applied Linguistics* 21. 112–126.

Horwitz, E. K., Horwitz, M. B., & Cope, J. A. 1986. Foreign language classroom anxiety. *The Modern Language Journal* 70(2). 125–132.

Hashimoto, Y. 2002. Motivation and willingness to communicate as predictors of reported L2 use: the Japanese ESL context. *Second Language Studies* 20(2). 29–70.

Hye-Kyoung J., Hiver, P., & Al-Hoorie, A. 2017. Classroom social climate, self-determined motivation, willingness to communicate, and achievement: a study of structural relationships in instructed second language settings. *Learning and Individual Differences* 53. 133–144.

Iwaniec, J. 2019. Language learning motivation and gender: the case of Poland. *International Journal of Applied Linguistics* 29. 130–143.

Joe, H.K., Hiver, P., & Al-Hoorie, A. 2017. Classroom social climate, self-determined motivation, willingness to communicate, and achievement: a study of structural relationships in instructed second language settings. *Learning and Individual Differences* 153. 133–144.

Kissau, S. 2006. Gender differences in second language motivation: an investigation of micro- and macro-level influences. *Canadian Journal of Applied Linguistics* 9(1). 73–96.

Krashen, S. 1982. *Principles and practice in second Language acquisition*. Oxford: Pergamon Press.

Lamb, M. 2017. The motivational dimension of language teaching. *Language teaching* 50(3). 301–346.

Lay, T. 2008. The motivation for learning German in Taiwan. A pilot study on the foreign language-specific motivation of Taiwanese learners of German. *Zeitschrift für Interkulturellen Fremdsprachenunterricht* 13(2). 1–17.

Li, M., & Zhang, L. 2021. Tibetan CSL learners' L2 Motivational Self System and L2 achievement. *System* 97. 102436.

Liu, H.-J., & Chen, T.-H. 2014. Learner differences among children learning a foreign language: language anxiety, strategy use, and multiple intelligences. *English Language Teaching* 7(6). 1–13.

Lu, Z., & Liu, M. 2011. Foreign language anxiety and strategy use: a study with Chinese undergraduate EFL learners. *Journal of Language Teaching and Research* 2(6). 1298–1305.

MacIntyre, P. D. 2002. Motivation, anxiety and emotion in second language acquisition. In P. Robinson (Ed.), *Individual differences and instructed language learning*, 45–68. Amsterdam: John Benjamins.

MacIntyre, P.D. 2007. Willingness to communicate in the second language: understanding the decision to speak as a volitional process. *The Modern Language Journal* 91(4). 564–576.

MacIntyre, P. D., Babin, P. A., & Clément, R. 1999. Willingness to communicate: antecedents and consequences. *Communication Quarterly* 47(2). 215–229.

MacIntyre. P. D., Baker, S. C., Clément, R., & Donovan, L. A. 2002. Sex and age effects on willingness to communicate, anxiety, perceived competence, and L2 motivation among junior high school French immersion students. *Language Learning* 52(3). 537–564.

MacIntyre, P. D., Clément, R., Dörnyei, Z., & Noels, K. A. 1998. Conceptualizing willingness to communicate in an L2: a situational model of L2 confidence and affiliation. *Modern Language Journal* 82(4). 545–562.

MacIntyre, P. D., & Gregersen, T. 2012. Affect: the role of language anxiety and other emotions in language learning. In S. Mercer, S. Ryan, & M. Williams (Eds.), *Psychology for language learning: insights from research, theory and practice*, 103–118. Berlin: Springer.

MacIntyre, P. D., Ross, J., & Clément. R. 2019. Emotions are motivating. In M. Lamb, K. Csizér, A. Henry & S. Ryan (Eds.), *Palgrave Macmillan handbook of motivation for language learning*, 183–197. Basingstoke: Palgrave.

MacIntyre, P. D., & Vincze, L. 2017. Positive and negative emotions underlie motivation for L2 learning. *Studies in Second Language Learning and Teaching* 7(1). 61–88.

Markus, H.R., & Nurius, P. 1986. Possible selves. *American Psychologist* 41(9). 954–969.

Maxwell, S. E., & Delaney, H. D. 2004. *Designing experiments and analyzing data: a model comparison perspective*, 2nd edn. Lawrence Erlbaum Associates Publishers.

McCroskey, J. C., & Baer, J. E. 1985. *Willingness to communicate: the construct and its measurement*. Paper presented at the annual convention of the Speech Communication Association.

Menezes E., & Juan-Garau M. 2015. English learners' willingness to communicate and achievement in CLIL and formal instruction contexts. In M. Juan-Garau & J. Salazar-Noguera (Eds.) *Content-based language learning in multilingual educational environments*, 221–236. Cham: Springer.

Mihaljević Djigunović, J. 2012. Dynamics of learner affective development in early FLL. *Studies in Second Language Learning and Teaching* 2(2). 159–178.

Mihaljević Djigunović, J. 2015. Individual differences among young EFL learners: Age-or proficiency-related? A look from the affective learner factors perspective. In J. Mihaljevic Djigunovic & M. Medved Krajnovic (Eds.), *Early learning and teaching of English: New dynamics of primary English*, 10–36. Bristol: Multilingual Matters.

Moksnes, U. K., Moljord, I. E., Espnes, G. A., & Byrne, D. G. 2010. The association between stress and emotional states in adolescents: The role of gender and self-esteem. *Personality and individual differences* 49(5). 430–435.

Munezane, Y. 2013. Attitude, affect, and ideal L2 self as predictors of willingness to communicate. In R. Leah, A. Ewart, M. Pawlak, & M. Wrembel (Eds.), *EUROSLA Yearbook 13*, 176–198. Amsterdam: John Benjamins.

National Agency for Education. 2021. Moderna språk som språkval 2019/2020 [Modern languages as language choice] Retrieved from https://siris.skolverket.se/reports/rwservlet?cmdkey=common&geo=1&report=moderna_sprak&p_ar=2019&p_hman=&p_lan_kod=&p_kommunkod=&

Nilsson, M. 2020. *Young learners' perspectives on English classroom interaction: foreign language anxiety and sense of agency in Swedish primary school* (PhD dissertation).

Norton, B. 2000. *Identity and language learning: gender, ethnicity and educational change*. Harlow: Pearson Education.

Oga-Baldwin, W.L.Q., & Fryer, L.K. 2020. Girls show better quality motivation to learn languages than boys: latent profiles and their gender differences. *Heliyon* 6, e04054.

Owens M., Stevenson J., Hadwin J.A., & Norgate, R. 2014. When does anxiety help or hinder cognitive test performance? The role of working memory capacity. *British Journal of Psychology* 105(1). 92–101.

Öz, H., & Bursalı, H. 2018. The relationship between L2 motivational self-system and willingness to communicate in learning English as a foreign language. *Journal of Language and Linguistic Studies* 14(4). 1–11.

Öztürk, G., & Gürbüz, N. 2013. The impact of gender on foreign language speaking anxiety and motivation. *Procedia – Social and Behavioral Sciences* 70. 654–665.

Papi, M. 2010. The L2 motivational self system, L2 anxiety, and motivated behavior: a structural equation modelling approach. *System* 38. 467–479.

Parrish, A. 2020. Modern foreign languages: decision-making, motivation and 14–19 schools. *Cambridge Journal of Education* 50(4). 469–481.

Prior, M. T. 2019. Elephants in the room: an "affective turn," or just feeling our way? *The Modern Language Journal* 103(2). 516–527.

Riis, U., & Francia, G. 2013. *Lärare, elever och spanska som modernt språk. Styrkor och svagheter –möjligheter*. Uppsala: Centre for Professional Development and Internationalisation in Schools.

Rocher Hahlin, C. 2020. *La motivation et le concept de soi: Regards croisés de l'élève et de l'enseignant de français langue étrangère en Suède*. (Doctoral dissertation). Études romanes de Lund, Lund University.

Sayehli, S., Österberg, R., & Granfeldt, J. 2021. *Does language matter? Attitudes and motivations in L3 learners of French, German and Spanish*. [Manuscript in preparation]. Department of Swedish language and Multilingualism, Stockholm: Stockholm University.

Shirvan, M. E., Khajavy, G. H., MacIntyre, P. D., & Taherian, T. 2019. A meta-analysis of L2 willingness to communicate and its three high-evidence correlates. *Journal of psycholinguistic research* 48(6). 1241–1267.

SOU. 2010. SOU: s betänkande om pojkar och flickor i skolan, könsskillnader (2010). Flickor, pojkar, individer. Om betydelsen av jämställdhet för kunskap och utveckling i skolan. Slutbetänkande för Delegationen om jämställdhet i skolan. *Statens offentliga utredningar, SOU betänkande 2010: 99*.

Sundqvist, P. 2009. *Extramural English matters: out-of-school English and its impact on Swedish ninth graders' oral proficiency and vocabulary*. Doctoral dissertation, Karlstad University.

Swain, M. 2013. The inseparability of cognition and emotion in second language learning. *Language teaching* 46(2). 195–207.

Swain, M., Kinnear, P., & Steinman, L. 2010. *Sociocultural theory in second language education: an introduction through narratives*. Bristol: Multilingual Matters.

Teimouri, Y. 2017. L2 selves, emotions, and motivated behaviors. *Studies in Second Language Acquisition* 39(4). 681–709.

Teimouri, Y., Goetze, J., & Plonsky, L. 2019. Second language anxiety and achievement: a meta-analysis. *Studies in Second Language Acquisition* 41. 363–387.

Tholin, J., & Lindqvist, A. 2009. *Språkval svenska/engelska på grundskolan: en genomlysning*. University of Borås, Department of Education, Borås.

Tuncel, F., Yapici, A., Akman, P., Elçi, A. C., Demiroglari, B.K., & Mahmut O. 2020. Foreign language anxiety of adolescent students. *African Educational Research Journal* 8(2). 164–169.

Wang, H., Peng, A., & Patterson, M.M. 2021. The roles of class social climate, language mindset, and emotions in predicting willingness to communicate in a foreign language. *System* 99 (102529).

Williams, M., Burden, R., & Lanvers, U. 2002. 'French is the language of love and stuff': student perceptions of issues related to motivation in learning a foreign language. *British Educational Research Journal* 28(4). 503–528.

You, C. J., Dörnyei, Z., & Csizér, K. 2016. Motivation, vision, and gender: a survey of learners of English in China. *Language Learning* 66(1). 94–123.

Debora Carrai
Secondary school pupils' language choice satisfaction in the L3 classroom: The roles of teaching, motivation, language choice and language classroom anxiety

Abstract: The present study explores the relation between pupils' L3 language choice satisfaction and the independent variables teaching quality, differentiated instruction, motivation, language choice, classroom anxiety, and pupils' perceptions of the learning environment. It comprises data from a representative sample of 1521 9th graders from 25 Norwegian lower secondary schools who answered a 142-item questionnaire that tapped into different aspects of course satisfaction, teaching, motivation, language choice and language classroom anxiety.

The study uses multiple linear regression to analyze how the dependent variable pupils' choice satisfaction covaries with independent variables such as motivation and teaching. It presents data for the entire sample, and separately for the three main L3 languages (French, German and Spanish). The results of the analysis show the importance of teaching quality, differentiated instruction and intrinsic motivation for pupil satisfaction.

Because of the non-mandatory status of L3 languages in the Norwegian school, this study concludes by arguing the need to improve L3 instruction and teacher professionalism, and the importance of ensuring pupils' motivation regardless of language choice.

Keywords: L3 choice satisfaction, motivation, teaching, learning, adaptation

1 Introduction: Background and rationale for the study

The present article investigates how teaching quality, differentiated instruction, motivation, language choice, classroom anxiety, and pupils' perceptions of the learning environment account for 1521 Norwegian lower secondary school pupils' satisfaction with their second foreign language choice (hereafter referred to as L3).

The L3 courses in lower secondary school, which start in grade 8 and last until grade 10, come in addition to their first foreign language and English (hereafter referred to as L2). The background for the correlational study (Carrai

2014), from which this article draws its data, is the complex dynamic involving competition between, and quality of teaching in the L3 languages and the competing elective subjects.

Prior to the 2006 *Knowledge Promotion Curriculum Reform* of *primary, lower secondary and upper secondary education and training* (hereafter referred to as LK06) (KD 2006a) the situation for the L3 language courses had long been deteriorating following the 1976 curriculum reform. This reform reduced their status to that of elective subjects that no longer counted for admission to upper secondary school. The L3 courses were characterized by a declining interest which reached its lowest level in school year 1995/96 (with only 66% of the pupils chosing an L3 language), and drop-out rates around 30% in school year 2000/01 (Speitz and Lindemann 2002). This trend was further exacerbated by having to compete against a practical subject called *Project work* with the same number of teaching hours, but almost no homework burden.

The LK06 reform partially reversed this situation, by changing the status of L3 language subjects from optional to semi-optional – by requiring pupils to choose between an L3 language or alternative, *In-depth studies* in Norwegian, English or Math and, later *Skills for Working Life*, a less academic subject. Both L3 languages and *in-depth studies* (or *skills for working life*) were intended for all three years of lower secondary school and had an equivalent number of teaching hours.[1] Despite this, the L3 languages under the LK06 reform still experienced a high and increasing *drop-out* rate during 8th and 9th grade in favor of the in-depth subjects, as well as the possibility to change subject during the first or second year. This was most probably due to the alternative subjects having less homework and to their being considered much easier by the pupils (Carrai 2014: 188–191). Indeed, the increasing drop-out rates in the main L3 languages, ranging between 9% and 11% (8th grade) and between 5% and 9% (9th grade) (Grunnskolens informasjonssystem, elaborated in Carrai 2014: 25), led to the 2012 decision to favor those who chose to specialize in the L3 languages in upper secondary school with extra credits counting for admission to higher education.

Currently, years after the LK06 reform and at the beginning of a curriculum revision called *Subject Renewal* (hereafter referred to as LK20) (KD 2019), we see a lower *drop-out* rate than before, but also a decreasing interest in choosing an L3 in favor of the competing subjects, with attrition rates increasing from 19% (in school year 2006–2007) to 26% (in school year 2020–2021) (Nasjonalt

---

[1] L3 languages and *in-depth studies* have the same amount of hours during lower secondary school (222 hours distributed over three years), which corresponds approximately to two 60-minutes lessons per week (KD, 2019. www.udir.no/lk20/fsp01-02/timetall).

Senter for engelsk og fremmedspråk i opplæringen 2021). In lower secondary school attrition due to the competition between the L3 languages (mainly French, German and Spanish) and their alternatives remains a problem, a key reason being that pupils still have the chance to change from L3 languages to other *in-depth* subjects during the 8th grade. Carrai found that quitting an L3 language in favor of an in-depth study subject could be due to low intrinsic and extrinsic L3 motivation, poor quality of the information about L3 languages, disappointed expectations, and a high level of difficulty compared to in-depth subjects (2014: 245).

In order to keep down attrition rates, it is therefore important to find out more about pupils' satisfaction with, or lack thereof, for the chosen L3 languages. Therefore, the main research aim of this article is to understand which choice-related motivational factors, as well as measures related to teaching, learning and learning environmental factors, play a key role with regard to the pupils' satisfaction with the chosen L3 language.

The main research question for the present article is therefore:

What are the factors that can predict pupils' satisfaction with the chosen L3 language?

To investigate this, this study draws upon the data from the first, large scale national study of L3 choice using a sample of 1521 9th grade pupils (Carrai 2014), i.e. pupils who after starting the subject in 8th grade can account for both their language choice (which takes place in 7th grade) and other factors important for their subsequent language choice satisfaction. The present study therefore could provide interesting information about pupils' choices that can contribute to our understanding of pupils' satisfaction, or dissatisfaction, with their respective L3 courses. Consequently, and indirectly, it could also provide information about the need for improved teacher professionalism.

2 Previous studies in the Norwegian school context

Little relevant research about pupils' L3 choices or L3 motivation has been carried out in Norway, and no studies have investigated pupils' satisfaction with their chosen language. The few existing studies can be divided into two thematical groups: the mapping of pupils' choices and attempts to understand the reasons behind these choices.

In the first group we find the annual reports by *The Norwegian National Centre for English and other Foreign Languages in Education* (Fagvalgstatistikk, Nasjonalt Senter for engelsk og fremmedspråk i opplæringen) and the more extensive study by Doetjes and Ryen (2009) who also attempted some inferences about the reasons behind the pupils' choices, despite the lack of a sampling instrument with motivational items.

The second group comprises two studies. During the years prior to the LK06-curriculum, Speitz and Lindemann (2002) studied the subject status and attempted an indirect non-causal analysis of the reasons behind the pupils' choices. This was followed by a quantitative longitudinal study of upper secondary school pupils' L3 motivation (Lindemann 2008). While the sample, however, is not representative, this is the only previous study that allows for (indirect) assumptions about pupils' satisfaction with their L3 choices.

Relevant contributions from outside Norway can otherwise be found in Henry (2011) and Henry and Apelgren (2009), who studied different aspects of L3 learning and motivational factors in the Swedish lower secondary schools. These studies are especially important for the Norwegian context because of the similarities between the contexts and curricula (Skolverket 2011).

As none of the mentioned Norwegian studies include large-scale studies and statistical analysis, the aim of the present article is to contribute towards filling this gap by presenting new research based upon further analysis of previously collected data from Carrai (2014). It is a large, quantitative, cross-sectional, correlational study with a representative sample, and is the first attempt at providing a database for the factors involved in L3 learning and teaching in the Norwegian lower secondary school. Carrai (2014) investigated the reasons behind pupils' choice of L3 subjects, the differences between the three main L3 groups of pupils (from the main languages French, Spanish and German) and their level of satisfaction with the L3 choice. It also included items to provide additional detail about the possible factors involved in their L3 choice satisfaction. Among the main findings were that pupils chose their L3 course based on both internal factors, i.e. instrinsic and extrinsic motivation as well as language attitudes, and external factors which could include poor or misleading information from schools, parents and peers. The pupils' experience with L3 courses was at least partially negative[2] (see section 5.2) with regard to their

---

[2] The overall satisfaction rate with the chosen L3 language is around 51%, with French having the most satisfied group (59% of positive answers) and Spanish the least satisfied (44% of positive answers). And the pupils with Spanish as L3 language are also the least satisfied with language teaching, teaching adaptation and their perception of learning (Carrai 2014: 153–158, 168–169).

satisfaction with the chosen language, their perception of learning, their experience of language teaching and the extent of adaptation to their level and needs (Carrai 2014: 244–245). Further, the comparison between L3 pupils and *drop-outs* (pupils who had changed from an L3 language to an in-depth subject between 8th and 9th grade) showed that the main reasons for changing subjects were clearly linked to their perceptions of L3 courses as not being interesting enough as well as too demanding (Carrai 2014: 245–246). Fortunately, the rich data from Carrai (2014), allowed for a more comprehensive statistical investigation of the relation between the pupils' L3 language choice satisfaction and a number of key variables like teaching quality, differentiated instruction, motivation, language choice, language classroom anxiety, and pupils' perceptions of both learning and the learning environment.

3 The factors in this study

The aim of this article is to see to what extent it is possible to explain variation in pupils' satisfaction with their chosen language. In the following I will concentrate on specific elements dealing with L3 languages in the classroom. As this article represents a further analysis of an already established data set, the aim of this section is to present the factors from (Carrai 2014) which have been taken into consideration in order to answer and discuss the research question. The chosen factors concern pupils' L3 motivation, the teacher and the teaching, including adapted or differentiated instruction, the pupils' perceptions of learning, the learning environment and language classroom anxiety. In the presentation of these factors, L3 motivation has a predominant role.

3.1 L3 choice satisfaction

Research into motivation in second language acquisition (SLA) has in recent years focused on the factors affecting second language (here, L3) learners' motivation. This article/study, however, concentrates on an analysis of pupils' satisfaction with their chosen L3 language course.

L3 choice satisfaction encompasses 9th graders' overall satisfaction with the chosen language after more than one year of experience (see Section 1) and, given this dynamic perspective, is to be understood as an *outcome* of motivation. The pupils in the sample are therefore required to answer questions about their initial *choice motivation* in the *pre-actional* phase – cf. Heckhausen and

Kuhl's definition (cited by Dörnyei & Ottó 1998: 43) – while they are currently in the *actional* or *post-actional* phase.

In this theoretical framework choice motivation comes *before* pupils' satisfaction, and in spite of the survey being cross-sectional, this is investigated as a dependent variable using specific questions about the two different moments in time: initial choice and later satisfaction.

With the motivational construct explaining L3 language choice and teaching and learning environment factors on the one hand, and pupils' satisfaction with the chosen language on the other, the focus of this study relies on elapsed time. This is because the design of the study – correlational and exploratory with only one survey – does not allow for the investigation of the natural development of, and changes in, motivation and satisfaction over time. Thus, a retrospective time perspective is not only inherent to the study design, but it also provides the justification for suggesting hypotheses about causal inferences that the design itself does not support. This is because it could be assumed that pupils who find themselves in the *post-actional* phase, can draw on an *a posteriori* vision when answering both about their own motivation *before* their language (or subject) choice, and about teaching and learning environment factors in the *actional* phase. According to this timeline logic they are also answering about their motivation *for*, as well as their satisfaction *with* that choice.

The above-mentioned variables were analyzed in order to explain pupils' satisfaction as a dependent variable.

3.2 L3 choice motivation

Language choice motivation is understood as the type of motivation that leads pupils to select one of the offered L3 language alternatives. It is based on Dörnyei's definition of motivation as providing "the primary impetus to initiate [L3] learning" (2005: 65). Choice motivation can also be regarded as *initiating* (Williams & Burden 1997), or even as *pre-actional* (Dörnyei & Ottó 1998) motivation.

L2, or, as in this case, L3 motivation being a wide field of investigation, I will limit this section to the theoretic framework relevant for the survey which is directly linked to the pupils' language choice in 7th grade, as pupils start learning their L3 in 8th grade.

When focusing on pupils' L3 choice in the present study, instead of concentrating on the classic opposition between intrinsic vs. extrinsic motivation (Deci & Ryan 1985; Pae 2008), I use Gardner's (1985a, 1985b, 2004) and Crookes and Schmidt's (1991) arguments for a less conflictive dualism. Regarding the opposition between instrumental (Dörnyei 2001: 49) and integrative (Dörnyei 2001: 48; 1999:

46) elements of extrinsic motivation, the items used in this survey are meant to tap into both types of elements, which are part of the intended extrinsic motivation.

The present study also follows Gardner's motivational construct regarding the pupils' attitudes towards learning the language, cf. *Attitude and Motivation Test Battery* (1985a: 2004), hereafter referred to as *AMTB*. Pupils' attitudes towards the learning situation (Gardner 1985b) in this survey are limited to their general language attitudes.[3]

In addition to the use of Gardner's motivational construct, Dörnyei and Ottó's *process model of L2 motivation* (1998) represents the theoretical framework which can support the study of motivation as seen in a dynamic perspective. According to their definition, it is possible to define motivation as changing over time, and this allows the construction of a timeline with different phases: *pre-actional, actional* and *post-actional* phases by which motivational elements can be analyzed according to whether we consider motivational development before starting to study the language, after a fixed time period, or after a school cycle. This theoretical framework allows the study of pupils' choice motivation in retrospect: Pupils in 9th grade are required to give reasons for their L3 choice motivation immediately before 8th grade. At the same time, they account for their satisfaction with the chosen language, as a motivational *outcome*, or *motivated learning behavior* (Csizér and Kormos 2009) shown by keeping their chosen L3 language after more than one year of experience. This time difference between choice motivation and L3 satisfaction allows for inferences about possible changes in motivation.

3.3 The teaching and the teacher

Both LK06 and LK20 curricula, following the trend established by The Common European Framework of Reference for Languages (Council of Europe 2018, 2001), are organized according to the expected goal achievement after levels 1, 2 or 3 (FSP1-01; KD 2006). The curricula do not specify which methods to follow in order to achieve the goals that are specified for subject's areas (*LK06*, KD 2006a) and core elements (*LK20*, KD 2019). This means that both the quality of L3 courses, the quality of teaching materials (which is not investigated in this study) and the chance to achieve goals rely on teachers' professionalism. The

---

[3] In the complete version of the survey (Carrai 2014) attitudes are divided into attitudes towards language learning and attitude towards the language teacher.

role of the teacher in L3 courses has been emphasized by a number of studies (Dörnyei 2018; Dörnyei and Kubanyiova 2014; Dörnyei 2001a; Dörnyei and Malderez 1999), and two measures of it (*Evaluation of the Language Instructor* and *Evaluation of the Language Course*) were included in Gardner's *AMTB* as components of pupils' *Attitude Towards the Learning Situation* (Masgoret, Bernaus & Gardner 2001: 283). Even if researchers underline the need for pupils to develop their own learning strategies as a step towards better control over their learning process (Dörnyei 2005: 110–114; KD 2006; KD 2019), there is consensus on the implications the teacher's role has for pupils' L3 motivation (Al Kanboody 2013; Dörnyei 2005; Dörnyei and Csizér 1998).

3.3.1 Adapted teaching and learning

A further step into teachers' responsibility is the concept of adapted or differentiated teaching and learning (hereafter adaptation), which is a key principle in the Norwegian school system, as established by The Education Act (Opplæringsloven § 1–1; KD 1998). According to this, teachers are required to adapt their teaching, as well as the activities in the classroom, to the needs of different groups or pupils, as stated by the *Læringsplakaten* (KD 2006a: 2, 4; KD 2006b). Consequently, Norwegian classrooms are by definition multilevel groups where teachers have both the freedom and the challenge to differentiate level, method, speed and materials. Since the Norwegian curriculum does not specify teaching methods and materials (see 2.2), the process of adaptation is often a challenge for teachers (Brevik and Gunnulfsen 2016). Moreover, the lack of proper adaptation, and failure in making the course relevant for the pupils, may affect pupils' motivation (Dörnyei and Csizér 1998: 217).

3.3.2 Pupils' perception of learning

The two previously mentioned curricula for L3 languages (LK06, KD 2006; LK20, KD 2019) strongly and openly encourage, learners to take an active role in their learning process. In LK06 one of the main areas, *Language learning*, claims that the pupils have to be able to express their learning needs and goals, and to describe and assess what they are learning (KD 2006: 6). We recognize some of the same encouragements in the corresponding core element *Language learning and multilingualism* in the new curriculum (LK20), according to which the pupils should explore their own learning process.

The path towards both autonomy in language learning and awareness of one's own learning needs is also highlighted by the *Language Portfolio* promoted by the *CEFR* (Council of Europe 2001), and harmonizes with the already mentioned principle of adapted teaching and learning. The thematic proximity to formative assessment theories (Black & Williams 2018) deserves mention, even if the limitations of this paper do not allow a thorough review of the field.

The freedom to choose how they want to learn is considered a prerequisite to pupils' motivation (Dörnyei 2001: 103–104), according to self-regulation theory (Benson 2001, in Dörnyei 2001: 103), and to increase pupils' involvement in the learning process is autonomy-supporting (Dörnyei 2001: 104).

In order to being able to express learning goals or choices, and to understand learning needs, it is necessary for the pupils to be cognizant of how they are doing, or how they think they are doing, i.e. the pupils' perception of learning. This perception can have consequences on future motivation depending on the balance between effort and achievements in the so-called *post-actional* phase, which is also a motivational retrospection (Dörnyei 2005: 84) and is clearly important to determine the level of satisfaction with the chosen language.

3.4 The environmental elements

According to Skaalvik & Skaalvik (2003: 139) and Brophy (1987, cited in Skaalvik and Skaalvik 2003), an environment where pupils feel at ease not only contributes to the pupils' well-being, but also facilitates the learning process. In the following I will present two of the environmental factors considered relevant in the process of understanding pupils' satisfaction with the chosen language.

3.4.1 Learning environment

There is wide consensus about the importance of the learning environment. Clément, Dörnyei and Noels (1994) underline the role of group cohesiveness for L2 motivation, other studies (Dörnyei 2001a: 81; Dörnyei and Kormos 2000: 280) confirm the connection between motivation and the role of the group. Given the contribution of group dynamics for succeeding in the L3 classroom (Dörnyei 1997), a pleasant and supportive atmosphere is always highly recommended (Dörnyei 2001).

Furthermore, in order to understand the importance of the learning environment and the possible impact on pupils' satisfaction, and, in the end, on learning, we have to consider the way Norwegian L3 classes are organized.

Most Norwegian lower secondary schools schedule L3 classes in the same time period, which means that most L3 classes comprise pupils from parallel classes. According to this system, L3 classes are the only mixed groups with pupils converging from the different permanent classes, although all are from the same grade level. This organizatory system may have repercussions on the learning environment, because L3 pupils don't know each other very well, and this can prevent the development of group cohesion.

3.4.2 Language classroom anxiety

In addition to the emphasis on group dynamics and environment, many studies have highlighted the importance of the so-called affective elements for understanding L2 or, as in this case, L3 learning. These elements in their complexity are called *language classroom anxiety*, defined as "anxiety reactions to situations in which one might make use of the target language" (Gardner and MacIntyre 1993: 2).

There seems to be general agreement on the fact that anxiety is part of the language learner's characteristics, and it is such a specific language related type of anxiety (Dörnyei 2005; MacIntyre 2002; MacIntyre and Gardner 1994) that it can be considered as a component of motivation (Clément and Kruidenier 1985). Furthermore, anxiety is recognized as the most obstructive affective factor to the learning process (Arnold and Brown 1999 in Dörnyei 2005: 198), with a negative effect on language performance (Oxford 1999: 59).

This phenomenon has been the object of several quantitative studies, and has been measured by a number of items included in Gardner's *AMTB* (1985b) and by the *Foreign Language Classroom Anxiety Scale* (hereafter referred to as *FLCAS*) (Horwitz, Horwitz and Cope 1986).

4 Method

4.1 Procedure and sampling method

The survey was conducted in the autumn term of the pupils' 9th grade, and was administered by the local teachers. It was given to 9th grade pupils from 25 lower secondary schools in Norway, who could answer the questionnaire based on their experience of the previous year.

The sampling criterion required pupils coming from public schools offering Spanish among their L3 languages.[4] Schools that met this criterion were then selected by choosing and contacting every 20th school on the Norwegian official school list *Pedlex* (2009) which follows a geographic distribution from south to north and from east to west. About 30 schools were needed to collect the planned number of about 2000 respondents. When a school opted not to participate, the choice fell on the next school on the list.

At the outset all the 9th graders from each school were intended as possible respondents, but in some cases not all pupils answered the questionnaire due to misunderstandings with the local survey administrators. Nevertheless, the survey ended up with 1512 respondents, giving a 69% response rate (Carrai 2014: 124–125). The sample obtained was an implicitly stratified, random sample, which qualifies as a probability selection (Hellevik 2002: 114–117) and allows for generalizability to lower secondary school pupils in Norway in general, and to a certain extent, to L3 pupils in comparable countries, i.e. countries with similar school systems, the Scandinavian countries in particular.

4.2 Participants

The sample includes 1521 pupils: 740 boys, 773 girls and 8 who didn't answer the gender question). About 68% of the respondents were studying an L3 language, and 31% Norwegian or English in-depth courses. Spanish represents the 38% of the L3 sample, followed by German (19%), and French (11%) (Table A2, Appendix A), while the in-depth-courses pupils were divided between in-depth Norwegian (10%) or English (21%). The distribution between the three main languages in the samples differs slightly from the same distribution on a national level because of the main sampling criterion, i.e. schools that offered Spanish in addition to French and German. However, the L3 languages sizes (in percentage) in the sample still correspond to those in the reference population where Spanish is the most popular language, followed by German and French.

The 25 schools were of different sizes, 10 were from larger or smaller cities, 14 from rural areas, and 1 is uncertain.[5] The schools are geographically distributed, and 17 of the 19 counties are represented in the sample (Table A1, Appendix A).

---

4 This is because the research project aimed to explore the possible reasons behind the L3 drop-out rate, which was higher in Spanish than in German and French.
5 The questionnaires were not labelled with the school name to ensure anonymity and were sent by post. Since the package from this particular school did not contain the sender's name, it was difficult to identify the school with certainty.

4.3 The instrument

The Norwegian language questionnaire was developed after an initial interview-cycle with six pupils, and was then tested and refined over three different surveys, a pre-pilot, a pilot, and the present survey. The questionnaire[6] comprises of 44 questions (142 items), most of these multiple-choice questions using 3 or 4-point Likert scales. The majority include several items: choice-motivational factors together with other factors interacting with both language choice and satisfaction (such as external sources for information about the languages), the influence of family and friends, background information (parent's knowledge and use of the language), teacher and teaching-related factors, language group factors (language classroom anxiety and pupils' perception of the learning environment). The questions have a section (questions 1–24) that are to be answered by all respondents, a section (questions 25–40) for those who have chosen a foreign language, and a last section (questions 41–44), for those who have chosen an in-depth study course in English or Norwegian instead of the L3. Since the latter comprises pupils who have dropped out of previously chosen L3 languages, two of the questions (43–44) tap into their reasons for quitting the L3 course. The corresponding questions in the questionnaire have been translated into English and can be found in Appendix B (Table A1–A6).

Due to the lack of similar instruments in the Norwegian context (Carrai 2014: 104), the formulation of items tapping into motivation required drawing upon acknowledged international instruments such as Gardner's well-known *AMTB* (Gardner 1985a, 1985b) which remains valid even after Gardner, Tremblay and Masgoret's revision of the motivational construct (1997). Another very relevant item-pool is also derived from Dörnyei's catalogue of the L2 motivation measurement instruments (2001: 260–269). As regards items about language classroom anxiety and learning environment, a useful source is Horwitz et al.'s recognized scale *FLCAS* (1986). The original items have been modified and adapted to the Norwegian school context.

4.3.1 L3 choice satisfaction

L3 choice satisfaction, i.e. the level of satisfaction with the chosen language in 9th grade, is measured by the single-item question *How satisfied are you with*

---

[6] The complete version of the questionnaire in Norwegian can be found in Carrai (2014): https://www.duo.uio.no/handle/10852/41477.

the subject you have chosen? (Table B1, Appendix B). This item, which is studied as a dependent variable in this article, is seen as the outcome of a number of other variables, and can be explained by the following model of the time dimensions taken into account in the questionnaire (Figure 1). This model is organized according to Dörnyei og Ottó's *process model of L2 motivation* (1998) (see 3.2) and is modified from Carrai (2014: 92).

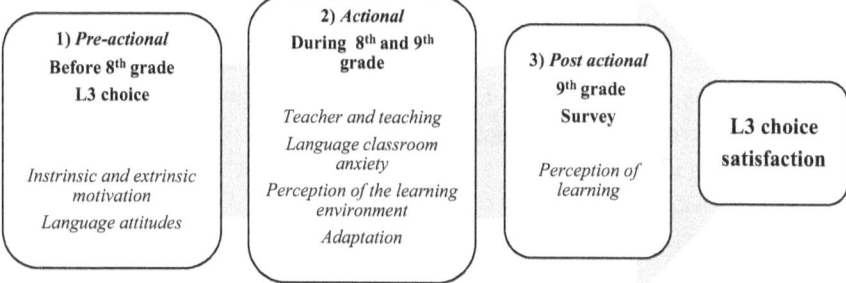

Figure 1: Model of the timeline of the measures in the study, with L3 choice satisfaction as outcome.

Figure 1 shows the timeline of the measures in this study, and places them in the three different phases. The *pre-actional* (phase 1) is the stage when the L3 was chosen, a choice based on motivational orientations and language attitudes. The *actional* (phase 2) is the period between 8th and 9th grade until the survey takes place, and it is when pupils experience their L3 in school and can form their impressions about the teacher, the teaching, language classroom anxiety, the learning environment and how the subject is adapted to their level and needs. The *post-actional* (phase 3) is the time for a critical retrospective evaluation about one's efforts and achievements, i.e. when the pupils can express their perception about learning. The survey takes place in this phase, when the pupils can, based on their experiences from the previous phases, express their level of satisfaction with their L3. The timeline also illustrates how L3 choice satisfaction can be considered an outcome of the already mentioned measures.

4.3.2 Multi-items measures used in the study

The following 5 multi-items measures were used in the study: *intrinsic* and *extrinsic motivation, language attitudes, language classroom anxiety, pupils' perception of the learning environment.* The corresponding questions in the questionnaire are reported and translated in Appendix B (Tables B2–B6).

Among the motivational factors *intrinsic motivation* (question 30) is partially derived from Dörnyei's questionnaire (2001: 261–263) and adapted to the Norwegian school context. *Extrinsic motivation* (question 29), comprises both *instrumental* and *integrative motives* and is derived from Gardner's *AMTB* (1985b). In addition to these, *language attitudes* (question 31) is derived from Gardner's definition of motivation as a complex synergy of attitudes towards learning the language, motivational intensity as well as desire to learn the language (1985a).

Confirmatory factor analysis was performed in order to make additive indices and construct indicators.[7] In all cases a principal component analysis was initially performed with the purpose of identifying underlying factors. Then direct oblimin rotation was used to achieve a simple factor structure, and the adequacy of the sampling was verified with the Keiser-Meyer-Olkin measure for the following measures[8] (see Tables A4–A8, Appendix A for the specific factor loadings):

1) *Intrinsic motivation.* In the questionnaire 8 items (question 30, Table B4, Appendix B) were designed to tap into the construct *intrinsic motivation*. The principal component analysis revealed only one underlying factor, with a KMO of .828. The construct had an explained variance of 43% and a good reliability (α=.77). However, the analysis highlighted that two items (30.1 and 30.8) could be eliminated to achieve higher reliability. This led to considerations about the possibly misleading formulation of the two items and to their elimination. A new principal component analysis of the 6 remaining factors achieved an explained variance of 54% with a KMO of .82 and a fairly high reliability (α=.83).

2) *Extrinsic motivation.* At the outset, 12 items (question 29, Table B3, Appendix B) were intended as indicators of *extrinsic motivation*. The principal component analysis revealed three underlying factors one of which (29.12) was the only with the highest loading on the third factor. The decision to eliminate this item was based on considerations about its content, and both varimax and oblimin rotations were used in an attempt to separate the other two factors, but with consistently identical results. This led to two different additive indices which account for two different components of extrinsic motivation. The first factor (*extrinsic motivation-career*, comprising

---

[7] A more detailed description of the performed analysis can be found in Carrai (2014: 198–297).
[8] In all the presented cases Bartlett's test of sphericity was significant.

items 29.1 to 29.3) (Table A4, Appendix A), with an explained variance of 58% and KMO of .74, is related to the chance to find a job by learning the language and therefore more instrumental and achieved a good reliability (α=.75). The second factor (*extrinsic orientation-free time*, comprising items 29.5 to 29.11) with a explained variance of 42% and a KMO of .78 is considered to be tapping into a more integrative side of language choice and showed a good reliability as well (α=.76).

3) *Foreign language attitudes*. The 4 items in question 31 (Table B5, Appendix B) are designed to tap into general language attitudes towards languages. The principal component analysis and the oblimin rotation revealed that the items are a homogeneous group loading on the same underlying factor (Table A7, Appendix A), with a KMO of .75 and an explained variance of 60%. and can be considered as indicators for different aspects of a general language attitude, with a good reliability (α=.78).

4) *Language classroom anxiety*. Language classroom anxiety was intended to be measured by the 6 items (question 40, Table B6, Appendix B). Principal component analysis was used and two underlying factors were identified, however the two items (40.1 and 40.3) loading on the second factor were eliminated because of considerations regarding the formulation of the question[9] (Carrai: 2014: 203–204). This led to a reduction of the number of items, as shown in Table A9 (Appendix A). Then an analysis of the remaining 4 factors was performed using both varimax and oblimin rotations with consistently identical results, with the 4 factors explaining 56% of the variance and a KMO measure of .723. The construct obtained a fairly high reliability (α=.78).

5) *Pupils' perception of the learning environment*. Originally 4 items (question 23, Table B2, Appendix B) were designed to be indicators for the perception of the learning environment, but the principal component analysis evidenced 2 different factors, with one item (23.1) loading on the second factor. An analysis of both content and formulation of the item,[10] concluded that the item was misleading for the respondents, and led to its elimination from the group. After an oblimin rotation, the remaining items achieved an explained variance of 59% with a KMO of .63, and a medium-sized reliability (α=. 65). (Table A8, Appendix A).

---

[9] The 2 items (40.1 and 40.3) seemed to point more at teacher activity then at pupils' feelings about the language classroom.

[10] The item content (*It is important for me to have my friends in the classroom*) could lead to various interpretations, and was considered to point at the importance of friends in itself, rather than to the friends' support in the learning environment.

The specific items and the Cronbach Alpha reliability coefficients for internal consistency are summarized in Table 1.

Table 1: Overview of additive indices created from the multi-items measures in the questionnaire with reliability coefficients for internal consistency.

Multi-items measures – additive indices	Items in the questionnaire	Cronbach alpha
Intrinsic motivation	30.2, 30.3, 30.4, 30.5, 30.6, 30.7	0.83
Extrinsic motivation-career	29.1, 29.2, 29.3, 29.4	0.76
Extrinsic motivation-free time	29.5, 29.6, 29.7, 29.8, 29.10, 29.11	0.75
Language attitudes	31.1, 31.2, 31.3, 31.4	0.78
Language classroom anxiety	40.4, 40.5, 40.6	0.78
Pupils' perception of the learning environment	23.2, 23.3, 23.4	0.65

4.3.3 Single-item measures in the study

In addition to L3 choice satisfaction, the 4 measures of *teaching, teacher, adaptation and pupil's perception of learning* are also single-item measures represented by the number of questions in the questionnaire, as specified in Table 2. The corresponding questions in the questionnaire are reported and translated in Appendix B (Table B1).

Table 2: Overview of single-items measures and corresponding questions in the questionnaire.

Single-item measures	Questions in the questionnaire
Teaching	13
Teacher	21
Adaptation	14
Pupils' perception of learning	16

The reason for the choice of single-items measures, despite their possible weakness from a measurement point of view, lies in the questionnaire-making process. During the pre-pilot and pilot phases,[11] it became clear that these

---

[11] The questionnaire underwent both a pre-pilot and a pilot process. The pre-pilot was conducted with a convenience sample of 30 respondents and followed by 6 interviews, and the

specific questions (originally formulated differently) had to be simplified and adapted accordingly to the respondents' level of comprehension. In particular, it was important to make the dependent variable L3 choice satisfaction (Table B1, Appendix B) more consistent with the timeline of the survey, and to make the respondents directly connect their L3 satisfaction in 9th grade with their own L3 experience in 8th grade.

4.4 Data analysis

The statistical analysis was carried out using SPSS and includes correlations, confirmatory factor analysis to make additive indices, and reliability study with Cronbach's alpha coefficients. *Independent sample t-test* is also used to test for statistically significant differences between the different L3 languages.

Finally, the research questions of this article are explored by using multiple regression analysis in order to analyze how the dependent variable L3 choice satisfaction covaries with a number of independent variables in the questionnaire.

5 Findings and analysis

In the following I examine the relationships between the dependent variable, L3 choice satisfaction and measures of the independent variables coming both from single-item questions in the questionnaire, as well as from constructs obtained by performing confirmatory factor analysis on the multiple items-questions in order to create additive indices (see 4.2). Since the present article uses a previously collected dataset, and has its starting point in a previous analysis, the choice of independent measures to explain variation in L3 choice satisfaction was based on the strongest correlations already found in Carrai (2014), which are repeated and summarized in Table A8 (Appendix A).

I start with a general overview of the findings regarding the sample, then I focus on the specific findings related to L3 choice satisfaction in the three main

---

pilot phase with a convenience sample of 189 respondents. During the pre-pilot it became clear that some of the questions were too complex, or too sensitive (this applies to the questions about the teacher and the teaching). The Likert scale was also adjusted according to the respondents' feedback. The validity of the new formulations was then confirmed by the consistent results between the pilot and the final version of the questionnaire (Carrai 2014).

L3 languages. Finally, I use multiple linear regression to test a model predicting variation in L3 choice satisfaction.

5.1 The drop-outs in the sample

The sample includes, as mentioned, 1521 9th graders. The number of *drop-outs* between 8th and 9th grade in our sample can be estimated to about the 10% of the total number of pupils (Table A3, Appendix A). This is comparable to the *GSI* (The national database about Norwegian lower secondary school) numbers for the country as a whole. The general trend is that drop-out pupils replace a foreign language with an in-depth course in either Norwegian or English, which are considered less demanding (Carrai: 2014: 184–185).

5.2 The general L3 choice satisfaction

L3 choice satisfaction, i.e. the level of satisfaction with the chosen language in 9th grade, is measured by a single item (question 5: *How satisfied are you with the subject you have chosen?*). Table 3 is modified from Carrai (2014: 149) and summarizes the differences between language groups.

Table 3: Distribution of L3 choice satisfaction within the three languages (N=1521).

How satisfied are you with the subject you have chosen?	French	German	Spanish
Not at all	11%	13%	18%
Enough	57%	57%	51%
Very satisfied	33%	29%	31%

As can be seen, the French group is the most satisfied with almost 90% positive answers (*enough* and *very satisfied*), while the Spanish group is the least satisfied with 18% answering *not at all*. Spanish also has a somewhat lower percentage, 82%, of positive answers. An independent *t*-test, however, revealed that the differences between the languages are not statistically significant ($p>0.05$).[12]

---

12 The differences among the three groups i.e. between French and German, French and Spanish as well as Spanish and German had all *p*-values over 0.05 (respectively $p=0.500$, $p=0.210$ and $p=0.487$).

5.3 Explaining L3 choice satisfaction

This study was conducted to determine which factors can influence pupils' satisfaction with their chosen L3 language. It was hypothesized that *teaching, adaptation, perception of learning, teacher, learning environment, language classroom anxiety, foreign language attitude, intrinsic and extrinsic motivation* would predict L3 choice satisfaction.

To test this hypothesis, multiple regression analysis is used to construct a model using L3 choice satisfaction as a dependent variable, and a pool of possible predictors chosen according to the strongest correlations with the dependent variable (see Table A10, Appendix A). These include measures of teaching quality, adaptation, intrinsic and extrinsic motivation, language attitudes, pupils' perception of learning, language classroom anxiety, and pupils' perception of the learning environment.[13]

The first attempted model included all the possible independent predictors shown in Tables 1 and 2, but the results allowed the exclusion of the two constructs extrinsic motivation (both *free-time* and *career*, see 4.2), foreign language attitude and language classroom anxiety because their unique contributions were not significant ($p>0.05$), this despite relatively strong correlations with the dependent variable.

A second multiple regression analysis (Table 4) was then used to test whether the remaining predictors can explain L3 choice satisfaction.

First, the explained variance for the items was $R^2 = 57.6\%$, that is to say the variation in L3 choice satisfaction that can be accounted for by the 6 predictors collectively [$F(6,961)=219.799$], $p<0.005$]. With regard to the unique individual contributions of predictors, the results show that teaching ($β=.385$, $t=11.696$, $p=0.00$), adaptation ($β=.055$, $t=2.401$, $p=0.017$), perception of learning ($β=.221$, $t=8.849$, $p=0.00$), teacher ($β=.076$, $t=2.469$, $p=.014$), perception of the learning environment ($β=.091$, $t=4.223$, $p=0.00$) and intrinsic motivation ($β=.218$, $t=8.443$, $p=0.00$) positively predict L3 choice satisfaction.

Furthermore, the results indicate that teaching, perception of learning and intrinsic motivation are the strongest predictors and have a significant effect on L3 choice satisfaction, while adaptation, teacher and perception of the learning environment contribute to a much lesser extent. In other words, the pupils who like the way teachers teach, who feel that they are learning the language and

---

[13] These measures correspond respectively to questions 13, 21, 14, 29, 30, 31, 16, 40 and 23 in the questionnaire (see Tables B1–B6, Appendix B).

Table 4: Results from a multiple linear regression model predicting L3 choice satisfaction.

Variables entered in the model	Unstandardized Coefficients		Standardized Coefficients	t	Sig.	95,0% Confidence Interval for B	
	B	Std. Error	Beta			Lower Bound	Upper Bound
1. L3 Choice satisfaction	.096	.080		1.200	.231	-.061	.254
2. Teaching	.274	.023	.385	11.696	.000	.228	.320
3. Adaptation	.020	.008	.055	2.401	.017	.004	.036
4. Pupils' perception of learning	.214	.024	.221	8.849	.000	.167	.262
5. Teacher	.052	.021	.076	2.469	.014	.011	.094
6. Pupils' perception of the learning environment	.123	.029	.091	4.223	.000	.066	.180
7. Intrinsic motivation	.278	.033	.218	8.443	.000	.213	.342

Note. Dependent Variable: L3 choice satisfaction, question 5 (*How satisfied are you with the subject you have chosen?*).

are intrinsically motivated towards language learning, are most likely to be satisfied with the L3 language that they have chosen.

6 Discussion and implications

The aim of this section is to discuss the results in relation to the research question, and in relation to other and similar studies. I will use the theoretical framework in order to answer the research question(s) and indicate their contribution to the field, e.g. their implications.

6.1 Predicting L3 choice satisfaction

This study has investigated the relation between pupil satisfaction and their chosen L3 as a dependent variable, and a number of independent measures. The choice of a theoretical framework was based on the need for a timeline that made it possible to tap into the pupils' satisfaction *after* their choice of L3, their motivation for this choice, and their classroom experience of L3 instruction.

Results show that a model based on the independent measures of intrinsic motivation, teacher, teaching, adaptation, perception of learning and perception of the learning environment explained R^2 = 57.6% of the variance in the dependent measure of L3 choice satisfaction as an answer to the research question. Moreover, the measures of teaching, perception of learning and intrinsic motivation can be considered the strongest predictors of L3 choice satisfaction.

6.1.1 The role of motivation

Research literature shows consensus about the importance of motivational factors for both L3 choice and L3 choice satisfaction (Hadfield and Dörnyei 2013; Lindemann 2008; Dörnyei 2001). In the present study, motivational factors can, on the one hand, provide an explanation for L3 choice, and, on the other, for L3 choice satisfaction. Although correlational studies do not directly allow for causal inferences, it is still possible to make hypotheses about the reasons behind pupils' language choice by reason of the logic of the time perspective offered by Dörnyei and Ottó (1998), this because of the mutable nature of motivation. It is therefore important to consider motivational factors as an *in progress* phenomenon which can be used to predict language choice (Dörnyei 2001: 187). This logic, also applied by Csizér and Dörnyei (2005a, 2005b) in a similar survey study, allows the characterization of L3 choice as a *motivated behavior*, i.e. an outcome of the motivational factors. This opens for considering them as factors affecting both pupils' choice, in a phase prior to their experience with the language, i.e. *before* beginning with the 8th grade, and during the learning process. It can be mentioned that Masgoret and Gardner (2003) also confirm the hypothesis that the motivational component can be taken into consideration not only in the *pre-actional* phase, but also in the general situation during the *actional*-phase.

The results of the regression analysis confirmed and highlighted the role of intrinsic motivation in predicting variation in L3 choice satisfaction. Moreover, it confirms L3 choice satisfaction as an outcome of both motivated behavior and of the learning experience, as stated by Dörnyei (2005: 107). Comparable results can be found in Ramage (1990) and Pae (2008).

However, it was an unexpected finding that the contributions of both extrinsic motivation and language attitudes were not significant (see Section 5.4). A possible explanation may be the stronger influence of intrinsic motivation when it comes to explaining persistence of pupils' effort in L3 learning. Another explanation may be that the borders between the motivational factors might be unclear. This would be supported by Dörnyei and Clément's redefinition of the motivational factors when they described *integrativeness* as a combination of "*affective motive, language attitudes, intrinsic motivation, attitudes toward L2 learning, enjoyment* and *interest*" (Dörnyei and Clément 2001: 423).

6.1.2 The importance of teacher and teaching measures

The model predicting L3 choice satisfaction includes three teacher related measures: the teacher, the way teachers teach, and to what extent they manage to adapt L3 to the pupils' different needs. These results are not unexpected considering the emphasis and agreement of several studies regarding not only the role of the teacher (Dörnyei 2018; Dörnyei and Kubanyiova 2014; Dörnyei 2001: 49, Dörnyei and Malderez 1999: 165, Masgoret, Bernaus and Gardner 2001: 283).), but also the implications this role has for pupils' L3 motivation (Al Kanboody 2013; Dörnyei 2005; Dörnyei and Csizér 1998). The fact that teaching is found to have a stronger single contribution than the teacher to L3 choice satisfaction, can be explained by arguing that pupils recognize and value teaching practice more than they express preference for the single teacher.

Furthermore, adapted teaching and learning add to the value of the act of teaching due to its function with regards to facilitating learning, and this is teachers' responsibility (see Section 3.3). It is therefore not surprising that adaptation, seen as the result of a professional approach to teaching, contributes to explaining pupils' satisfaction with the language that they teach. On the other hand, the process of adaptation is still problematic for experienced as well as for novice teachers (Brevik and Gunnulfsen, 2016).

6.1.3 Pupils' perception of learning

Pupils' perception of learning can be seen both as pupil-based, and as a function of teacher professionalism, since pupils and teachers together are responsible in making the pupils able both to express learning needs and to monitor the learning process.

Consequently, it is not surprising to find that pupils' perception of learning, as a retrospective evaluation of the results of their effort (Dörnyei 2005: 84), is among the strongest predictors of their satisfaction with L3 choice. In the specific case of L3 languages, however, pupils' perception of learning, and especially negative perceptions, could also be affected by pupils' expectations about learning the language. Carrai (2014: 146–148) found that unfulfilled expectations, that in part could be due to misleading information about L3 courses before secondary school start, could reduce the pupils' satisfaction.

6.1.4 The environmental elements

Of the two classroom environmental measures considered, namely language classroom anxiety and the pupils' perception of the learning environment, the regression model found that language anxiety did not contribute to explaining L3 choice satisfaction. This was surprising, given the important role the theory attributes to this affective factor for language learning (Arnold and Brown 1999 in Dörnyei 2005). However, it is possible that the recognized, though low, predictive contribution given by the pupils' perception of the learning environment might have compensated for the negative effect of anxiety. Moreover, it is possible to argue that the two factors have much in common, since they both tap into the importance of the classroom, of group cohesiveness, and of the way the environment may affect learning (Dörnyei 2001). Another possible explanation is that pupils with high levels of language anxiety might have chosen one of the competing courses.

In this case, as in the case of adaptation, I am inclined to interpret pupils' perception of the language environment as, at least partially, dependent on the teacher's role in the classroom, since the teacher is responsible for creating a supporting atmosphere and cohesion (Dörnyei and Kormos 2000). The low contribution of the environmental elements could be therefore a result of the individual contribution of the teaching measure, which proved to be the strongest predictor ($\beta=.385$).

6.2 Implications

In the following I will address the possible implications of the findings of this study, first mentioning the implications the predicting model of L3 choice satisfaction has for the L3 choice in general, and second, the implications for the teacher's role and for teacher professionalism.

6.2.1 Intrinsic motivation in Norwegian lower secondary school

L3 languages have, as briefly mentioned above, a semi-optional status at the lower secondary school level. Being subject to the competition with less demanding in-depth subjects, pupils' motivation for L3 languages has been object of discussion in the media as well as at a more institutional level for over a decade. This discussion relates to both the general use pupils can have for L3 languages in school and in the Norwegian society (European Commission 2003; KD 2007–2008; Hellekjær

2007), as well as for the future use they might have for one of the most frequent offered ones, i.e. French, Spanish or German.

One important contribution of the present study is therefore its confirming of the role played by the motivational factors in general and, more specifically, the predominant role played by intrinsic orientations in explaining not only L3 choice satisfaction as well as L3 choice in the first place. This points towards a less instrumental and more genuinely intrinsic interest for the chosen language, at the expense of the discussion about the practical use pupils can make of the different languages. Intrinsic motivation can therefore be considered a key factor for L3-choice as well for the whole learning process.

Finally, in the light of the above mentioned current decline in overall L3-choice in lower secondary school (see Section 1), it is of vital importance to keep in mind the importance of L3 choice and pupils' intrinsic motivation while discussing the status of L3 languages in Norway. This discussion should also question to what extent it is necessary to apply special measures to strengthen L3 languages in school in order to comply with the indications of the European Commission (2003) regarding language needs in Europe.

6.2.2 The role of the teaching

The other important implication, given the non-mandatory status of L3 in lower secondary school and especially since pupils are given a chance to exchange the L3 with less demanding subjects, is the importance of the teachers for L3 satisfaction. Given the importance of directly teacher-related measures, as well as less directly related measures such as the pupils' perception of the learning environment, one can state the predominant role that teachers have not only for predicting pupils' satisfaction with their chosen L3 language, but also for preventing the dissatisfaction with the subject that increases the *drop-out* rate. Unsurprisingly, previous studies have stressed the general need for further education (Christiansen 2006) and for a better integration between L3 teachers' disciplinary knowledge and pedagogical content knowledge (Llovet Vilà 2018).

With this in mind, and when in addition considering the freedom of teaching methods and materials established by curricula (see Section 3.3) and the key principle of adaptation in Norwegian schools, it is clear that the success of L3 teaching hinges upon teaching quality. It is therefore necessary to draw attention to the need for an increased L3 teacher professionalism, an issue that needs to be addressed by both school authorities and teacher education institutions.

7 Conclusion and further research

The present study contributes to the existing international research on language learning by providing new information on L3 choice satisfaction. At the same time, it is the first attempt to examine L3 choice satisfaction at the lower secondary level in the Norwegian, as well as the Scandinavian context.

The regression analysis revealed a clear relation between L3 choice satisfaction and measures of motivational, teaching and environmental factors that jointly accounted for 57.6 percent of the variance in pupils' satisfaction with the chosen L3 language. This means that they are strong predictors, and this clearly highlights the teacher's role and the importance of motivation. With respect to motivation, the analysis has also shown the preeminence of the intrinsic over extrinsic as well as attitudinal factors. This can have implications both for motivation as a research field – since it confirms the results of several international studies – and for pupils' overall language motivation in the Norwegian school system.

The survey design and the formulation of items according to the selected theoretical framework, have provided a database on L3 languages which is suitable for further studies.

Moreover, since the findings make it possible to compare language groups, they can help understanding the variation and the quality in pupils' motivation in the different L3 languages and, hopefully, also provide more information to adjust language teaching to the pupils' needs and expectations.

With regard to further research, it could be highly interesting to compare these findings with data from a new survey, and elaborate on the present study using qualitative studies. This could provide useful information in order to understand if the findings are confirmed in a new study. Furthermore, a comparable large-scale survey at the upper secondary school level could prove interesting as well as useful.

Appendices

Appendix A: Tables

Table A1: Geographic distribution of the sample.

Norwegian counties represented in the survey (17 out of 19 are represented)	Number of schools	Number of pupils
Østfold	1	69
Akershus	3	129
Oslo	1	44
Hedmark	1	70
Oppland	1	17
Buskerud	2	96
Vestfold	1	90
Aust-Agder	1	53
Vest-Agder	2	257
Rogaland	1	42
Hordaland	1	42
Sogn og Fjordane	1	38
Møre og Romsdal	1	60
Sør Trøndelag	1	52
Nord Trøndelag	2	77
Nordland	1	105
Troms	3	210

Table A2: Distribution of 9th grade pupils per subject (S)(N=1521) and distribution of pupils from the whole country (C).

	French		German		Spanish		Norwegian in-depth		English in-depth	
	S	C	S	C	S	C	S	C	S	C
Boys	67	3 631	143	8 139	244	8 709	91	2 988	182	8 555
Girls	104	5 161	138	7 140	575	10 246	66	1 953	128	6 138
Unknown	1		1		–		1		3	
Total	172	8 792	282	15279	574	18955	158	4 941	313	14693
Total (%)	11	14	19	24	38	30	10	7.8	21	23

Table A3: Pupils' drop out in number of pupils and percentage in the sample (N= 1512) and in the whole country.

	Fransk		Tysk		Spansk		Ford. i norsk		Ford. i engelsk	
	U	L	U	L	U	L	U	L	U	L
Number of pupils	−10	−619	−35	−1500	−54	−1904	+50	+1614	+46	+2528
Percentage according to the sample	− 0.6	−1	−2.3	−2.4	−3.6	−3	+ 3.3	+2.5	+ 3	+4
Percentage according to number of pupils in each L3 language	−5.5	−6.6	−11	−8.9	−8.6	−9.1	+ 46	+49	+17	+21

Table A4: Additive index for extrinsic motivation-career with factor loadings for the 3 items in in question 29 (How important is it for you that . . . ?).

Extrinsic motivation-career	Factor loadings
29.1 I can use the foreign language in further studies	.839
29.2 I can use the foreign language in a job context	.865
29.3 This foreign language will make it easier for me to find a job	.769

Table A5: Additive index for extrinsic motivation-free time with factor loadings for the 7 items in in question 29 (How important is it for you that . . . ?).

Extrinsic motivation-free time	Factor loadings
29.5 I already speak the language a bit	.523
29.6 I can use the language to communicate with family or relatives	.622
29.7 This language can help me to communicate on holidays	.705
29.8 When on holiday, I like to speak the local language or to be able to communicate.	.726
29.9 I can use the language with friends from other countries	.715
29.10 I would like to live in a country where they speak this language	.576
29.11 Speaking a foreign language is important in order to find new friends	.637

Table A6: Additive index for intrinsic orientation with factor loadings for the 6 items in question 30 (To what extent do you agree with the following statements about the language course you are attending?).

Intrinsic motivation	Factor loadings
30.2 I like the sound of this language	.689
30.3 I have a good impression of people who have this language as a mother tongue	.640
30.4 Foreign language is a funny/enjoyable subject	.837
30.5 Foreign language is an interesting subject	.840
30.6 I like to participate actively in the language class	.746
30.7 I am more at ease in the language class than in the other ones	.623

Table A7: Additive index for language attitudes with factor loadings for the 4 items in question 31 (How much do you agree on the following assumptions about foreign languages in general?).

Language attitudes	Factor loadings
31.1 I would like to learn several languages	.732
31.2 I am interested in language and culture from other countries	.850
31.3 It is important to me to get in contact with people and experience other cultures	.800
31.4 It is thrilling to hear myself speak a foreign language	.714

Table A8: Additive index for learning environment with factor loadings for the 3 items in question 23 (How important are these elements for your well-being in the classroom?).

Learning environment	Factor loadings
23.2 That noone laughs when someone makes a mistake	.706
23.3 That there is no confusion during the lesson	.828
23.4 That the atmosphere is relaxed	.769

Table A9: Additive index for language classroom anxiety with factor loadings for the 3 items in question 40 (To what extent do you agree with the following statements?).

Language classroom anxiety	Factor loadings
40.4 I feel unsure when I have to speak the language in front of the classroom	.832
40.5 It is embarrassing to speak a foreign language	.805
40.6 I am afraid of look like a fool in the language classroom	.866

Table A10: Overview over the correlations between the variable L3 choice satisfaction (Pearsons r) and the other measures in study. **correlations are significant at the 0.01-level, * correlations are significant at the 0.05-level.

L3 choice satisfaction	French	German	Spanish
Intrinsic motivation	.59**	.54**	.58**
Extrinsic motivation-career	.28**	.30**	.29**
Extrinsic motivation-free time	.34**	.41**	.35**
Language attitudes	.31**	.29**	.27**
Language classroom anxiety	−.18*	−.18**	−.20**
Pupils' perception of the learning environment	.26**	.13*	.20**
Teaching	.65**	.66**	.67**
Teacher	.55**	.50**	.56**
Adaptation	.28**	.59**	.33**

Appendix B: English translation of selected questions in the questionnaire

Table B1: Overview of the questions corresponding to single-items measures in the study.

Topic	Question number	Question
Pupils' L3 choice satisfaction	5	*How satisfied are you with the subject you have chosen?*
Teaching	13	*How satisfied are you with the teaching in your (L3) language?*
Adaptation	14	*How well do you feel that the teaching is adapted to your level?*
Pupils' perception of learning	16	*How much do you feel that you are learning in your (L3) language?*
Teacher	21	*How satisfied are you with the teacher's way of teaching in your (L3) language?*

Table B2: Items in question 23 (How important are these elements for your well-being in the classroom?) tapping into learning environment.

Learning environment
Question 23: How important are these elements for your well-being in the classroom?
23.1 That I have some friends
23.2 That noone laughs when someone makes a mistake
23.3 That there is no confusion during the lesson
23.4 That the atmosphere is relaxed

Table B3: Items in question 29 (To what extent do you agree with the following statements about learning a foreign language?) tapping into extrinsic motivation.

Extrinsic motivation
Question 29: To what extent do you agree on the following statements about learning a foreign language?
29.1 I can use the foreign language in further studies
29.2 I can use the foreign language in a job context
29.3 This foreign language will make it easier for me to find a job
29.5 I already speak the language a bit
29.6 I can use the language to communicate with family or relatives
29.7 This language can help me to communicate on holidays
29.8 When on holiday, I like to speak the local language or to be able to communicate.
29.9 I can use the language with friends from other countries
29.10 I would like to live in a country where they speak this language
29.11 Speaking a foreign language is important in order to find new friends

Table B4: Items in question 30 (To what extent do you agree with the following statements about the language course you are attending?) tapping into intrinsic motivation.

Intrinsic motivation
Question 30: To what extent do you agree with the following statements about the language course you are attending?
30.1 It is important to learn this language
30.2 I like the sound of this language
30.3 I have a good impression of people who have this language as a mother tongue
30.4 Foreign language is a funny/enjoyable subject
30.5 Foreign language is an interesting subject
30.6 I like to participate actively in the language class
30.7 I am more at ease in the language class than in the other ones
30.8 I listen to music in the language that I study

Table B5: Items in question 31 (To what extent do you agree with the following statements about foreign languages in general?) tapping into language attitudes.

Language attitudes
Question 31: To what extent do you agree with the following statements about foreign languages in general?
31.1 I would like to learn several languages
31.2 I am interested in language and culture from other countries
31.3 It is important to me to get in contact with people and experience other cultures
31.4 It is thrilling to hear myself speak a foreign language

Table B6: Question 40 (To what extent do you agree with the following statements?) tapping into language classroom anxiety.

Language classroom anxiety
Question 40 (To what extent do you agree with the following statements?)
40.1 I speak only when the teacher asks me a direct question
40.2 I speak only when I think that what I am going to say is correct
40.3 I like that the teacher explain the subject in Norwegian
40.4 I feel unsure when I have to speak the language in front of the classroom
40.5 It is embarrassing to speak a foreign language
40.6 I am afraid of look like a fool in the language classroom

---

References

Al Kanboody, Mastoor. 2013. Second Language Motivation; The Role of Teachers in Learners' Motivation. *Journal of Academic and Applied Studies* 3(4). 45–54.

Arnold, J., & H.D. Brown. (1999) A map of the terrain. In J. Arnold (Ed.), *Affect in Language Learning*, 1–24, Cambridge: Cambridge University Press.

Benson, P. (2001). *Teaching and researching learner autonomy in language learning.* London, England: Longman.

Black, Paul & Dylan Williams. 2018. Classroom assessment and pedagogy. *Assessment in Education: Principles, Policy & Practice* 25(6). 551–575. DOI: 10.1080/0969594X.2018.1441807

Brevik, Lisbeth M. & Ann Elisabeth Gunnulfsen. 2016. *Differensiert undervisning for høytpresterende elever med stort læringspotensial* [Differentiated instruction for high achieving students with higher learning potential]. *Acta Didactica Norge* 10(2). 212–234. https://doi.org/10.5617/adno.2554

Brophy, J. (1987). Synthesis of research on strategies for motivating students to learn. *Educational leadership, 45*(2), 40–48.

Carrai, Debora. 2014. *Fremmedspråk på ungdomstrinnet. En analyse av motivasjon og andre faktorer involvert i elevenes fagvalg og tilfredshet med faget.* [L3 languages at the lower secondary school level. An analysis of motivation and other factors involved in pupils' language choice and language choice satisfaction]. Oslo: Oslo University thesis. DUO Vitenarkiv. https://www.duo.uio.no/handle/10852/41477

Christiansen, Ane. 2006. *Kunnskapsløftet og videreutdanning i spansk.* [The curriculum for the Knowledge Promotion and further education in Spanish]. *Uniped* 2006(3). 32–37. http://hdl.handle.net/11250/295510

Clément, Richard & Bastian G. Kruidenier. 1985. Aptitude, attitude and motivation in second language proficiency: A test of Clément's model. *Journal of Language and Social Psychology* 4. 21–37.

Clément, R. Dörnyei, Z., & Noels, K.A. (1994). Motivation, self-confidence, and group cohesion in the foreign language classroom. *Language learning, 44*(3), 417–488.

Council of Europe. 2018. *Common European Framework of Reference for Languages: Learning, teaching, assessment. Companion Volume with new descriptors*. https://rm.coe.int/cefr-companion-volume-with-new-descriptors-2018/1680787989 (accessed 6 May 2022)

Council of Europe. 2001. *Common European Framework of Reference for Languages: Learning, teaching, assessment*. https://rm.coe.int/1680459f97 (6 May, 2022)

Crookes, Graham & Richard W. Schmidt. 1991. Motivation: Reopening the Research Agenda. *Language Learning* 41(4). 469–512.

Csizér, Kata & Zoltan Dörnyei. 2005a. Language Learners' motivation Profiles and Their Motivated Learning Behaviour. *Language Learning* 55(4). 613–659. https://doi.org/10.1111/j.0023-8333.2005.00319.x

Csizér, Kata & Zoltan Dörnyei. 2005b. The Internal Structure of Language Learning Motivation and Its Relationship with Language Choice and Learning Effort. *The Modern Language Journal* 89(1). 19–36. DOI:10.1111/j.0026-7902.2005.00263.x

Csizér, Kata & Judit Kormos. 2009. Learning Experiences, Selves and Motivated Learning Behavior: A Comparative Analysis of Structural Models for Hungarian Secondary and University Learners of English. In Zoltan Dörnyei & Ema Ushioda (eds.). *Motivation, language identity and the L2 self*, 98–111. Multilingual Matters.

Deci, Edward L. & Richard M. Ryan. 1985. *Intrinsic Motivation and Self-Determination in Human Behaviour*. New York: Springer.

Doetjes, Gerard & Else Ryen. 2009. *Språkvalg på ungdomsskolen. En kartlegging*. [Language choice at the lower secondary school level]. In Johanne Onstad (ed.) *Fokus på språk*, 16. Halden: Fremmedspråksenteret.

Dörnyei, Zoltan. 1997. Psychological processes in cooperative language learning: Group dynamics and motivation. *Modern Language Journal* 81. 482–493. https://doi.org/10.2307/328891

Dörnyei, Zoltan. 2001. *Teaching and researching motivation*. Harlow: Longman.

Dörnyei, Zoltan. 2005. *The Psychology of the Language Learner. Individual differences in Second Language Acquisition*. New York: Routledge.

Dörnyei, Zoltan. 2018. Motivating Students and Teachers. In John I. Liontas, Margo Delli Carpini & TESOL International Association (eds.) *The TESOL Encyclopedia of English Language Teaching*. Hoboken, NJ: Wiley Blackwell. https://doi.org/10.1002/9781118784235.eelt0128

Dörnyei, Zoltan & Richard Clément. 2001. Motivational characteristics of learning different target languages: results of a nationwide survey. In Zoltan Dörnyei & Richard Schmidt (Eds.), *Motivation and Second Language Acquisition*, (Technical report #23), 399–426. Honolulu: University of Hawai'i Press.

Dörnyei, Zoltan & Kata Csizér. 1998. Ten commandments for motivating language learners: Results of an empirical study. *Language Teaching Research* 2(3). 203–229. DOI:10.1191/136216898668159830

Dörnyei, Zoltan & Judit Kormos. 2000. The role of individual and social variables in oral task performance. *Language Teaching* 4(3). 275–300. DOI:10.1191/136216800125096

Dörnyei, Zoltan & Magdalena Kubanyiova. 2014. *Motivating Learners, Motivation Teachers. Building Visions in the Language Classroom*. Cambridge: Cambridge University Press.

Dörnyei Zoltan & Angi Malderez. 1999. The role of group dynamics in foreign language learning and teaching. In Jane Arnold (ed.), *Affect in language learning*, 155–169. Cambridge: Cambridge University Press.

Dörnyei, Zoltan & István Ottó. 1998. Motivation in action: A process model of L2 motivation. *Working papers in Applied Linguistics* 4. 43–69.
European Commission. 2003. *Special Educational Needs in Europe. The Teaching and Learning of languages*. https://eurlex.europa.eu/LexUriServ/LexUriServ.do?uri=COM:2003:0449:FIN:en:PDF (accessed 9 May 2022)
Gardner, Robert C. 2004. *Attitude/Motivation Test Battery: International AMTB Research project*. University of Western Ontario. http://publish.uwo.ca/~gardner/docs/english amtb.pdf (accessed 9 May 2022)
Gardner, Robert C. 1985a. *Social psychology and second language learning: The role of attitudes and motivation*. London: Edward Arnold Publishers.
Gardner, Robert C. 1985b. *Attitude/Motivation Test Battery: Technical Report*, University of Western Ontario. http://publish.uwo.ca/~gardner/docs/AMTBmanual.pdf (accessed 9 May 2022)
Gardner, R. & Peter D. MacIntyre. 1993. A students' contribution to second language learning. Part II: Affective variables. *Language Teaching* 26. 1–11.http://publish.uwo.ca/~gardner/docs/AMTBmanual.pdf (accessed 9 May 2022)
Hadfield, Jill & Zoltan Dörnyei. 2013. *Motivating Learning*. New york: Pearson.
Hellevik, Ottar. 2002. *Forskningsmetode i sosiologi og statsvitenskap*. [Research methods in sociology and political science]. Oslo: Universitetsforlaget.
Hellekjær, Glenn.O. 2007. *Fremmedspråk i norsk næringsliv – engelsk er ikke nok*. [Foreign Language use i Norwegian business – English is not enough]. *Fokus på språk*, 3, G. Doetjes & B. Trandem (red.). Halden: Fremmedspråksenteret.
Henry, Alastair. 2011. *L3 motivation*. Göteborg: Göteborg University Thesis. GUPEA: http://hdl.handle.net/2077/28132
Henry, Alastair & Britt M. Apelgren. 2009. Young learners and multilingualism; A study of learners'attitudes before and after the introduction of a second foreign language to the curriculum. *System* 36(4). 607–623. DOI:10.1016/j.system.2008.03.004
Horwitz, Elaine K., Michael B. Horwitz & Joann Cope. 1986. Foreign Classroom anxiety. *The modern Language Journal* 70(2). 125–132. https://doi.org/10.2307/327317
Kunnskapsdepartementet [KD] [Norwegian Ministry of Education and Research]. 2019. *Læreplanverket for Kunnskapsløftet 2020*. [The curriculum for the Knowledge Promotion 2020]. Udir. https://www.udir.no/laring-og-trivsel/lareplanverket/ (accessed 9 May 2022)
Kunnskapsdepartementet [KD] [Norwegian Ministry of Education and Research]. 2007–2008. *St. Meld. nr.23 Språk bygger broer. Språkstimulering og språklæring for barn, unge og voksne*. [Report to the Storting (white paper) nr. 23 Languages build bridges. Language stimulation and learning for children, young and adults] https://www.regjeringen.no/no/dokumenter/stmeld-nr-23-2007-2008-/id512449/ (accessed 9 May 2022)
Kunnskapsdepartementet [KD] [Norwegian Ministry of Education and Research]. 2006a. *Læreplanverket for Kunnskapsløftet* [The curriculum for the Knowledge Promotion] Udir. https://www.udir.no/laring-og-trivsel/lareplanverket/fagfornyelsen/ (accessed 9 May 2022)
Kunnskapsdepartementet [KD] [Norwegian Ministry of Education and Research]. 2006b. *Forskrift til Opplæringslova* [Regulations to the Education Act] FOR-2006-06-23 nr 724. https://lovdata.no/dokument/SF/forskrift/2006-06-23-724 (accessed 9 May 2022)

Kunnskapsdepartementet [KD] [Norwegian Ministry of Education and Research]. 1998. *Lov om grunnskolen og den videregående opplæringa (Opplæringslova)* [Education Act] (LOV-1998-07-17 nr 61). https://lovdata.no/dokument/NL/lov/1998-07-17-61 (accessed 9 May 2022)

Lindemann, Beate. 2008. *Læring av fremmedspråk og motivasjon for språklæring etter innføringen av Kunnskapsløftet* [Foreign language learning and motivation after the introduction of the Curriculum for the Knowledge Promotion]. In Gerard Doetjes & Beate Trandem (Eds.). *Fokus på Språk* 11. Halden: Fremmedspråksenteret.

Llovet Vilà, Xavier. 2018. Language Teacher Cognition and Curriculum Reform in Norway: Oral Skill Development in the Spanish Classroom. *Acta Didactica Norge* 12(1). 12. https://doi.org/10.5617/adno.5443

Macintyre, Peter D. 2002. Motivation, anxiety and emotion in second language acquisition. In Peter Robinson (ed.), *Individual differences in second language acquisition*, 45–68. John Benjamins. https://doi.org/10.1075/lllt.2.05mac

Macintyre, Peter D. & Robert Gardner. 1994. The subtle effects of language anxiety on cognitive processing in the second language. *Language Learning* 44. 283–305.

Masgoret, Anne-Marie & Robert C. Gardner. 2003. Attitudes, Motivation and Second Language Learning: A Meta-Analysis of Studies Conducted by Gardner and Associates. *Language Learning* 53(1). 123–163. https://doi.org/10.1111/1467-9922.00212

Masgoret, Anne-Marie, Mercè Bernaus & Robert C. Gardner. 2001. Examining the role of attitudes and motivation outside of the formal classroom: A test of the Mini-AMTB for children. 281–296. In Zoltan Dörnyei & Richard Schmidt (eds.), *Motivation and Second Language Acquisition*, (Technical report #23), 399–426. Honolulu: University of Hawai'i Press.

Nasjonalt senter for engelsk og framandspråk i opplæringa [The Foreign Language Centre]. 2021. *Notat 01/2021. Elevane sitt val av framandspråk på ungdomsskulen 2020–2021.* [Note 01/2021. Pupils' foreign language choice at the lower secondary school level]. https://www.hiof.no/fss/sprakvalg/fagvalgstatistikk/elevane-sine-val-av-framandsprak-i-ungdomsskulen-20-21.pdf (accessed 9 May 2022).

Oxford, Rebecca. 1999. Anxiety and the language learner: new insights. In Jane Arnolds (ed.), *Affect Language Learning*, 58–67. Cambridge: Cambridge University Press.

PEDLEX Norsk Skoleinformasjon. 2009. *Adressebok for skoleverket 2009.* [Address book for the school system 2009]. Otta: Pedlex AS.

Pae, Tae-Il. 2008. Second Language Orientation and Self-Determination Theory: A Structural Analysis of the Factors Affecting Second Language Achievement, *Journal og Language and Social Psychology* 27(5). 5–27. https://doi.org/10.1177/0261927X07309509

Ramage, Katherine. 1990. Motivational Factors and Persistence in Foreign Language Study. *Language Learning* 40(2),189–219. https://doi.org/10.1111/j.1467-1770.1990.tb01333.x

Skolverket [The Swedish National Agency for Education]. 2011. *Kursplaner for gründskolan* [Curricula for primary school]. https://www.skolverket.se/undervisning/grundskolan/laroplan-och-kursplaner-for-grundskolan/kursplaner-for-grundskolan (accessed 9 May 2022)

Skaalvik, Einar & Sidsel Skaalvik. 2003. *Selvoppfatning, motivasjon og læringsmiljø.* [Self-perception, motivation and learning environment]. Oslo: Tano Aschehaug.

Speitz, Heike & Beate Lindemann. 2002. *Jeg valgte tysk fordi hele familien min ville det, men jeg angrer. Status for 2. Fremmedspråk i norsk ungdomsskole.* [I chose German because the whole family wanted it, but I regret. Status for foreign languages in Norwegian lower secondary school]. Rapport 03/02. Notodden: Telemarksforskning. https://teora.hit.no/handle/2282/556

Williams, Marion & Robert L. Burden. 1997. *Psychology for language teachers. A social constructivist approach.* Cambridge: Cambridge University Press.

Internet pages

Grunnskolens Informasjonssystem (GSI) [Primary school Information System]: https://gsi.udir.no/ and www.wis.no/gsi

Norsk samfunnsvitenskapelig datatjeneste (NSD) [Norwegian Agency for Shared Services in Education and Research]: http://www.nsd.uib.no/

Statistisk Sentralbyrå [Statistics Norway]: www.ssb.no

Statistical Package for the Social Sciences (SPSS) version 27 http://www-01.ibm.com/software/no/analytics/spss/

Index

Action research 179
Adaptation. See differentiated instruction
Affective. See emotions
Affective filter 204
Age 4, 6, 95, 112–114, 117, 119, 123–124, 133, 135, 139–140, 145–150, 205
ANOVA 114, 117, 119, 214
Anxiety 5, 7, 158–159, 162, 165, 169, 178, 180–182, 188, 192, 194, 196–197, 203, 205, 207–208, 212, 214–219, 225, 229, 234, 236–237, 239, 243, 247
Apathy 162, 165
Aptitude 1, 3, 7, 10–12, 25, 43, 53, 65–70, 73–76, 78–81
Attitude 1, 92, 101, 104, 204, 206, 212, 228, 231–232, 237–239, 243, 245, 249
Audiovisual materials 66–67, 80
Authentic communication experience 4, 179
Autonomy 4, 155–159, 161, 163–164, 166–170, 233
– Autonomous learning behavior 4, 7, 155–159, 161, 164, 166–167
– Autonomous use of technology 4, 155–159, 161, 164, 166–167, 169–170

Basic interpersonal communication skills (BICS) 20
Behavior management 22–24
Bilingual program 12
Boredom 162, 165–167

Choice satisfaction. See satisfaction.
Classroom context. See formal setting
Classroom environment. See learning environment
Classroom observation 17
Cluster 133–135, 140–143, 145–150
Cognate linguistic distance 88, 103
Cognateness 71
Cognitive ability 11, 24, 67
Cognitive academic language proficiency 20
Cognitive development 1, 7
Cognitive disability. See learning disability

Cognitive theory of multimedia learning 66, 77
Community of practice 89
Concreteness 71
Confirmatory factor analysis 238, 241
Confusion 4, 162, 165–167, 169
Constant comparative method 186
Curiosity 155, 162, 165–170

Deficit thinking 9, 14–15, 18, 25
Developmental disorder 12
Differentiated instruction 5, 225, 229, 232, 240, 242, 244, 246–248
Digit span 33
– Backward digit span task 31, 35, 54
– Forward digit span task 52
Digital consumers 102
Dual coding theory 66, 77

Educational activities 109, 117, 119–120, 124–126
Elementary school. See primary school
Elicitation 141
Emic 87–88, 90, 104
Emotions 4–5, 7, 10, 100, 102, 155–159, 161, 163–164, 166–170, 178, 203–206, 208–212, 214, 216–219, 234
Engagement 90, 97, 99, 103–104, 112
English language development (ELD) services 12–13, 15, 17–18, 20
Enjoyment 4, 158–159, 161, 165, 167, 169–170, 181, 190–191, 194, 197, 208
Ethnographic 9, 17
Exchange program 4, 7, 177, 184, 193, 195, 197
Excitement 205
Explicit instruction 72, 75–77
Exposure 1, 3, 7, 11–13, 21, 65, 69–71, 74, 76–77, 79–81, 87–88, 103, 148–149
– Out-of-school exposure 1, 3–4, 6, 88–89, 91–93, 95, 103–104, 109–110, 112–117, 119–120, 123–127, 149, 164, 183
Extensive viewing 66–68, 77, 80–81

Extramural exposure. See (out-of-school) exposure

Feelings. See emotions
Focus group discussion 87, 90, 92–93, 97, 100–101, 104
Foreign language classroom anxiety. See anxiety
Formal setting 1, 32, 50, 65–66, 70, 79, 81, 87–91, 103, 110, 127
Form-meaning link 66
Frequency of occurrence 71
Frustration 190–191, 194–195, 197

Gaming 1, 3–4, 6–7, 87–89, 91–93, 95, 97, 103, 109–110, 112, 117, 120–121, 124–127
Gender 95, 139, 205, 208–211, 214, 216–217
Generalised linear model 74
Grammar 3, 7, 31–33, 35–37, 40, 42, 45, 47–51, 53–55
– Productive grammar 3, 31, 41, 54
– Receptive grammar 3, 31–32, 41, 48–49, 54–55
Grammatical sensitivity 68

Hapax legomena 145, 149–150
Hope 159, 162, 165, 169–170

Ideal L2/L3 self 5, 158–159, 161, 163, 166–167, 169, 206–209, 212, 214–219
Incidental learning 81
Inclusionary classroom 22, 24, 26
Individual difference
– External individual difference 1–2, 4, 6–7, 9–10, 12–15, 18, 22, 24–25, 79, 228
– Internal individual difference 1, 4–7, 10, 15, 18, 20–22, 24–25, 228
Inductive language learning ability 68
Informal setting 1, 6–7, 67, 110, 124, 126–127, 177
Input 17, 148
Instructed foreign language learning 34, 170
Instruction 1, 12, 148
Interaction 17, 186–188, 190–191

Intercultural communication 177, 190, 195–196
International posture 182, 196
Internet 87
Interview 17

Joy 158, 205

Kruskal Wallis test 93, 95

Language aptitude. See aptitude
Language balance 115
Language choice 5, 225, 227–230, 236, 245, 247–248
Language impairment 12, 15
Language learning autonomy. See autonomy
Learner satisfaction. See satisfaction
Learning disability 2–3, 6–7, 9–26
Learning environment 2, 5, 7, 10, 12–14, 17–18, 22–26, 91, 148, 206, 225, 227, 229–230, 233, 236–239, 243–244, 247, 249
Learning experience 4, 159, 161, 163, 166–167, 169, 232–233, 245–246, 248
Learning gains 11, 74
Lexical availability 134–135, 139–141, 148
Lexical coverage 71
Lexical fluency task 4
Lexical output 133, 139
Lexical profile 4
Lexical retrieval. See word retrieval
Limited capacity theory of bilingualism 11–12, 25
Lingua franca 88, 98
Linguistic self-confidence. See self-confidence
Listening
– Active listening 109, 117, 119–121, 124–125
– Listening to music / songs 87–89, 91–93, 95, 99, 103, 109–110, 117, 120–121, 124–126
Locus of control 180

Mann-Whitney U-test 74–75
Matthew effect 78

Media 3, 91, 99, 112–113, 117, 125
Mental lexicon 134, 149–150
Middle school 9
Motivated learning behavior 156, 158, 161, 163, 166–167, 169–170, 231, 245
Motivation 1, 4–7, 89–91, 93, 97–98, 100, 102–104, 127, 155–160, 163, 166–167, 169, 177–183, 186, 189–190, 194–197, 203–212, 214, 216–219, 225, 227–234, 236–238, 244–249
– Extrinsic motivation 227–228, 230–231, 237–239, 243, 249
– Instrumental motivation 158, 206, 212, 214–218, 230, 238, 248
– Integrative motivation 158, 182, 206, 208, 218, 230, 238, 245
– Intrinsic motivation 5, 7, 208, 225, 227–228, 230, 237–238, 243–245, 248–249
Multimodal input 65–66, 69, 71, 77, 80–81, 87
Multiple case study 9, 15, 17

Nervousness 188–189, 193–194
Non-verbal intellgence 39, 42–45, 47–49, 51
Non-word repetition (NWR) 3, 31, 34–37, 39, 43–45, 47–55

Ought-to L2 self 158–159, 161, 163, 169
Output 17

Phonemic coding ability 68
Phonological loop 32–33, 52–53
Phonological processing 3, 7, 34, 50–52, 54–55
Phonological short-term memory 31–34, 36–37, 42–44
Pride 159, 162, 165–167, 169–170
Primary school 2–3, 12, 38, 42–43, 69–70, 91–92, 109–110, 112–114, 140, 150, 177–179, 183
Principal component analysis 238–239
Prior knowledge 52
Process model of L2 motivation 237
Prototype theory 149

Reading 91–93, 95, 103, 112, 127
Recall 78
– Form recall 65, 71–72
– Meaning recall 65, 71
Recognition 78
– Meaning recognition 72
Regression analysis 43, 47–49, 120, 155, 163, 166–167, 215, 225, 241–243, 245, 249
Rote memory 68

Satisfaction 5, 7, 225, 227–231, 233, 236–237, 240–249
School type. See type of education
Second foreign language (L3) 5, 203–204, 210, 211, 216–217, 219, 225–229, 232, 234–235, 241, 244, 246–249
Second language motivational self system (L2MSS) 155, 158, 206–207, 211, 218
Secondary school 2, 5, 140, 155–156, 160, 163, 209, 225–228, 234, 247–249
Self-concept 208
Self-confidence 4–7, 112, 126, 177–183, 186, 191–197
Self-efficacy 179–182, 195
Self-evaluation 181
Self-perception 179
Self-regulation 156–157, 170, 233
Semantic categorization task 133
Semantic category 135, 139, 141, 145, 148
Semantic domain 6, 133–134
Semantic fluency task 133, 135, 140–141
Semantic memory 140, 150
Semantic organization 135, 140
Semilingual 21
Shame 158, 162, 165, 169
Social cognitive theory 179
Social media 1, 3, 87, 89, 91–93, 95, 97, 99, 102–103
Socio-educational model 206, 212
Speaking 87, 89, 92–93, 95, 97, 103, 124
Status 91, 104, 204, 228
Strategy 139
Subtitles 3, 65–67, 69–71, 74–77, 80, 88, 91–93, 95, 99, 103, 109, 117, 120–121, 124–126

Switch 133–135, 140–143, 146–148

T-test 74–75, 142, 163–164, 241–242
Task-based language teaching (TBLT) 14
Teacher 5, 7, 9, 16–17, 20, 22, 25–26, 225–226, 229, 232, 236–237, 240, 242, 244, 246–249
Teaching. See teacher
Technology 7
Television viewing 3–4, 7, 65–67, 70, 76–77, 79, 87–89, 91–93, 95, 99, 103, 124, 126–127
Token 142
Type 142, 144–145
Type of education 114, 117, 119–122, 126

Vocabulary 3, 4, 7, 31–37, 40–45, 47–49, 51–55, 65–70, 74–80, 109–110, 112–114, 117, 120–123, 125–127, 150
– Productive vocabulary 133, 135, 140
– Receptive vocabulary 3, 31, 33, 37, 43, 45, 47, 50, 52, 54
– Vocabulary size 70–71, 149–150

Wilcoxon rank-sum test 93, 95
Wilcoxon signed-rank test 74–75
Willingness to communicate (WTC) 5, 7, 182–183, 195–196, 203–204, 207–208, 210–212, 214–219
Word association 133–134, 139–142, 144–145, 147, 149–150
Word production 134–135, 139, 140–141, 143, 145, 148–150
Word retrieval 133–134, 140, 149–150
Word search 133, 140
Word storage 134
Working memory 3, 31–32, 35–37, 42, 45, 47–48, 52, 54–55
– Verbal working memory 31–33, 36, 39
– Working memory span 32–33, 35–37, 39, 47–51, 53–54

www.ingramcontent.com/pod-product-compliance
Lightning Source LLC
Chambersburg PA
CBHW030231170426
43201CB00006B/184